EDUCATION AND RACE
FROM EMPIRE TO BREXIT

Sally Tomlinson

P

First published in Great Britain in 2019 by

Policy Press
University of Bristol
1-9 Old Park Hill
Bristol
BS2 8BB
UK
t: +44 (0)117 954 5940
pp-info@bristol.ac.uk
www.policypress.co.uk

North America office:
Policy Press
c/o The University of Chicago Press
1427 East 60th Street
Chicago, IL 60637, USA
t: +1 773 702 7700
f: +1 773-702-9756
sales@press.uchicago.edu
www.press.uchicago.edu

© Policy Press 2019

British Library Cataloguing in Publication Data
A catalogue record for this book is available from the British Library

Library of Congress Cataloging-in-Publication Data
A catalog record for this book has been requested

ISBN 978-1-4473-4584-8 paperback
ISBN 978-1-4473-4582-4 hardcover
ISBN 978-1-4473-4585-5 ePub
ISBN 978-1-4473-4586-2 Mobi
ISBN 978-1-4473-4583-1 ePdf

The right of Sally Tomlinson to be identified as author of this work has been asserted by her in accordance with the Copyright, Designs and Patents Act 1988.

The statements and opinions contained within this publication are solely those of the author and not of the University of Bristol or Policy Press. The University of Bristol and Policy Press disclaim responsibility for any injury to persons or property resulting from any material published in this publication.

Policy Press works to counter discrimination on grounds of gender, race, disability, age and sexuality.

Cover design by Robin Hawes
Front cover image: istock

Contents

Acknowledgements

This book uses work from social and imperial history, politics, educational policy, and the politics of race, ethnicity and education. So many thanks to all colleagues with whom over the years I have been able to discuss and argue over the issues and learn from them. Special thanks to Tahir Abbas, Kalwant Bhopal, Linda Akomaning, Sue Caudron, Danny Dorling, Dave Gillborn, Carol Vincent, Geoffrey Walford, and Brian Tomlinson for the tech stuff. Thanks again to Jo-Anne Baird, Head of Department, for the hospitality of the Department of Education, University of Oxford, while this book was being written. The book is dedicated to the late Professor John Rex, who made it his intellectual life's work to destroy racism in all its forms, and to Baroness Doreen Lawrence, who fought a murderous racism.

Permissions

Thanks to Colin Schindler for kind permission to quote from his book *National Service* (2012). Thanks also to Linda Akomaning for permission to quote from her PhD thesis, 'The educational experiences of Ghanaian children in England' (2018).

List of abbreviations

APPG	All-Party Parliamentary Group
BIS	Department for Business, Innovation and Skills
CATE	Council for the Accreditation of Teacher Education
CEA	Conservative Education Association
CNAA	Council for National Academic Awards
CRC	Community Relations Commission
CRE	Commission for Racial Equality
CTCs	City Technology Colleges
DCFS	Department for Children, Schools and Families
DCMS	Digital, Culture, Media and Sport Committee
DES	Department for Education and Science
DfE	Department for Education
DIUS	Department for Innovation, Universities and Skills
DUP	Democratic Unionist Party
EAZ	Education Action Zones
EBacc	English Baccalaureate
EBD	Emotionally and behaviourally disturbed
ECHR	European Court of Human Rights
ECJ	European Court of Justice
EEC	European Economic Community
EHRC	Equalities and Human Rights Commission
ESG	Education Support Grant
ESN	Educational subnormality
EU	European Union
FSM	Free School Meals
GCSE	General Certificate of Secondary Education
GDP	Gross Domestic Product
GM	Grant-maintained
HEFC	Higher Education Funding Body
HMC	Headmasters' and Headmistresses' Conference
HMI	Her Majesty's Inspectorate
LEA	Local education authority
MEP	Member of the European Parliament
NCC	National Curriculum Council
NODM	National Organisation of Deported Migrants

NUT	National Union of Teachers
OECD	Organisation for Economic Co-operation and Development
OFFA	Office for Fair Access
Ofsted	Office for Standards in Education
ONS	Office for National Statistics
PFI	Private Finance Initiative
PISA	Programme for International Student Assessment
PLASC	Pupil Level Annual School Census
QCA	Qualifications and Curriculum Authority
SEU	Social Exclusion Unit
SMSC	Spiritual, moral, social and cultural
TTA	Teacher Training Agency
UKIP	United Kingdom Independence Party
WTO	World Trade Organization

Introduction

Every country depends on its sense of identity, on a story about itself.... I have witnessed, and indeed been part of, many attempts to construct a post-imperial story. (Brown, 2017: 22)

You could tell from the way they did call them – Froggies, Eyeties, Dagoes – the only way we'd describe them was that they were all beneath you. (Elderly man, quoted in Humphries, 1981: 43)

This book covers the period from the height of the British Empire, from 1870, to 2018, when it became clear that 'Brexit' – the vote to leave the European Union – had increased hostilities towards racial and minority ethnic groups and migrant workers, raising sharp questions about national identity. Will a populist view prevail that there should be a 'British identity' underpinned by unproblematic British values and culture, largely excluding minorities? Or will arguments based on equality, human rights and economic needs prove more powerful in challenging the idea of a white, monocultural British identity unencumbered by immigrants and refugees? Will a Scottish, Welsh or Irish identity be more inclusive than an English one, assuming that the United Kingdom of Great Britain and Northern Ireland continues to be formed out of four nations? What part will education play in future scenarios when, for over a century-and-a-half, there has been a dismal failure at all educational levels to alleviate ignorance and xenophobia?

Most white British people, including the supposedly well-educated, know little about the Empire their grandparents were born into, which post Second World War turned into a Commonwealth of some 53 nations, 31 of these with fewer than 3 million people. They also know little about the often brutal processes of decolonisation and the reasons for the arrival of immigrants from the Caribbean, the Asian subcontinent and other post-colonial countries. The incorporation of now settled citizens and their descendants into the British class structure continues to be regarded as a problem, especially if they are Muslim. Indeed, it was only in 2018 that the full story began to emerge of the deliberate creation by the Home Office of a 'hostile environment' towards migrants that led to the deportation of some of the early Caribbean migrants – the 'Windrush generation' – some after 70 years having worked in the UK (Elgot, 2018).

The presence of migrant workers from European countries and other parts of the world, despite the economic need for migrant labour, remains contentious. Populist politicians encourage those who perceive themselves to be victims of a globalisation that has out-sourced jobs outside the country, or been taken by migrants inside, to feel dispossessed. Many who regard themselves as 'rightful' national residents turn on those regarded as 'not British'. Migrants and refugees from global conflicts, often created by former imperial wars and action, are made scapegoats, with race and migrant hatreds intensifying. This book attempts to cover something of the politics and ideologies of empire, the arrival of immigrants from the former colonial countries, antagonisms to their settlement, links with Europe and the free movement of labour, the arrival of refugees and asylum-seekers from global conflicts, and growing hostility to aspects of the EU – linking all this to education and racial politics and policies over the years.[1]

Age was an important factor in the Brexit decision, with a majority of those over 45 voting to leave the EU, rising to 60% of those over 65. The elderly respondent who told Stephen Humphries that he and his contemporaries felt superior to all other Europeans (Humphries, 1981: 43), and children who in the 1970s were nostalgic for the British Empire and a country without 'coloureds' (Jeffcoate, 1979), were those voters. Older people had experienced in various forms an ethnocentric jingoistic curriculum, still resonant with late 19th- and 20th-century consciousness of 'empire'. This book covers a period when popular imperialism was at its height, which coincided with the time when mass education was developing and a value system based on military patriotism, xenophobia and a nationalism that excluded minorities, colonials and foreigners was filtering down from the upper-class public schools to the middle-class grammar schools and the elementary schools attended by the working classes.

In 1902 a history textbook recommended by the Board of Education extolled *Men of renown* who had conquered and plundered countries inhabited by 'savage crowds eager to slay Englishmen' (Finnemore, 1902: 254). In early juvenile literature the noble Tarzan was forever fighting in jungles against wicked black men, a new Tarzan film being released in 2016. In 1948 an *Empire Youth Annual* included an article on an exciting train journey from Delhi to Lahore without mentioning the horrors of the previous year's partition of India (Fawcett, 1948). This *Annual* also extolled an 'Enormously Exciting Venture' – the British government's groundnut scheme, which was an attempt to grow groundnuts (peanuts) in East and West Africa to make margarine. The scheme was funded by a subsidiary of Unilever and supported by the Ministry of Food. The article described how 'native women' threshed the plants and 'native dockers' bagged the nuts and carried them on their heads. It told its youthful readers – the grandparents of today – that 'This great scheme will give work to and raise the standard of life of the natives in these British possessions, and keep valuable money within the Commonwealth and Empire' (Fawcett, 1948: 66-7). The expensive scheme was a total failure, abandoned in 1951: 'The scheme and its spectacular failure was to become emblematic of the fallacies (or fantasies) of late colonial developmentalism' (Rizzo, 2006: 207).

Schools and textbooks were largely places of myth-making and evasions of the truth. Until the 1960s, maps of the world still had large sections coloured pink because the countries 'belonged to us', and a curriculum tacitly supporting the merits of empire and silent on exploitation and cruelty was the norm. Race and empire shaped the concept of national citizenship, and resentment of immigration shaped the view of who should belong or should be excluded. It is not surprising that a YouGov poll in 2016 reported that over 40% of respondents thought the British Empire was a 'good thing', and 'an unwillingness to engage with the warts and all of imperial history makes Britain particularly blind to how governments and people of other countries view British society' (Owen, 2016). In social class-bound Britain, racism and xenophobia have no class boundaries, and include those who have attended the prestigious English public (non-state) schools. In 2017 the 4th Viscount St Davids was jailed for racially abusing Gina Miller, a businesswoman who won a legal challenge over the government on voting for Brexit. He was convicted for describing her as 'a boat jumper ... if this is what we expect from immigrants, send them back to their stinking jungles' and offering money for anyone who would 'accidentally run over this bloody troublesome immigrant' (Rawlinson, 2017; see also O'Carroll, 2017).

The pronouncement of former Eton-educated Foreign Secretary Boris Johnson, that 'The African continent is a blot, but it is not a blot on our conscience. The problem is not that we were once in charge, but that we are not in charge any more', suggests that the colonial mentality that characterised the attitude of the British State to the rest of the world still survives (Msimang, 2016). Even before he became Foreign Secretary, Johnson had a reputation for making derogatory remarks about post-colonial countries and their people. Journalist Ashitha Nagesh wrote ironically of '11 things Boris has said that makes him the perfect foreign secretary' (Nagesh, 2016). Boris, also when Foreign Secretary, boasted that 'Of the 193 present members of the UN, we have conquered or at least invaded 90% of them' (quoted in Brown, 2017: 27).

The aim of this book is to provide information on the ideological and political beliefs deriving from imperial days, which for well over a hundred years have formed the background to policies and practices concerning race, ethnicity and education in Britain. It discusses the education structures and curricula in place that have only minimally engaged with the realities of a multiracial and multicultural society, and describes the incorporation of minority young people into a largely hostile society over the years, from the high point of the British Empire to the Brexit vote. A pressing question in 2016 seemed to be, 'Brexit has its roots in the British Empire – so how do we explain it to the young?' (Tomlinson and Dorling, 2016; Dorling and Tomlinson, 2019). While there is a large and expanding literature on the settlement of post-1950s immigrant minorities and their education, there is less on the failures of education for a white majority, with the report by Lord

Swann, *Education for all* (Lord Swann and Committee of Inquiry into the Education of Children from Ethnic Minority Groups, 1985) being ridiculed or ignored. Resentments were fulled when those described as white working-class boys supposedly achieved less well in schools than some minorities (Gillborn, 2010; Gillborn et al, 2017). The chapters in the book cover the imperial and post-imperial ideologies, policies and immigration legislation over the decades, from Victorian times to the present, and an education system which, despite attempts at multicultural and anti-racism education, left untouched a 'whitewashing' of the past and the post-imperial values of empire.

Delusions of empire

The long and contentious discussions over the form Brexit and global trade will ultimately take demonstrated a reluctance to engage with current 21st-century realities. As journalist Bhanuj Kappal pointed out, the idea that the UK can 'bring all its former colonies back into the fold of a warm free-trade loving family is based on delusions about empire' (Kappal, 2017). While in some respects Britain is a relatively successful multiracial and multicultural country, education at all levels has done little to prepare all young people to answer the question raised by French sociologist, Alan Touraine, who asked, *Can we live together?* (Touraine, 1997). Living together means understanding the past. In what, from 1922, become a United Kingdom of Great Britain and Northern Ireland, there is universal ignorance of much that is important to the survival of future generations in a connected world. In the UK we have more successful 'schooling' in terms of testing and examination passing, but we do not have successful education. We continue to manufacture ignorance of the past in a divided and fragmented education system in which neither the present nor the future can be clearly understood.

There is also a manufacture of ignorance about globalisation, as governments have spread the belief that they cannot control economic competition between countries, the movement of transnational businesses around the world to find cheaper labour, or the disappearance of local, regional or national industry and jobs. One of the earliest and more pessimistic writers on globalisation, Ulrich Beck, described a 'jobless capitalism' in Western societies with precarious forms of work, lower wages and widening inequalities (Beck, 2000). Unregulated markets lead to national and global inequalities, unemployment or low-wage employment and to greater social and economic insecurities. Danny Dorling (2018) has described in detail the rising inequality in Britain over the past four decades, and the ways in which the very rich try hard to live away from the poor, and keep money in tax havens overseas, mainly in the 14 small overseas territories remaining in the British Commonwealth. Elites no longer inhabit the same economy or society as the mass of people, and separate themselves and their families into private enclaves, including schools.

Richard Sennett (2006) drew attention to the worrying consequences of the insecurities generated by current capitalism, where whole populations are frightened and project their anxieties onto migrants and foreign workers rather than on governments. After the vote to leave the EU in 2016 it became clear that many politicians encouraged a 'Leave' vote by stoking up existing fears of immigrants and immigration. The print media colluded in this. Out of the 14,779 newspaper and magazine articles published in newspapers in the 10 weeks up to the referendum, almost all included negative coverage of immigration. In his autobiography in 2017, former Prime Minister Gordon Brown wrote that, for many years 'we have been dealing with the fall-out from the end of Empire and how Britain could reposition itself' (Brown, 2017: 22). He, too, blamed globalisation, and marketisation that took the form of state shrinking, tax cutting and free market fundamentalism through which many suffered the pain of unemployment, poverty and being left behind. He was, however, less candid about the responsibility Labour governments, as well as Conservative governments, had for producing anti-immigrant policies.

Empire and a long good-bye

A favourite book of the 19th-century Victorian educated classes was Edward Gibbon's *The history of the decline and fall of the Roman Empire* (1781), even as their own empire expanded. A voluminous literature on empires, especially the British Empire, has ensued, with historians often divided into those who regard the empire as a 'good thing', as in Niall Ferguson's *Empire: How Britain made the modern world* (Ferguson, 2004; and see Chapter Seven, this volume) to those who are more sceptical. John Newsinger dramatically documented the atrocities of empire in *The blood never dried: A people's history of the British Empire* (Newsinger, 2006). Jeremy Paxman, taking time off from his television career, perhaps represents the more sceptical and amusing point of view that the empire and decolonisation is in a long irreversible decline, and the 'sound chaps' and their Home Counties wives enjoying sundowners on the veranda and suet puddings on the colonial dinner table have long since retired. Even the imperial sport of cricket, once governed by the Marylebone Cricket Club (MCC), is now run by an international committee in Dubai (Paxman, 2012). Paxman suggested that the native British had been cushioned from reality for so long, because the empire gave such comforting illusions about their place in the world, a 'stupid sense that they were born to rule' (Paxman, 2012: 285). Bernard Porter has noted that whatever the arguments about the empire being good or bad, each 'side' accepts the old imperialist view of the importance and 'greatness' of empire, especially in terms of the global power wielded. The actual notion of a British Empire conjured up images of domination and pride, assisted by the pink bits of maps on school walls into the 1960s, which, using the Mercator projection, actually exaggerates the area of land of the colonies and dominions (Porter, 2015).

Another view could be found in the six-year-long study by Piers Brendon, who, emulating Gibbon, produced *The decline and fall of the British Empire 1781-1997* (Brendon, 2007). Covering in detail the history of the decline of the British Empire from the loss of the American colonies in 1781 to the handing over of Hong Kong to China in 1997, he concluded that while on the debit side there was indeed arrogance, violence, exploitation, jingoism and racism, which were a betrayal of the civilised values the British claimed to espouse, 'the lust for conquest is part of the human condition, and the spirit of imperialism is not dead' (Brendon, 2007: 656). Bruce Gilley (2017) appeared to endorse this view, and made out a case for recolonising some weak states and even creating new Western colonies. His article led to demands that his paper be retracted (*Times Higher Education Supplement*, 2017). However, there had been a number of claims that in 2007 the then Prime Minister Tony Blair discussed with the Army Chief of Staff the possibility of invading Zimbabwe, a country that finally obtained its independence in 1980, as he disliked, as many of its citizens did, the behaviour of the then Prime Minster Robert Mugabe (Smith, 2013). If followed through this certainly would have been a recolonisation. In 2017, another suggestion by a Conservative MP was that Ireland, first colonised by the English in 1169, had made a mistake leaving a union with Britain in 1922, and should rejoin (Macshane, 2017).

Historians of empires have produced much entertaining literature on a variety of aspects of imperial behaviours. Deana Heath's book *Purifying Empire* (Heath, 2010) provides interesting information on the attempts to regulate what the upper classes and colonists regarded as 'obscenity' in Britain, India and Australia, and attempted a moral regulation of the English working classes, and those colonised. Literature in particular must be kept 'pure' – the obscene engravings and carnal literature of India and the 'aesthetic pornography' produced by eminent writers in Britain were equally shocking to the moralists, and attempts to regulate the obscene in 19th-century Britain were transformed into an imperial project.

The start of what is referred to as the 'first British Empire' is debatable. The first actual takeover of land is usually claimed to be the island of Bermuda following a British shipwreck there in 1609. Ironically it is now a tax haven for wealthy individuals and multinational companies. Lizzie Collingham has claimed that 'The British Empire was born on Newfoundland's stony beaches' (Collingham, 2017: 13). By the 1540s West Country fishermen were sailing past Iceland to catch cod in Newfoundland waters, primarily to feed the Royal Navy. Eventually, through conquests and exploitation of other countries, Britain emerged as a major sea power and trading nation. The East India Company, forerunner of the imperial conquest of India, was sending millions of tons of spices by the mid-18th century, when around half of imported goods into Britain were foodstuffs, especially sugar produced by slave labour in the Caribbean.

The East India Company was a corporation with an army. By 1765 it had taken over Bengal and other states from the Mughal Emperors, later sending out Robert Clive, 'an unstable sociopath' (Dalrymple, 2015: 25), to run the Company, loot the country and enrich himself. A Mughal official lamented that 'he had to take orders from a handful of traders who had not yet learned to wash their bottoms' (Dalrymple, 2015: 26). Clive was one of the *Men of renown* included in the 1902 history textbook (Finnemore, 1902). The East India Company has been described as a model of corporate efficiency, and violence: 'For all the power wielded today by the world's largest corporations, Exxon, Mobil, Walmart or Google, they are tame beasts compared with the ravening territorial appetite of the militarised East India Company' (Dalrymple, 2015: 27).

The way in which territories were casually added to the Empire can now seem breath-taking. In 1849 *The Times* newspaper proudly recorded 'The Annexation of the Punjab', by which this area was now to be part of the British Empire of India, the local Maharaja having to hand over his province to the British and 'solicit clemency of the British government' (*The Times*, 1849). By the mid-19th century, Britain had embraced an industrial revolution, and during the period regarded as the 'second British Empire', described itself as 'the workshop of the world'. Much of this industrial revolution and its raw materials depended on slave and indentured labour overseas. British imperialists pursued an ideology of free trade and attempted to break down protectionism – how countries protect the export and import of their goods and services – to open up markets for British goods and ensure economic control. The rail network the British built in India was mainly to transport goods for export, and by 1900, a fifth of Britain's wheat imports came from India. Collingham has recorded that between 1875 and 1914, some 16 million Indians died in famines, and a colonial government did little to alleviate the misery, insisting this was nature's way of keeping a check on the Indian population (Collingham, 2017: 221).

As this book briefly covers the period from the later 19th century, it is worth noting here that the high point of imperialism in the 1920s and 1930s, and trade up to the Second World War, was a period when successive governments were abandoning notions of free trade and introducing 'imperial preference' that imposed taxes on goods from outside the Empire. In 1924 the Empire Exhibition in London aimed to persuade people to buy food and other goods from the Empire's colonies. A major item of interest was a life-sized statue of the Prince of Wales on horseback made entirely out of Canadian butter (Paxman, 2012: 247). This melted quite easily. In 1926 the government set up an Empire Marketing Board that produced 72 reports in 10 years extolling imperial trade. Examples of such reports were *A calendar of fruits and vegetables from the Empire* and a report on *Why every woman should buy British (and Empire)*. In this last was a recipe for an Empire Christmas pudding with ingredients to be sourced from all corners of the colonised countries. A filmed ceremony was held on 20 December 1926 in the headquarters of the London Overseas League, with turbaned Indian servants carrying in the required currants, sultanas, flour and suet, candied peel and spices, with even Irish eggs and Cyprus brandy included. As a symbol of national and imperial pride the Royal family were induced to eat the pudding at Christmas (Collingham, 2017: 270). The official caterer for the Indian pavilion at the Empire Exhibition was Mr Veeraswamy, who later opened the first Indian restaurant in Regent Street in London, noted for preparing Balti (bucket) food. The restaurant became popular with fashionable society. By 2017 immigration officials were questioning the arrival of Indian chefs to carry on cooking what has become some of the nation's favourite food.

Brexit after Empire

In the decolonisation of the 1950s and 1960s Britain abandoned its protection of post-imperial goods, although instigating a lucrative and sometimes illegal arms trade. The British Empire was finally considered to be dying after 1956, with the debacle over trying to retain the Suez Canal in Egypt after President Nasser nationalised what was considered a high road to India for shipping (Lloyd, 1984). In 1972 the country joined the European Economic Community (EEC), which was finally voted for in a referendum in early 1975. Conservative politicians, as veteran Tory MP Kenneth Clarke recorded, were eager to join the

European trading block (Clarke, 2016), although many Labour MPs were opposed. Forty years later, in a U-turn Margaret Thatcher would not have approved of, since she signed the 1986 Act that created a Single Market for European trading, the Conservative Eurosceptics and those campaigning to leave the EU seemed convinced that leaving the EU and its trade arrangements would be a marvellous opportunity to renew imperial trade.

When the British public were asked in 2016 whether to leave the EU after some 40 years or remain in what had become a 'club' of 28 member states, the United Kingdom Independence Party (UKIP) claimed in its election literature that, 'Outside the EU the world is our oyster and the Commonwealth the pearl within'. In 2017 the then Foreign Secretary Boris Johnson published his 'Vision for a bold, thriving Britain after Brexit' as 'we will be able to get on and do free trade deals, not least with the fastest growing Commonwealth economies' (Johnson, 2017a). Negotiations over the years of Brexit have been dominated by claims and counter-claims over the trade benefits offered by EU membership as against benefits from global trading, although as Jonty Bloom (2017) and others have pointed out, things have changed since European empires crumbled, and UK trade would be subject to global trade rules that could take years to negotiate.

If schooling from the 19th century presented the British Empire as a romanticised and seemingly permanent entity that was mainly a force for good, and whose demise was to be regretted, no such romanticism was ever attached to the EU by the British. Those in other European countries may have been romantic enough to think, as did Václav Havel, the playwright imprisoned under Soviet rule, and the first President of a free Czechoslovakia in 1989, that 'Europe is attempting to create a new kind of order through the process on unification, in which no one more powerful will be able to suppress anyone less powerful' (quoted in Albright, 2018: 4). But few British political leaders were really enthusiastic for a 'European Project', and opposition to closer ties with near neighbours remained strong. The British government refused to join the moves towards European economic union in the 1950s, and then both Conservative and Labour leaders made unsuccessful attempts to join in the 1960s and 1970s, vetoed by the French President General de Gaulle. In the 1970s, after long negotiations, the country voted for what was then a European Economic Community (17.3 million in favour, 8.4 million against). Mrs Thatcher disputed levels of British contributions to the EEC but signed up for a Single Market in 1986. In 1988 she made a speech in Bruges opposing any further integration, with some leading Conservatives embracing 'Euroscepticism' and keeping up a permanent opposition. Despite this, former Prime Minister John Major signed the Maastricht Treaty in 1992, creating a European Union.

As Chancellor of the Exchequer in a Labour government, Gordon Brown kept the country out of the European common currency – the euro – but in 2003 Tony Blair made a speech declaring that while Britain must remain a close ally of the USA, which included joining wars in the Middle East, 'Britain must be at the heart of Europe' (Blair, 2003). He was one of only three leaders in EU countries in 2004 that allowed more free movement of labour. The demands made by UKIP and its Member of the European Parliament (MEP), Nigel Farage, tended to drown out any positive measures membership of the EU brought, and the persistent opposition to EU migrant workers was considered to be a major reason for the 'Leave' vote in June 2016. The 'Leave' campaigners secured a victory of 51.9% of the vote, 17.4 million in favour of leaving, 16.3 million in favour of remaining, and 28% of the electorate did not vote at all. There was considerable debate after the vote as to which groups voted 'Remain' or 'Leave'. A poll by Lord Ashcroft suggested it was the young, the old and northerners who were most in favour of leaving the EU (Speed, 2016). Further analysis found that many of the young did not or could not vote, and it was mainly middle-aged and older Conservative voters who were most in favour of leaving. Scotland, Northern Ireland and the Welsh-speaking areas of Wales voted to 'Remain', as did London, including poorer areas of London (Hennig and Dorling, 2016). Two years after the vote, it was becoming clear just how much money had been spent by rich men on trying to influence the vote, especially by digital advertising (Moore and Ramsey, 2017).

The Brexit vote and subsequent debates and legislation have been dominated by the perpetuation of a generalised hostility to 'immigrants'. The post-war arrival at the instigation of the government and businesses of labour from the Caribbean and the Asian subcontinent, as colonised countries gradually won their independence, were joined over the years by refugees and asylum-seekers from global conflicts. These included workers from European countries under the free movement of labour after 1992. All these groups have long been persistently lumped together as unwanted immigrants, despite their contribution to the UK economy and culture. The majority of people in these groups are British citizens who are the Black British or British Asian descendants from post-war migration. As Paul Warmington has eloquently pointed out,

> The term "black" has a complex history. It can, depending on context, denote either people of African/African-Caribbean descent or, via discourses of "political blackness", the wider assembly of African, African-Caribbean, Asian, Arabic and mixed race people constructed in the post-war period of immigration – something akin to the collective referred to in the USA as people of colour. (Warmington, 2014: 5)

Antagonism to different skin colours was joined from the 1990s with antagonism to economic migration from European countries under the EU rules of free movement of capital and labour. Such hostility was encouraged by Eurosceptic politicians, much of the media and others, influencing many people to vote to leave the EU. Scare stories of immigrants and foreigners taking resources, jobs, benefits, homes, schools and health facilities could be traced back to the 19th century, and continued to influence the Brexit debates.

Legends of imperial triumphs and conquests formed the basis for a widespread belief in a superior British heritage, and the pervasive notion, shared across all social classes, that the white British had economic, moral and intellectual superiority over the former colonised people, and indeed, over all 'foreigners'. This is perhaps the most damaging legacy of the long good-bye of empire. Central to the future education of all young people must be some understanding of the rise and fall of the British

Empire, and the way that current race, class, migration and trade conflicts are rooted in imperial and colonial history. Most (white) British writing on empire assumes that whether good or bad, the British Empire was 'Great' in terms of its power and importance.

Post-imperial views

There is now a growing literature, produced by many black and minority scholars, documenting the past and current experiences of racial and cultural groups who are of immigrant descent, and for whom the British Empire and its aftermath was not 'Great'. A post-colonial literature is documenting the consequences of empires (Bhambra and Narayan, 2016; Chantiluke et al, 2018), and increasingly published are the stories of those regarded as *Bloody Foreigners* (Winder, 2004), Black British settlers (Fryer, 1984; Olusoga, 2016), the future of multiculturalism after empire (Gilroy, 2004), and the black intellectuals and activists who have acted as agents for social change in Britain (Warmington, 2014). There are also analyses of 'British identity' from the point of view of the previously colonised (Mishra, 2017), how *White privilege* works (Bhopal, 2018) and *Why I'm no longer talking about race* (Eddo-Lodge, 2017), plus writing revealing negative policy towards British Islam and the demonisation of Muslims as an 'enemy within' (Warsi, 2017). These, and many more, are now part of post-imperial literature.

University students in 2017 were calling for a decolonisation of English literature syllabuses, and eminent black and minority ethnic writers produced their list of books for essential reading (Kureishi et al, 2017). Increasingly, on social media and in blogs and articles, journalists, activists and academics from the former colonised countries and those settled in Britain are recording their views that British government perceptions of the future place of the country in the world is based on delusions of empire and an unwillingness to recognise a diminished role in the world, especially in the current debates on immigration. To repeat Kappal, 'The UK cannot harbour dreams of being a global Britain while closing its doors to the world' (Kappal, 2017). Increasingly, in a world where non-black people are in a minority, there is no white exceptionalism except in the minds of white supremacists.

Structure of the book

There are large literatures on the British Empire, the Commonwealth, the incorporation of post-colonial immigrants, other migrants, refugees and asylum-seekers, and education history and policy. This book, as in every history book, is necessarily selective of significant events. Chapter One notes that explanations for the 2016 Brexit vote, trade wars, race and migrant antagonisms and hatreds must start with the British Empire, especially in the later 19th century, when power, wealth and dominance were concentrated in a white world. There is much ignorance among young and old about empire, decolonisation and global migrations. Racial arrogance and assumptions of national superiority have continued into the 21st century. The chapter discusses the development of education in England in the late 19th and early 20th century, combined with events associated with imperialism and its ideologies. It records the way British values and invented traditions, imbued with nationalism, militarism and racial arrogance, were filtered down from elite 'public' schools to secondary and elementary schools, and comments on the teaching, textbooks and youth literature that reflected and entrenched beliefs in the superiority of white people and a distrust of foreigners.

By the 21st century the whole notion of a United Kingdom, the Union with Scotland, Ireland and Wales, was called into question. These countries had been internally colonised by the English in much the same way that the British Empire's overseas colonies had been created. Chapter Two takes the form of a brief overview of the way in which the subjects of these Celtic areas were taken over and regarded as socially and culturally backward, while being dominated politically and exploited for labour. Northern Ireland has emerged as crucially important to the Conservative government after the Brexit vote and the 2017 General Election, as Prime Minister Theresa May became dependent on the votes of the Protestant Democratic Unionist Party (DUP) to put the law required for Brexit in place. The chapter briefly covers the conquest of the countries and attempts to Anglicise them through religion, language and education, the secession of 22 counties to form the Republic of Ireland, and the six remaining counties that included both Catholic and Protestant people. It also notes the ignorance in England of Irish affairs – it took an episode on television on the life of Queen Victoria (ITV, 2017) to rouse interest on social media from people who knew nothing about the Irish famine and the deaths of over a million and emigration of 2 million in the late 1840s. The chapter also notes that the English working class were subject to similar assumptions of intellectual and cultural inferiority, but were encouraged to regard the 'Irish and Blacks' as inferior.

Chapter Three covers the period from 1945 to the 1960s, linking the collapse of the British Empire as former colonies fought for or gained their independence, some with brutality and war, and some more peacefully, with the education systems emerging post Second World War in Britain. While Labour Prime Minister Attlee agreed to Indian independence in 1947, Winston Churchill was opposed to decolonisation and immigration, and even considered the slogan 'Keep Britain White' for the 1955 General Election. Employment needs for labour and the migration of workers from the former colonies set the racist terms for subsequent discussion of immigration and citizenship rights. Immigration legislation enacted during the 1960s was an attempt to control immigration. There were other anti-discrimination Acts attempting to control racism. The period covers the expansion of education from 1945 and the incorporation of immigrant minorities into a class-based education system. While initial notions of assimilation gradually gave way to assertions of cultural pluralism and racial co-existence, the school system did little to inform young people about the realities of decolonisation and why black, Asian and other minority people had arrived in the country. This surely was a period of education for ignorance. Any discussion of the brutalities of decolonisation was missing from public discourse as well as the school and university curriculum. The Commonwealth was claimed by government as an example of international cooperation, but the response to those migrating to work in what they had regarded as the 'mother country' was largely negative. It was also becoming apparent that the British class system embodied a caste-like barrier between citizens of the 'mother country' and those of the British Empire, and all social classes were, to some extent, united in hostility to the arrival of former colonial migrants. By the end of the 1960s politician Enoch Powell was claiming that a sense of being a persecuted minority was growing among working-class people, and middle-class Conservative Associations were firmly against colonial immigration.

By the 1970s any conservative beliefs in paternalistic imperialism, liberal notions of human rights and socialist ideals of a brotherhood of unionised labour had disappeared. Chapter Four documents the ways in which former colonised subjects with a variety of backgrounds, languages and religions were openly regarded as a threat to British identity. Political moves included more immigration control, campaigns for repatriation and politicians claiming British culture was being 'swamped'. Although the country voted early in 1975 to support entry into a European Economic Community, and there was a further anti-discrimination Act, the early 1980s saw violent clashes between the police and young minorities. The chapter records changing education policies, with moves towards comprehensive education, anxiety that education was failing to prepare young people for work, subsuming minorities under the label 'disadvantaged' and worries about their low school achievements. Although a Green Paper in 1977 had asserted that 'the curriculum appropriate to the imperial past cannot meet the requirements of modern Britain' (DES, 1977), there was little curriculum change until the 1980s, when attempts by teachers, local authorities and academics to change policies in a multicultural and anti-racist direction were met with hostility. Criticism was especially directed at Lord Swann's report, *Education for all*, which suggested focusing on educating all young people and teachers for a multicultural society. The public schools and universities educating many current politicians and civil servants were not notable for embracing curriculum change. Although the Labour Party claimed in 1989 that 'Britain is manifestly a multiracial society with a plurality of cultures', as the country moved from imperial to national status, debates on national identity intensified (Labour Party, 1989).

Chapter Five demonstrates that in a short period of time in the 1990s, more issues and tensions emerged over immigration after the signing of the Maastricht Treaty on European Union in 1992, which guaranteed free movement of capital, services and people. There was also a surge in numbers of refugees and asylum-seekers from global conflicts and more migration of non-Europeans to fill professional and service jobs. Political ideologies of a white indigenous nation became more closely tied to assertions that a white majority were missing out in housing, education and health services. The 1991 Census was the first to include an 'ethnic' question, and the geographical spread of settlement became clearer, with settled minorities mainly embracing notions of Western individualism as well as ethnic assertion. The first Gulf War led to more popular racism directed at Islam, neo-Nazi parties continued to recruit young whites, and the murder of student Stephen Lawrence in 1993 became a focus for the effects of racism. The chapter documents the education legislation from 1988 to 1996 that encompassed almost every aspect of education, and turned education into a marketplace, stressing parental choice and competition between schools and students. New disadvantages for minority young people emerged. The government took control of the curriculum and assessment, and multicultural dimensions were summarily dismissed. Teacher preparation and university courses on race and education disappeared over the decade and multiculturalism was derided. Prime Minister John Major left office in 1997, asserting that policies must be colour-blind, and that they must just tackle disadvantage.

New Labour came to power in 1997 asserting a commitment to social and racial justice, affirming that a modern nation valued diversity and recognised the rights of settled minorities and the inequalities they faced. Chapters Six and Seven note initial equitable policies – a Human Rights Act, state funding for Muslim schools alongside other faiths, the Stephen Lawrence Inquiry and an Ethnic Minority Achievement Grant – but New Labour continued Conservative policies of choice and competition that exacerbated social and racial segregation. The introduction of academies in 2002 eventually led to a breakdown in a national democratic system of state education. Rioting in northern towns led to further assertions that 'multiculturalism has failed' and that community cohesion should be stressed. A focus on attainment in basic school subjects was not accompanied by much curriculum change to help young people to understand their world, apart from a Black History Month that underlined the marginalisation of minorities. A report from The Runnymede Trust on *The future of multi-ethnic Britain* (Parekh, 2000), commissioned by Jack Straw, then Home Secretary, was attacked in the right-wing media and promptly disowned by the government.

Prime Minister Blair supported seven wars during his tenure. The invasion of Afghanistan in 2001 and Iraq in 2003 helped to radicalise a small number of young Muslims and led to a scapegoating of all Muslims. Blair's ending of restrictions on Eastern European migrants led to more antagonism to economic migration, an important factor in the Brexit vote. Settled minorities continued to be conflated with new migrants and asylum-seekers. The Blair–Brown governments implemented further immigration control. In 2010, a Borders, Citizenship and Immigration Act was passed at the same time as an Equalities Act, which notionally targeted discrimination by race, religion, gender and sexual orientation, disability and unequal pay. Declared goals of preparing all young people for an ethnically diverse society was not matched by action, and the education of minorities was set against that of a white working class. A Labour-instigated review led to university fees being raised to £9,000 a year by the succeeding Coalition government, which resulted in a whole generation of young people being landed with debt virtually for life.

Chapter Eight covers the Coalition/Conservative period of government to 2010-15 and the Conservative government from 2015 to June, 2016, which was notable for austerity policies that affected working-class people, whether white or minority. There was no acknowledgement that Britain had become a rich country by exploiting the Empire, and austerity was justified by blaming previous Labour governments, unions, immigrants and the poor claiming benefits. The country was becoming more divided than ever into richer and poorer areas, with education 'choice' making this worse. David Cameron, having declared in 2009 that he would never hold a referendum on leaving the EU, changed his mind, and after trying to 'reform' EU rules, decided to hold a referendum. The government was especially taken up with condemning riots and violence by young people, especially if they were poor or minorities or both, with measures to prevent young Muslims being radicalised. The demonisation of Muslims and Islam reached a peak during the period, with a hysterical reaction to a supposed 'Trojan Horse' infiltration of schools by Islamists. British values were to be taught in schools while the whole system was becoming more undemocratic via academies, free schools and the control of teachers. University education was reformed by increasing tuition fees and creating a private company to administer student loans. Curriculum 'reforms' introduced by Education Secretary Michael Gove ensured a narrowing of the curriculum and more competitive testing. The distortion of the realities of empire and colonialism and the lack of support for education policies and practices that might have alleviated racism, xenophobia and hostility directed against minorities and 'foreigners' became more evident. The absorption of migrants and minorities into what was now a contentious 'United Kingdom' continued to be contested. Education continued to reflect a hierarchical and status-based class system, with competitive jockeying for position encouraged by a diversity of schools, higher education and employment chances.

Chapter Nine covers the period from June 2016 to 2018, surely one of the most turbulent periods in British political history, as parties, individuals and the EU slugged it out to present some kind of Brexit to the British public, who were divided by nation, class, age, race, gender and geography. Those tasked with an exit from the EU appeared at first to have little understanding of the past or present realities, with civil servants joking that an 'Empire 2.0' could be created. There can be no conclusions in this book to the situation created by the self-interest of politicians and the confused xenophobia of the public. After two years of often vicious argument between 'hard Brexiteers' and more moderate Conservative MPs, in July 2018 Prime Minister Theresa May produced a scheme for a 'soft Brexit', which promptly caused the resignation of a number of ministers including the Foreign Secretary Boris Johnson. There can be no answers as to whether future sovereignty and national identity will include or exclude racial and minority ethnic groups, or how the country will function without migration. Black and other minorities have made advances into a plural co-existence in a reluctant society, and some younger people appear to be 'learning to live together' and turning to political parties that do not appear so ethnocentric. But there are few signs that those in charge of education at all levels are able or willing to think through what an education system for a globally oriented, racially and socially just education system would look like. There is little evidence in schools or higher education that the content of learning has come to terms with a post-imperial role and Britain's changed position in the world. Recent government interventions suggest an adherence to an imperial version of the past, with no plans to challenge political or public ignorance, and the misinformation that was evident during the Brexit vote and beyond. The consequences of xenophobic and racist understandings of past decades will not be changed by teaching questionable 'British values' and continuing to blame migrants and minorities for social and economic ills that are the consequences of long-term policies and austerity programmes that impoverished millions of working people. Ignorance of the past and presentation of a mythological future, where Britain is 'Great' again, are more likely to lead to a perpetuation of unpleasant, nationalist sentiment and a continuation of racial and migrant scapegoating as the country comes to terms with the status of a 'third country'.

Note

[1]   There is a large international literature discussing the concepts of race and ethnicity from the time of the pseudo-science of the 19th century to the 21st-century behavioural geneticists. Much of the imperial literature assumed the superiority of a white 'race', and later much has been devoted to explaining the falsity of this ideology. This book does not review this literature but see, for example, Gould (1981), Rex (1986), Rose and Rose (2012) and Cole (2018). It uses the changing terminology of the periods discussed, and takes for granted that the problems of racism and xenophobia are major problems facing the world at the present time. As Cole has noted, 'racism is a frighteningly real, burning and omnipresent issue' (Cole, 2018).

1

Empire and ethnocentric education

> What is Empire but the predominance of Race … do we not hail in this, less than the energy and fortune of a race, than in the supreme direction of the Almighty? (Lord Rosebery, 1900)

> The unbroken life of the English nation over a thousand years or more is a phenomenon unique in history … from this continuous life of a united people in its island home spring … all that is peculiar to the gifts and the achievements of the British nation. (Enoch Powell, quoted in Lord Howard of Rising, 2014: 146)

Trying to explain the British Empire to most young people, unless they have specifically 'done a module' on some aspect, is to invite incomprehension. Even older people, schooled during decolonisation, have little knowledge about it, the Commonwealth or recent global migrations, although regrets for a lost empire still linger. But explaining the 2016 Brexit vote, trade wars and race and migrant antagonisms must start with the British Empire, specifically in the later 19th century, when power, wealth and trade dominance were concentrated in a predominantly white world. Any early 19th-century humanitarian notions, which had influenced legislation ending slavery, gave way, as more countries were added to the Empire, to beliefs that 'black and brown subjects were natural inferiors' (Lloyd, 1984: 180). Beliefs that God was in favour of white supremacy and imperial expansion were widely embraced, as Lord Rosebery, in his inaugural address as Rector of the University of Glasgow in 1900, indicated. Queen Victoria was proclaimed Empress of India in 1877, and there was a 'scramble' for imperial control of African countries by major European powers in 1884. American historian David Goldberg wrote that by the late 19th century, race 'had assumed throughout the European orbit a sense of naturalness … a more or less taken for granted marking of social arrangements … an assumed givenness and inevitability in the ascription of superiority and inferiority' (Goldberg, 2009: 3). But he also noted that it took hard work to reproduce social and racial arrangements. Science and literature, scripture and law, culture and political rhetoric were co-opted to establish assumptions of white superiority.

Although in 1805 Prime Minister William Pitt and Emperor Napoleon Bonaparte were famously lampooned via a cartoon of a plum pudding representing the globe for dividing the world up between them, the 1880s to the 1930s was the high point of imperial conquests and trade that benefited Britain. Imperial expansion by this time was dedicated to capturing markets and claiming natural resources in colonised countries for exploitation. An ignorance of the actual territories comprising the British Empire continued into the 20th century, some people being confused in 1982 when the Argentineans invaded the Falkland Islands, which many thought were Scottish islands. Imperial arrogance was evident during this war, with naval officer David Tinker writing that, 'The navy felt that we were British and they (the Argentineans) were wogs, and that made all the difference' (Tinker, 1982: 178). David was killed aged 26, in the war.

Although she never visited, Victoria was interested in India, and in 1895 she formed a friendship with her Indian servant Abdul Karim ('the Munshi') which shocked her courtiers, a film of this being released in 2017.[1] But it was Victorian beliefs in racial superiority, underpinned by pseudo-scientific rationalisations for political and economic takeovers and exploitation of other countries, plus renewed militarism and notions of patriotism, that created the English assumptions of nationalistic superiority that survives to the present day. Enoch Powell (of whom more in later chapters) could, in a speech in 1961, refer to distant continents and strange races even while colonies in those continents were fighting for independence and Britain was becoming more multiracial, multicultural and multireligious. His appeal was as a major advocate of an imperialist ideology and a popularist nationalism that, in the 21st century, has found expression in right-wing politics in and out of parliaments, and in a resurgence of white supremacist activities in Europe and the USA.

The aim of this chapter is to link some significant events in the development of education in England in the 19th and 20th centuries with imperial events and ideologies. This was a period when, as Aminul Hoque noted, a rhetoric of coloniser versus the colonised, powerful versus powerless, civilised versus uncivilised, modern versus backward, educated versus uneducated, helped shape and institutionalise race, class and gender relations between white people and those from the 'dark continents' of Africa and Asia (Hoque, 2015). The chapter indicates the way in which 'British values', imbued with nationalism, militarism and racial arrogance, were filtered down from public schools to secondary and elementary schools through an imperially oriented curriculum, textbooks and juvenile literature that reflected and entrenched beliefs in the superiority of white people and a distrust of foreigners.

Education and empire

In Andrea's Levy's novel *Small island*, the child Queenie is taken by her father to the Empire Exhibition in 1924. Watching a black woman skilfully weaving cloth, she was told that 'We've got machines to do that' and 'They're not civilised, they only understand drums' (Levy, 2004: 5). In the real world at this time, an African-American classical pianist Florence Price was composing her Symphony No 1 in E minor, in which she incorporated some drumming, drums being forbidden under slave regimes in case secret messages were transmitted. Price's symphony was premiered by the Chicago Symphony Orchestra in 1932, and in 2018 featured in a concert by the Cheltenham Philharmonic Orchestra in England. There has always been more interest in how the British Empire influenced education in colonised countries than in how schools taught about empire to the children of the imperialists in Britain (McCulloch, 2009). Lord Macaulay did his best by asserting that he had not found one Orientalist 'who could deny that a single shelf of a good European library was worth the whole literature of India and Arabia' (quoted in Moorhouse, 1984: 77). Connecting imperial events and education developments, and the ideologies and beliefs that imbued imperialists and educators in Britain from the high point of empire to eventual decline, is important, as whatever the outcome of the vote to leave the EU, what was a United Kingdom will be a much diminished and disunited country. The point to be made, sustained in future chapters, is that education at all levels has never come to terms with the imperial xenophobia, arrogance and ignorance that continues to be demonstrated before and after the Brexit vote and subsequent negotiations to leave the EU.

The 1880s through to the 1930s was a time when, after vast areas of Africa and Asia were taken over, the empire was at its height, and a range of invented imperial traditions were developing. The period coincided with a social class-based expansion of mass education in England. Historians of education agreed that the struggle to deliver education to the working classes over the 19th century mirrored a hierarchical social structure that placed their schooling firmly within the lower layers of the social class pyramid. Brian Simon, in his studies of education from the 18th to the 20th centuries, noted that after universal secondary education developed, class and interest group conflicts persisted, but what was actually taught in schools was always influenced by the public (non-state private) schools attended by the upper-class young. The values underpinning schooling filtered down from public to grammar to elementary schooling (Simon, 1960, 1990). With some prescience, he noted that from the later 19th century the role of examinations became more important, especially in these public schools. As one maths textbook of 1892 pointed out, 'many persons who are supposed to have received the best education the country affords, are in matters of numerical information ignorant and helpless, in a manner which places them far below members of the middle classes' (Colenso, 1892: introduction). Future engineers and merchants of the British Empire needed to be able to work out the gross annual receipts and dividends to British shareholders who invested in railways, especially in India, where money needed to be converted to and from rupees, and they needed to be examined on their knowledge.[2] While upper-class boys were being trained to run the empire, the imperial subjects were not so lucky. Some elite schools in colonial countries, set up along the lines of English public schools, were educating colonial elites, but the masses had little or no schooling. When the British finally did leave India, the illiteracy rate was 80-85% across the country.

Significant events

1864	Report of the Clarendon Commission on English public schools
1868	Schools Inquiry Commission
1869	Francis Galton (*Hereditary genius*) and the rise of Social Darwinism
1870	Education (Elementary) Act
1885/89	Egerton report on defective children
1899-1902	Boer War and concern over (white) racial deterioration
1902	Education Act
1905	Aliens Act
1906	Labour Party formed
1914-1918	First World War
1916	Sykes–Picot Agreement
1917	Balfour Declaration
1919	Scheme to distribute land in Kenya to white European officers
1919	Jallianwalla Bagh massacre; Indian Independence movement
1922	Labour Party manifesto, *Education for all* (school leaving age raised to 14)
1924	Empire Exhibition at Wembley
1926	Empire Marketing Board set up
1931	Mahatma Gandhi visits Lancashire
1930s	42 million British subjects, 500 million imperial subjects
1939-1945	Second World War

In 1864 the Clarendon Commission reported on the top nine public schools. It was chaired by the Earl of Clarendon, whose family owned land in Jamaica and who had been connected to slavery and the sugar trade. Recommendations were made to improve the organisation and curriculum of the schools, a culture of athleticism was encouraged, and the schools encouraged belief in the superior moral virtue of the upper-class boys they were educating. Cheltenham College claimed it was a training place for defenders of the empire; Haileybury and Marlborough schools were praised as places where those going out to rule the Empire 'lived and died as officers and gentlemen' (Simon, 1960: 328). Commissions and reports on the then existing grammar schools for the middle classes and on elementary education led to the conclusion that 'the different classes of society … require different teaching' (Schools Inquiry Commission, 1868). Although public schools retained their emphasis on the classics, their schools and those for the middle classes were to have a grounding in maths, science, English, history and geography.

An 1870 Education Act created mass elementary education for the working classes, concentrating on literacy, numeracy, moral and manual training, although it was not until 1876 that schooling to age 12 was made compulsory. A Moral Instruction League was influential enough for a syllabus for moral teaching to be placed into the 1906 Code of Regulations for elementary schools. There were similar intentions behind sending missionaries out to moralise to the colonised and teaching the working class to be well behaved and moral. Francis Galton, a cousin of Charles Darwin, through his writings on *Hereditary genius* (1869), helped to popularise Social Darwinism and eugenic theories, through which it was eventually suggested that low ability, mental defect, delinquency, crime, prostitution, illegitimacy and even unemployment were inherited tendencies in the lower social classes (RCCCFM, 1908). A Royal Commission was set up in 1885 to report on the education of those considered physically and mentally defective, chaired by Lord Egerton, whose family had also become wealthy by interests in the West Indian sugar trade (Egerton Commission, 1889). Eugenic theories underpinned beliefs in the inferior intellect of the lower classes and of the colonised.

Passion for the classification of supposed races along biological lines developed around the same time as eugenic theories were spreading. A white Caucasoid 'race' was supposedly superior to Mongoloid and Negroid 'races'. In 1866 John Langton Down explained Mongolism (later Down's syndrome) as having an appearance similar to what was described as a Mongoloid race (Tomlinson, 2017: 33). The stereotypes of the defective, ignorant and idle lower working classes in England were similar to the stereotypes of lazy and stupid 'natives' overseas. Assumptions of biological and cultural deficiencies in the lower classes and in other supposed races persisted into the 20th and 21st centuries. In 1899 the British government became concerned about a 'degenerate' working class while recruiting for the Boer War against Dutch settlers in South Africa. Army recruits were discovered to be weak and malnourished, and in the final wars of imperial expansion, demonstrated to an Edwardian elite a deterioration of what was termed the (white) 'British race'. Efforts were made to improve the health of school children – a schools medical service was set up in 1907. Baden Powell created his Boy Scout movement in 1908 with the intention of transforming 'pale narrow-chested miserable specimens who smoked, loafed and practised self-abuse' into a healthy race (quoted in Brendon, 2007: 226), although recruits to the 1914 First World War infantry were deemed not as healthy as some of the soldiers who had arrived from the Empire to help fight a European war.

Despite the war being won with the help of recruits from the Empire, especially from India and African countries, and with labourers from China, in 1918 the government set up a scheme to distribute some of the best land in Kenya to white Europeans who had fought for 'King and Country' (Best, 1979). In 2018 the artist William Kentridge set up a project in the Tate Modern Turbine Hall in London, to illustrate that the spread of the First Word War cost millions of African lives, as many people were conscripted by force to join, and the British were eager to take over the German colonies in East Africa. Ironically, some Africans joined in the war thinking that if they took part alongside white soldiers, they would be regarded as equals and given rights afterwards (Kentridge, quoted in Aspden, 2018). Meanwhile, in 1916 the Sykes–Picot Agreement, named after the British and French diplomats who signed it, carved up the Middle East territories between these countries, setting the stage for a perpetuation of conflicts into the 21st century. The 1917 Balfour Declaration concerning Palestine and a Jewish Homeland similarly set up future conflicts over land. Hostility to immigrants and a closing of free movement from Europe was evident via the Aliens Act 1905. This gave the Home Office responsibility for immigration, and was introduced to control the numbers of Jewish settlers arriving from Eastern Europe and Russia, who settled in the poor areas in London's East End. This Act was partly in response to claims that 7 million immigrants would swamp British shores (although in the previous two decades 2 million Britons had emigrated). In 1900 a British Brotherhood League collected 45,000 signatures on a petition against immigration and to 'stop Britain being a dumping ground for the scum of Europe' (Benewick, 1969: introduction). This League was subsequently overtaken by an Immigrant Reform Association and Oswald Mosley's National Union of Fascists.

Labour and education, 1900-39

By the early 1900s there were signs that Western European imperialism might be faltering. Denis Lawton, in his study of the Labour Party and education from 1900, wrote that the Boer War indicated to Gandhi that the British were not invincible and could be opposed in India (Lawton, 2005: 18). The Russian Revolution, First World War and the ending of the Hapsburg Empire suggested that empires and their colonies could not last for ever. But English education, dominated by a public school-educated aristocracy and civil service, persisted in its role of propping up the social structure and imperial overtones. In the 1890s, only around 2.5% of young people, largely upper and middle class, received a secondary education. Some elementary schools had developed a higher elementary education for working-class children with grants from local school boards. A legal judgment put a stop to this in 1900, and local school boards were abolished in 1902. The Duke of Devonshire, one of the country's richest landowners, had, along with other aristocrats, worried that local school boards and trade unions were demanding a secondary education for all children rather than a narrow selection of 'scholarship' children. Another rich Irish landowner, the Marquis of Londonderry, appointed as President of the National Board of Education in August 1902, oversaw the (Balfour) Education Act 1902. This was largely the work of civil servant Robert Morant, whose views on education were essentially based on upper-class assumptions of social stability (Lawton, 2005: 12). The Act ensured that only those working-class children, with what was considered to be of exceptional ability, could join children whose parents could pay secondary school fees.

The Labour Party, formed in 1906, led the movement for secondary education for all, with the school-leaving age raised to 14 in 1922, although some in the Party still argued for selective schooling. Another Lord to chair the Board of Education, Lord Eustace Percy from the Duke of Northumberland's wealthy family, also suggested that secondary education ought to remain exclusive. The Hadow Consultative Committee reported on *The education of the adolescent* in 1926, and recommended selection by 'differentiation' – a secondary modern school would have a four-year course 'with a realistic and practical trend' (Board of Education, 1927: 95), while grammar schools would pursue a literary and scientific curriculum. Technical and trade schools should develop to cater for the needs of local industry. Any possibility of comprehensive schooling disappeared for some years, and by 1939 and the start of the Second World War, 88% of young people had left school by the age of 14. The governments formed after 1931 were more interested in the structures of education and the eventual separation of children through the Education Act 1944 into different kinds of secondary schooling than in the content of what was actually taught, apart from general agreement that grammar schools should be 'academic'. Secondary modern schools were for children who 'would not need any measure of technical skills or knowledge' (Ministry of Education, 1946: 13).

While the Empire was beginning to decline, the 1919 Jallianwalla Bagh massacre in Amritsar in India, when troops fired on an unarmed crowd gathered in response to Mahatma Gandhi's campaign for passive resistance to British rule, created unease among the working class in England. In 1931, when Gandhi visited Britain, he was welcomed ecstatically by mill workers in Lancashire, who recognised a connection between imperial rule and their class position. During the 1920s and 1930s, trade with the Empire, encouraged by protectionism and 'imperial preference', at least ensured the working classes were fed, and there were attempts to boost patriotism through Empire Days and the Empire Exhibition at Wembley. Despite the Empire Christmas pudding that the Royal family were induced to eat, enthusiasm for empire needed nourishing, and imperial propaganda and education served this purpose.

History, values and curriculum

What constitutes a curriculum at all levels in education is a product of the values and decisions of the dominant social and political groups of the time. What developed as 'the curriculum' in English state schools, despite constant changes and political interference, continued to be influenced by a period of imperial enthusiasm and a final expansion of the British empire, and certainly excluded discussion of the more unpleasant realities of British rule. Raymond Williams, a perceptive analyst of cultural values in education, noted in the 1960s 'the fact about our present (school) curriculum is that it was essentially created in the 19th century' (Williams, 1965: 171). It was during this period that many aspects of what is regarded as 'British culture and values' came to be reflected in the curriculum. What was acceptable curriculum knowledge would now be regarded as ideological manipulation, as the selection of what passes for curriculum knowledge at any one time depends on the values of controlling elites and their views and interests. It is not surprising that imperial values permeated education and curricula for so long. Keith Joseph, leaving office as Secretary of State for Education in 1985, reiterated a mythologised view of British values. Referring to a government policy for an ethnically mixed society, he wrote that:

> British history and cultural traditions are, or will become, part of the cultural heritage of all who live in this country ... schools should be responsible for trying to transmit British culture, enriched as it has been by so many traditions. (Joseph, 1986: 8)

The problem remains that many of the traditions and values were and are highly questionable in terms of democracy, tolerance and justice, with imperial contacts largely taking the form of military conquest, appropriation of land and wealth, slavery, forced labour and denial of human rights. Close scrutiny of 'the stories we tell ourselves', as Fred Inglis (1985) pointed out, are often too uncomfortable and disgusting. Just 20 years before, in the early 1960s during African opposition to a white-dominated Central African Federation, captured African fighters had heavy stones tied to their penises for hours (Williams, 2011), presumably not something Joseph would have wished school children to know about.

The 19th- and early 20th-century view of the world was not traditional at all, but spread by education and imperial propaganda into popular consciousness. Propaganda took many forms; a major visual effort to impress visiting dignitaries to the London Foreign Office was the commissioning of a series of grand murals, the final one depicting 'Britannia Pacificatrix', intended to demonstrate a victorious Britain upholding peace. Imperial subjects and the colonised may have had different views of British peace-keeping, but these did not figure in the English school curriculum, and alternative views continued to be resisted. During the 20th and into the 21st century, teachers in schools, and increasingly in universities, have been subject to more political direction and control, and the ethnocentric nature of schooling has only changed slowly. School pupils may now be less likely to enquire of Zimbabwean actors, as they did of those visiting Gloucestershire schools in 1988, whether they were cannibals (Dorras and Walker, 1988), and they may even know that Zimbabwe is a country in Africa, but they are less likely to know some of the more unpalatable history and consequences of imperialism.

Public school influence

The social and political values of the upper classes in England in the 19th century came to influence mass education in England via the public schools, and the world views implicit in the curriculum in these schools filtered into the developing state elementary and secondary schools in the early 20th century. In a 2018 analysis of the privileges that still come with a public school education, Robert Verkaik pointed out that 'Public schools have helped to write British history. They have been cheerleaders for colonialism and controlled the narrative of Empire' (Verkaik, 2018: 45). A clear illustration of this was provided by John Lawson Walton, an exponent of the duties of government to empire, who wrote in *The Contemporary Review* in 1899 that 'since the energies of the British race had given them their empire' and as 'British rule of every race brought within its sphere has the incalculable benefits of just law, free trade and considerate government', it was the duty of public schools to provide competent rulers (Lawson–Walton,

1899: 306). In his studies of images of empire in Victorian and Edwardian public schools, Mangan (1980, 1986) concluded that the British Empire was run by public school boys and the values imbibed by public school boys eventually influenced all school pupils. An awareness of empire among public school boys, allied to themes of militarism and patriotic self-sacrifice, were instilled by public school head teachers and staff, most of whom were committed imperialists.

W.H. Moss, Head of Shrewsbury School from 1872 to 1908, believed that God had entrusted England with the task of creating a Christian Empire held together by military means, and set up one of the first Cadet Corps with competitions in shooting and drill. He invited serving Generals to review the boys' parades. He also recommended training Army officers so that 'boys with brains and character would be would be available for the preservation of English dominions in times of war', and their public school ideals would permeate down the ranks of soldiers (Mangan, 1986: 119). J.E.C. Weldon, Head of Harrow School, was another enthusiastic proponent of empire. He read a paper to the Royal Colonial Institute in 1895 on 'The Imperial aspects of education', arguing that 'The boys of today are the statesmen and administrators of the future, in their hands is the future of the British Empire.' He believed in the moral superiority of white people to govern their 'racial inferiors' and to demand 'instinctive obedience' from imperial subjects, and on one occasion approved of a boy beating up an Egyptian fellow student who had 'said something bad about the British race' (quoted in Mangan, 1986: 121). One of Weldon's recent pupils, Winston Churchill, was some 60 years later to suggest that 'Keep Britain White' might be a slogan in the 1955 General Election campaign.

In Scotland, H.H. Almond, Head of Loretto School in Edinburgh from 1862 to 1903, also reflected the values of imperial government, militarism, moral and religious superiority over imperial subjects and the healthy discipline acquired on the games field. He delivered an annual lecture on 'The divine governance of nations', in which he asserted that God's purpose for the British was to guide world history, and the major purpose of a public school was to create neo-imperial warriors. In the school magazines of Eton, Haileybury and Cheltenham College, the public school boy was defined as a warrior patriot, a role enthusiastically embraced by Fettes, the Scottish public school opened in 1870. From 1966 to 1971 Anthony Charles Lynton Blair, later the British Prime Minister, attended this school, and although he was reportedly more interested in rock music than militarism, he actually led the country into seven wars during his ministerial tenure. The school magazine, *The Fettesian*, with a first edition in 1878, excelled in 'strident jingoism' (Mangan, 1986: 123):

> When once she knows her cause is right.
> Britannia never shuns the fight
> Then Victory crowns the race
> Unconquered country every way
> Britannia o'er the land holds sway
> Britannia rules the waves.
> (*The Fettesian*, 1 April 1878: 13, quoted in Mangan, 1986: 123)

The public schools 'traditions' of military self-sacrifice and imperial patriotic duty gave rise to a host of organisations with these values. These included the Boy Scouts, the Boys' Brigade, the Empire Youth Movement, the Navy League, the League of Empire, the Girls' Patriotic League and many others. The 'traditions' were especially promoted by Eton-educated Reginald Brabazon, 12th Earl of Meath, who was associated with a variety of patriotic organisations, including a Duty and Discipline Movement, and a Lads' Drill Association, intended to prepare a fit and healthy working class. His series of papers on *Essays in duty and discipline* included some eminent contributions from the Archbishop of Canterbury, Winston Churchill, Baden Powell and others, and he was severe on the moral deterioration of women who were failing in their marital and childrearing duties (Lord Meath, 1910).

Eugenics and motherhood came together in movements aimed at women, with the Labour-supporting Fabian Society being keen to educate British girls in motherhood, and the 1904 Board of Education Regulations placing needlework, laundry and cooking for girls in the elementary curriculum. For boys, a

National Service League was formed in 1899, which proposed compulsory military service, and eventually incorporated the Lads' Drill Association, school cadet corps and rifle clubs. The League intended to include working-class boys and its programmes were 'designed to improve national physique and instil a sense of citizenship among the young as well as cleanliness, punctuality, order and discipline in order to improve the industrial and commercial efficiency of nation and Empire' (MacKenzie, 1984: 155). In 1912 it held a conference of Teacher Associations, set up an Imperial Union of Teachers and prepared a series of textbooks and atlases of the British Empire. A more political organisation was the British Empire Union (BEU) founded in 1915 'to increase knowledge of Empire ... and make our people increasingly empire-minded' (quoted in MacKenzie, 1984: 157). This organisation linked empire to capitalism and conservatism, attacked socialism and communism, and survived until 1959, arguing against decolonisation and for protected Commonwealth trade. The BEU, as were many of the imperial organisations, was supported by a public school-educated aristocracy of Dukes, Earls, Lords and Admirals, and also over the years by commercial firms including Castrol, Firestone, Hoover, Morris Motors, Tate & Lyle and Typhoo tea.

Verkaik (2018) pointed out that minor public schools also trained many of the middle classes who were to become the 'bureaucratic workhorses' of the Empire, administering large tracts of imperial lands, but still imbued with the sense of racial and class superiority. He noted that Robert Clive, described by historian Dalrymple (see the Introduction, this book) as a sociopath, attended a grammar school then, briefly, Merchant Taylor's public school in London. Although expelled from the school, their website still places him on a list of 'great men' it has schooled.

Imperial values, education and social class

Historians of the left and right have argued over how far imperial values affected the working class, but in the early 20th century it was becoming clear that the emergence of new nationalisms created a need for new rituals and invented traditions to solidify working-class support for the state. There was a need for more justification for colonial wars, expansion and conquests than was catered for by Social Darwinist ideologies of racial superiority. Glorification of empire found expression in pageantry, school textbooks and juvenile literature, and a filtering down of the imperial values from public schools. It was due to Lord Meath that an Empire Day was created, a Court journal in 1910 explaining that Meath's self-sacrificing devotion to empire was a noble idea to be instilled into the minds of the young (Guest, 1910). There were also Empire Weeks that included patriotic plays, pageants, songs, poems, flags and speeches, and Empire Day persisted until 1958, when it became Commonwealth Day. To a young Robert Roberts, brought up in a Salford slum in the early 20th century, school was a 'gaunt, blackened building, made exciting by learning that there were five oceans and five continents … most of which seemed to belong to us' (Roberts, 1971: 140). The teachers were fed on patriotism helped along by the popular imperialistic book *The expansion of England* (Seeley, 1883) and especially the heroic works of Rudyard Kipling.[3] The children welcomed Empire Day, and the flag waving, processions, bands, uniforms, free mugs and chocolate that accompanied Royal visits.

Roberts detailed the way state school teachers copied their public school 'superiors' in fostering an ethnocentric view of imperial greatness and racial superiority. The public school ethos, distorted by myth, set standards and ideals for slum boys (Roberts, 1971: 142).

In a further study of early 20th-century working-class youth, Humphries (1981) noted that the ideologies of imperialism had a direct appeal to working-class boys, as it reflected any number of their cultural traditions – fighting, gang warfare over street territory, superiority over foreigners and assertion of masculinity. Upper-class beliefs in the social inferiority of the working class and the racial inferiority of the colonised came together, in a language of 'slum monkey', 'brute savages' and 'aping' others. Later in the century, Paul Willis (1977) documented the ways in which fighting, racism and sexism were still part of the values espoused by working-class boys, although these values were similar for upper- and lower-class boys. The major importance of the cultural values that were disseminated from the upper to the working class was that through the influence of imperial propaganda and a distorted school education, the 'lower classes' were encouraged to believe in their economic, political, social and racial superiority over the rest of the Empire. The domestic underclass could become the imperial overclass, and all classes could unite in a comforting, national patriotic solidarity. This (white) class solidarity has demonstrably persisted into the 21st century, and goes some way towards explaining the xenophobia and racism still part of the British heritage and British 'values'.

The influence of textbooks[4]

Justification for imperial expansion, colonial wars and conquests, and the continued dominance over colonised people, was reproduced on a large scale in late Victorian and Edwardian textbooks and juvenile literature, with an Education Code of 1892 recommending ways of teaching about British colonies. The Geographical Society proposed the study of empire geography for secondary schools in 1896, and school geography, history, English and religion all became vehicles for imperial propaganda. This stressed heroic military adventures, great voyages, missionary activity and the subjugation of those Rudyard Kipling eloquently described as 'lesser breeds without the law' (Kipling, 1940). Oxford Professor A.J. Herbertson, a prolific writer of geography textbooks, his *Junior geography* selling over a third of a million copies, urged teachers to make use of geographical manuals and even daily newspapers. His series on *Commercial geography* was intended for students of empire, and of 'non-British civilised lands'. Higher and complex economic civilisations could induce the colonised to produce goods where the inhabitants previously only needed to supply themselves. Thus, 'the intervention of a higher economic civilisation can be seen in parts of Africa, … here the native is not displaced, for he alone can healthily perform the necessary manual labour, but his work is organised by the Europeans, who also ensure the peace without which sound economic progress is impossible' (Herbertson, 1910: 56). His wife, having attended Cheltenham Ladies College, was also a keen geographer, producing *Descriptive geographies from original sources* that echoed these sentiments. Joseph Stembridge's *The world: A general regional geography* (1939) was still used in classrooms in the 1960s, and his paternalistic view stressed the civilising and beneficial influence of Britain's role in helping Africa to modernise:

> Under the guidance of Europeans, Africa is steadily being opened up … doctors and scientists are working to improve the health of the African and missionaries and teachers are educating the people. The single fact remains that the Europeans have brought civilisation to the peoples of Africa, whose standard of living has been raised by their contact with white people. (Stembridge, 1956, 7th edn: 347)

History, introduced into the public school curriculum by Matthew Arnold at Rugby, did not become compulsory in senior and elementary schools until 1900. This was a time when a single ideological slant was introduced into school texts (MacKenzie, 1984: 177). The slant was a convergence of ideas of military conquests, patriotic support for imperial dominance and racial superiority. The past was manipulated to fit current ideals. In textbooks the American Civil War and slavery were glossed over, and moral responsibility for conflict shifted to the colonial countries. Omissions, half-truths and lies encouraged pupils to believe that the territorial and commercial wars fought were ultimately for the benefit of the colonised.

The popular history book recommended by the Board of Education in 1902 suggested that *Men of renown* (the book included three women – all Queens) was a suitable way to teach history to higher elementary classes (Finnemore, 1902). In this text the presentation of 'natives' who fought to resist imperial rule as possessed by evil ill feeling towards their benevolent rulers was a persistent theme, and their cruelty towards women and children was stressed. Sir Henry Havelock and Lord Roberts were described as suppressing the Indian Mutiny of 1857 (known in India as the First War of Independence) in which 'English women and children were called upon to suffer horrors and torture to which one cannot give a name' (Finnemore, 1902: 237). The emotive language of this book, the 'pluck, endurance and heroic bravery' of British troops, was contrasted with the 'fiends incarnate' who were resisting British rule.

The thrill of history (Magraw, 1919), which went into seven editions to 1959, contained chapters extolling men such as David Livingstone and Cecil Rhodes in Africa, Lawrence of Arabia and even Gandhi. In one chapter it describes an old Matabele woman meeting Rhodes who she says is a great chief who will bring peace, justice and plenty to the Matabele. Rhodes is now regarded generally as an imperialist who looted South Africa's diamond mines and oversaw the founding of Rhodesia. He believed the Anglo-Saxon race was the finest in the world (MacFarlane, 2007). Rudyard Kipling and his co-author produced *A school history of England* in 1911, which even then was criticised for its racial overtones, Africans in the West Indies being described as 'lazy, vicious and incapable of serious improvement' (Fletcher and Kipling, 1911: 240), and the Irish came in for strictures on their incapacities.

Kipling's writings, prose and poetry have been influential through the decades, living through films and musicals such as *The Jungle Book* and *The Lion King*, but he specialised in propaganda for empire, his poem 'The White Man's Burden' exemplifying the labour of running an empire (Kipling, 1940). His poetry apparently continued to be popular in public schools. In January 2017, the then Foreign Secretary Boris Johnson, on a visit to Burma (now Myanmar), colonised by the British from 1824 until 1948, attempted to recite the poem 'Mandalay' while in front of a statue of the Buddha at a sacred Buddhist site.[5] The embarrassed British ambassador managed to stop him before the lines 'Bloomin idol made of mud, Wot they call the Great Gawd Budd' (Booth, 2017).

In *New world geographies: Europe* (Stembridge, 1951) – a book still in use in Sussex Down Preparatory School in 1976 – pupils were told on page one that 'Mankind is usually divided into three races: (1) the Caucasian or White Race, (2) The Mongoloid or Yellow Race, (3) The Negro Race.' The Foreign Secretary who quoted Kipling's poetry in a manner likely to offend his hosts was at his preparatory school in the 1970s in East Sussex. An understanding of the world, both in private and in state schools, was influenced by xenophobic geographies and histories and imperialistic poetry, texts that were not the best way to understand Britain's changing place in the world.

University influence

In 1905 a young lecturer at the University of Oxford told his class that instead of Greek that morning they were to study a most important historical event, 'the victory of a non-white people over a white people' (Zimmern, 1926). This was the defeat of Russia by the Japanese in the Russia–Japan war. But in general, university influence on imperial racial superiority could not countenance such a situation, and the white race continued to be presented as superior. Most of the school textbooks and influential literature in the late 19th and early 20th centuries were produced by men who had studied at Oxford or Cambridge, as had their publishers. Universities colluded in the celebration of empire and preferential colonial trade. Professor Herbertson, in his *Commercial geography of the world* (1910) noted above, gave detailed statistics on the imports and exports of 'British Possessions', exports from British South Africa being mainly gold bullion, diamonds and ostrich feathers, the latter presumably to decorate Edwardian ladies' hats.

A Rhodes Chair of Imperial History was set up in 1919 to celebrate a man now regarded as having looted South Africa and Rhodesia. In Oxford, Rhodes House is still named after him. In 2017 Oxford students attempted to have his statue removed from outside Oriel College, but the university was not amused and the statue still stands, as does his portrait in the Department for International Trade in London. Groups of scholars in Oxford and in Cape Town, South Africa, set up movements called 'Rhodes Must Fall'. The book *Rhodes must fall: The struggle to tear out the racist heart of empire* (Chantiluke et al, 2018) noted that this was not simply about pulling down a symbol of British imperialism; it was about confronting the toxic inheritance of the past, and the pernicious influence of colonialism in education to the present day. Professor Halford MacKinder, one of the founders of the London School of Economics and Political Science (LSE), set up a School of Geography in Oxford in 1899, and developed a series of empire lectures for teachers in the 1920s. The Empire

Marketing Board endowed a Professorial Chair at LSE in Imperial Economic Relations in 1926, which was intended to promote protectionist trade and that Empire Christmas pudding. Cambridge-educated Henry Fox-Wilson, first working in South Africa with Cecil Rhodes, and later an MP, set up the Empire Resources Development Committee to protect and develop imperial trade.

Literature for youth

From the 1880s the expansion of popular publishing and the creation of wider readerships came at the same time as the development of mass education and improved literacy. A publishing market that made millions until well after the Second World War was the juvenile literature market of children's magazines, story books and comics. Much of this literature took the form of an adventure tradition full of militarism and patriotism, where 'violence and high spirits became legitimised as part of the moral force of a superior race' (MacKenzie 1984: 199). The adventure literature was mainly designed for boys and many of the fictional tales were set in public schools, which provided another way by which imperial values could be spread. Roberts (1971) wrote of the way he and his friends in back-street Salford became avid for the fictional world of the public school, especially 'Greyfriars', the public school invented by Frank Richards, which was the setting for stories in the popular magazines *Magnet*, *Gem* and *The Boys' Own Paper*. Rudyard Kipling's book *Stalky and Co* (1899) extolled the high spirits, patriotic pride and intrepid bravery of the public school boys destined to be leaders of empire, and this book was the basis for a television series filmed in the 1980s.

An influential magazine produced from the 1880s to 1933 was *Union Jack*, whose editor G.A. Henty had fought in colonial wars. He employed well-known writers for the magazine, including Conan Doyle (of Sherlock Holmes fame), Jules Verne and Robert Stevenson. Henty's schoolboy heroes exhibited both class snobbery and racism, and their superior morality was associated with their superior education and Nordic complexions. Many of the stories were openly anti-black and anti-Semitic, black people being presented as unfit to govern themselves, and the energy and self-reliance of Northern Europeans contrasted with the lethargy and ignorance of 'the natives'. Imperial arrogance became an acceptable value. The Tarzan stories, written by Chicago-born Edgar Rice Burroughs, offered an example of this view of the world, the stories being presented on film, television and in magazines and comic strips. Tarzan's aristocratic breeding (he is really Lord Greystoke) enabled him to be an educated gentleman in the jungle, continually fighting treacherous savage natives. His breeding apparently allowed him to kill black people with deliberate cruelty. In *Tarzan the untamed* Tarzan could not 'resist the pleasures of black-baiting, an amusement and sport in which he grew ever more efficient' (Burroughs, 1919: 29). This included torturing and killing men. Tarzan was called back to the jungle in a film released in 2016, although one review of this film described it as a myth wrestling with history in the mud. But the imperial adventure stories, in which intellect was not prized and physical power and fighting were more important, ensured that 'The world became a vast adventure playground in which Anglo-Saxon superiority can be repeatedly demonstrated vis-à-vis all other races, most of who are depicted as treacherous and evil' (MacKenzie, 1984: 204).

Other stories stressed the romance of empire, which went along with the starched uniforms and plumed hats of British officers and officials. The Seeley Service Library included such titles as *The romance of savage life* and *The romance of missionary heroism*. In these stories the bravery of heroic, white individuals was a constant theme, with naval adventure stories in particular stressing role of the brave Royal Navy:

> England is a gallant little nation, whose power and conquests are obviously the reward of merit, since all opponents are bigger and uglier than she is.… The British tar is superhuman in his bravery, endurance and discipline … the officers are wonderfully good at inspiring their men and able to carry out audacious manoeuvres under the noses of lumbering befuddled foreigners. (Bratton, 1986: 83)

There are parallels here with the Navy's views of the Falklands campaign in 1982. To be white and British provided the moral and ethical base for judging foreigners and races who were always found wanting. While many of these publications went out of print by the 1920s, other publications came to replace them, particularly the comics *Rover* (1922), *Skipper* (1933) and *Hotspur* (1933), and later the *Dandy* and *Beano*, which, in the 1950s, had a circulation of around 2 million. Girls were not well catered for, their major magazine being *Sunny Stories*, mainly written by children's author Enid Blyton until the 1940s. Her story in the first issue in January 1937 introduced a character called the Tricky Golliwog which featured in further stories. The popular writer Angela Brazil, in her stories of girls' boarding schools, wrote a tale of 'A patriotic schoolgirl' in 1918, and Katherine Hughes has documented the 'Dorm feasts and red-hot pashes' that figured in many of Brazil's novels (Hughes, 2015). But in imperial literature girls and women were usually home bodies, admiring men or in need of rescue.

Summary

This chapter has indicated the way in which the development of state education, its values and teachings were inextricably tied up with the ideologies of imperialism, and the values of nationalism, militarism and racial arrogance that filtered down from public schools to secondary and elementary schools to both the middle classes and the 'slum' boys, and that still form the base for many 21st-century views of other nations, races and 'foreigners'. It underpins beliefs that somehow an 'Empire 2.0' will be created after Brexit (Olusoga, 2017). The intensity of ethnocentric beliefs in the glories of empire, and white racial superiority, uncritically reflected in textbooks, university writings, youth literature, films and later television, were reinforced by teaching that did little to combat unthinking acceptance of a value-laden imperial curriculum. To many older people, when questioned about their post-Second World War understandings, a major view was, 'we didn't think about it, the Empire was just there' (personal communication). Imperial nationalism created a unity across social classes, and gave all classes a sense of owning the world.

Earl Attlee, former Labour Prime Minister, a Major in the First World War, Deputy Prime Minister in the Second, and creator of the welfare state, gave the Chichele Lectures at Oxford in 1960. For his first lecture he chose 'Empire and Commonwealth'. In common with Robert's 'slum' boys, he described the excitements of youthful imperialism and 'the great map with large portions coloured red, [which] was an intoxicating vision for a small boy ... we believed in our great imperial vision' (Attlee, 1961: 5). Political opposition to decolonisation persisted until well after the Second World War, as did opposition to educating all children beyond the age of 15. A school-leaving age of 16 was not implemented until 1973, but visions of imperial greatness persisted in the curriculum into the 21st century. Countries colonised internally by the English over the centuries, Ireland, Wales and Scotland, also had mixed relationships with their imperial masters, and this is discussed in the next chapter, when the post-war period of decolonisation and the arrival of former colonial immigrants into Britain is taken up, and those landladies' signs of 'No Dogs, Blacks or Irish' began to appear.

Notes

[1] The film, *Victoria and Abdul*, was released in 2017 by 20th Century Fox (Abdul was known as 'the Munshi', meaning 'teacher').

[2] 'Of the whole cost of constructing a railway, 5/7 is held in shares, and the remaining £400,000 borrowed on mortgage at 5%. Find what amount of gross annual receipts – of which 40% will be required for the working expenses of the line, and 8% for a reserve fund – will yield to the shareholders a dividend of 4.5% on their investments' (Question 24, p 206; Colenso, 1892). (The answer was given as £125,000.)

[3] Rudyard Kipling (1865-1936), poet, novelist and imperialist, wrote poems describing Africans and Asians as 'lesser breeds without the law', and urged his readers to 'take up the white man's burden' (Kipling, 1940). He was awarded the Nobel Prize for literature in 1907.

[4] University College London (UCL)/Institute of Education, University of London, is creating an archive of old school textbooks in a Special Collection.

[5] Kipling, born and later working in India, spent only three days in Burma. He subsequently wrote the poem 'Mandalay' depicting a British soldier thinking about his Burmese girlfriend:

By the old Moulmein Pagoda
looking lazy by the sea
There's a Burmese girl a-setting
And I know she thinks of me ...

And I see'd her first a-smoking
Of a whacking great cheroot
An a-wasting Christian kisses
On an eathern idol's foot
Bloomin idol made of mud
Wot they called the Great Gawd Budd.
(Kipling, 1940)

2

Internal colonialism
and its effects

> I am haunted by the human chimpanzees I saw along
> hundreds of miles of that horrible country ... if they
> were black one would not feel it so much, but their
> skins, except where tanned by exposure, are as white
> as ours. (Charles Kingsley on Ireland, quoted in Curtis,
> 1968: 84)

The United Kingdom is not a country. Currently it is composed
of four countries – England, Wales, Scotland and Northern
Ireland. The people in the whole of Ireland, Wales and Scotland
were internally colonised by the English over the centuries, both
before and after England colonised overseas countries. The notion
of internal colonisation was used by Lenin to describe groups
in Tsarist Soviet Russia, by Gramsci to describe Southern Italy
and by other writers to describe the conquest and attempted
annihilation of American Indians (Hechter, 1975). But it also
describes the way English elites variously conquered, laid claim
to and took over these three countries, with subsequent conflicts
over governance, land, culture, language and religion. It was 1707
before an Act of Union joined England and Scotland, and only
in 1922 that a United Kingdom of Great Britain and Northern
Ireland came into being, Wales having been annexed by England
in 1536. It has already been noted that an understanding of the
imperial past and how people think Britain is now seen by the
rest of the world is largely a product of nostalgia and myths. Many
'traditions' in the three countries, as in the British Empire, were
invented by rulers imposing their cultures and beliefs or by groups
claiming or trying to sustain an identity (Trevor-Roper, quoted
in Hobsbawm and Ranger, 1983). Education fostered the myths
of heroic deeds that made a 'Great' Britain, but governments
are still in the business of denying what actually went on during

colonial times by removing or 'losing' archival material. Even files relating to the Falklands War in 1982 and 'The Troubles' in Northern Ireland from the 1970s have apparently been 'lost' (Cobain, 2017).[1]

This brief chapter is not in any way a definitive history, but it is included because there is much ignorance about the creation of a 'Great Britain' and the internal wars, conflicts and atrocities that took place as it was all notionally united. Some understanding of the past and present is important as after the General Election in 2017 the Conservatives were only kept in government and able to pursue leaving the EU with the support of 10 votes from the Democratic Unionist Party (DUP) of Northern Ireland. There is a general ignorance in England about Irish history and affairs. After an episode in the television production on the life of Queen Victoria (ITV, 2017), when she exhibited concern about the Irish famine in 1845, there was widespread sharing on social media from people who knew nothing about the death of over a million and the emigration of 2 million from the island. It also notes that the often vicious denigration of the people in these internal colonies in the 19th century was similar to that accorded to the overseas colonised, and also extended to the English working classes. English elites especially regarded the Welsh and Irish and the 'natives' overseas with the same arrogant contempt they accorded to the English working classes. But there were also similar fears of uprisings and challenges to authority: 'Discontented natives in the colonies and labour agitators in the mills were the same serpent … much of the talk of barbarism and darkness which it was Europe's mission to rout, was a transmuted fear of the masses at home' (Kiernan, 1969: 316).

Significant events

1169	Norman invasion of Ireland
1177	Henry II makes his son, John Lackland, Lord of Ireland
1282	Edward I invades and conquers Wales
1536	Henry VIII calls himself King of Ireland
1536	England annexes Wales; English law, language and church imposed
1614	An Irish parliament in Dublin with a Catholic majority
1641-53	Oliver Cromwell conquers Ireland for 'British Commonwealth'
1690	Battle of the Boyne; Protestant William of Orange defeats deposed King James II
1707	Act of Union with Scotland

1745/46	Jacobite rebellion in Scotland; defeat at Culloden
1801	Irish Parliament dissolved; Act of Union with the United Kingdom
1845-49	Irish potato famine; population reduced from 8 to 4 million
1914	Home Rule (Ireland) Act passed and then suspended
1916	Easter Rising; Partition created with 22 Free counties and 6 Union counties
1921-22	Anglo-Irish Treaty; Irish Free State becomes a Dominion of the Commonwealth
1921-72	Northern Ireland becomes a Protestant province within the UK
1968/69	Civil disturbances and 'The Troubles' in Northern Ireland; British troops brought in
1971	Ian Paisley sets up the Democratic Unionist Party (DUP)
1972	(January) Bloody Sunday
1998	Good Friday Agreement in Belfast (opposed by the DUP)
1999	Devolution of governing powers to Scotland, Wales and Northern Ireland
2016	In the referendum a majority in Northern Ireland vote to remain in the EU (the Irish Republic is part of the EU); DUP Leader Arlene Foster makes an informal agreement with the Conservative Party
2017	In the UK General Election the DUP wins 10 seats and agrees to support Theresa May's minority Conservative government
2018	Brexit negotiations debate the issue of the border between Ireland and Northern Ireland. A White Paper (Department for Exiting the European Union, 2018) was criticised by Eurosceptic MPs. The government went into its summer recess with no agreement on the border

What the Romans did for us

Most children still learn about the Roman conquest of Britain and Julius Caesar's invasion. Then, after 43 AD they learn that the country became a Roman province known as Britannia. Less well known is Caractacus, a Welsh Chief, who fought against the Romans, or the history of the Celts, whose lives, cultures and languages in Wales, Ireland and Scotland were eventually taken over as the countries were internally colonised by the English. A major difference between these conquests and the oppression that followed was that, as Charles Kingsley, University of Cambridge historian and author of the famous children's book *The water-babies* (1863) helpfully pointed out, the Celtic people were white. Despite this, the ethnic racism and denigration of the cultures and languages meted out, especially to the Welsh and Irish, was similar to the treatment of colonised black people. Kingsley was another fervent believer in the superiority of the white English race. Primary school children still learn (and older people remember) that after the Romans, what is now called

'England' was made up of immigrant Saxons, Angles, Jutes, Vikings and Danes all fighting each other, until Cnut (Canute), who is remembered for sitting in the sea and ordering the waves back, married a Norman French woman.

Then we remember '1066 and all that', when William the Conqueror defeated Harold, and from then on all the Kings and Queens were of French, Dutch or German descent. The Normans invaded and colonised Ireland in 1169, and Henry II handed the country over to his son. Edward I, now called an English King, invaded Wales in 1282, and there has been an English Prince of Wales ever since. A GCSE textbook in 2016 claims that the Normans were 'foreign invaders taking over a proud country' (Clarke, 2016: 22). This is a myth or invention as no one can know how 'proud' the majority of peasant inhabitants were, and Saxon Lords would presumably have been keener to keep their own wealth and property than feeling proud. At least the Normans documented who owned the country's wealth in 1086 in their Doomsday Book.

In 1536, Henry VIII, in between getting rid of his second wife and marrying a third, titled himself King of Ireland, and married his sister Margaret to the Scottish King. Scotland, with its warring clans, was always a harder country to colonise. It was not until 1707 that there was an Act of Union between England and Scotland, and in 1715 the English Parliament tried to ban the Scottish kilt, on the grounds that it was indecent when men bent down! The mass-produced kilt with its varied tartans was actually created by an English Quaker from Lancashire (Trevor-Roper, 1983). As noted in the Introduction, a major reason for early colonisation was the search for food, especially to feed urban populations and expanding armies and navies. This also applied to Wales and Ireland, where, from the 1500s, their grain and cattle fed the English (Tilly, 1976). It was only in the later 1700s that the myth of a 'Great Britain' began to emerge, as the German Hanoverian Kings took over and the early empire was emerging. A poem by a Scottish poet was set to music by Thomas Arne in 1740. This was 'Rule Britannia', which is one of the many patriotic songs still sung, especially at the end of the Last Night of the Proms broadcast world-wide from London. The poet, James Thompson, was given a pension for patriotism by the then Prince of Wales (German-speaking Frederick Ludwig of Bavaria, who only arrived in England in 1728). No other country calls itself 'Great'; the nearest any other European state gets to giving itself a superior label is the Grand Duchy of Luxembourg.

Internal colonialism and its effects

The Celtic peoples of Ireland and the Scottish Highlands were originally close politically and economically. Trevor-Roper has claimed that the Highlanders of Scotland were 'simply the overflow from Ireland' (Trevor-Roper, 1983: 15), and arguments as to which were the original invaders continued until the 1700s. Scotland soon claimed that it had the original Celtic culture, and rivalries have continued to be played out in literature, and especially in football. If you are a supporter of Glasgow Celtic, you are likely to be Catholic and/or Republican. A Glasgow Rangers fan is likely to be Protestant and Unionist. Although the Scots made a bid for independence from England in 1745, the Jacobites were defeated at the battle of Culloden, and it was not until 2014 that Scottish nationalism was resurrected in a referendum for independence that was also defeated. A majority in Scotland voted in the 2016 Referendum to remain in the EU.

The fierce fighting of the Scots was noted by the English government of Prime Minister Pitt the Elder, who encouraged the creation of Highland regiments to fight in imperial wars. Ironically, a major effect of the colonising of the three countries was to supply armies to fight in the wars to take over the overseas colonies of the British Empire. Highland and Irish regiments fought to claim and retain imperial land in India and South Africa, and Irish-American soldiers fought on both sides of the American Civil War during 1861 to 1865. Historians of internal colonisation have documented the expansion of an English state as it attempted to anglicise the countries. There was a 'political incorporation affecting the course of developments in the Celtic fringe by contributing to its economic, cultural and political dependence on England' (Hechter, 1975: 80; see also Brendon, 2007). As England benefited from this dependence, it is not surprising that hostilities and antagonisms between the three countries and the English persist to the present day. The Scots probably made the best of their colonisation, after James VI of Scotland became James I in 1603, calling himself King of Great Britain, France and Ireland. Scotland had its own parliament and legal system, was largely Protestant, and developed a profitable banking and investment system.

After the Act of Union between Scotland and England in 1707, local elites were co-opted to run the country, and a colonial policy successfully applied to the Empire as 'indirect rule', although one positive effect in Scotland was that local elites were prepared to help develop a national education system that served all communities. After devolution of powers to the Scottish Parliament in 1999, the country had control of its whole education system, setting up a Department for Education and Life-long Learning. By 2014 Scotland was noted by the Institute for Fiscal Studies as the most highly educated country in Europe, although it had private schools based on the English public schools that served both Scottish and some English elite members. Prince Charles was educated at Gordonstoun (boarding fees now £33,252 per annum); Prime Minister Tony Blair at Fettes (boarding fees now £33,480); while former Education Secretary Michael Gove had to content himself with being a day pupil at Robert Gordon's College (fees now £12,710). In a blog in 2013, a former pupil at the Scottish public school Glenalmond described the way the activities in his school, typical of the British public school system, functioned to build 'the class solidarity of the British elite'. All the sport, uncomfortable beds and spartan diet were originally designed to produce generations to run an empire now vanished. In his view, it later functioned to produce a culture that exuded confidence, created old boys' networks and sneered at the working and middle classes: 'The middle classes are taught to believe they will succeed through hard work and gumption. The upper classes know this is nonsense' (Ramsey, 2013: 8).

The Welsh had a tougher time than the Scots under their colonisation. Even before the Act of Union with England in 1536, Welsh people were forbidden to buy much land, could not officially carry arms, fortify their houses, hold assemblies, become judges, and any Englishman marrying a Welsh wife was deemed to be Welsh. Any Celtic traditions were outlawed, and after Union, the Church of England was the official religion, although many non-conformist groups continued to hold services in Welsh. The Welsh language came in for particular denigration. A Commission in 1846 reported to the English Parliament that 'Because of their language the mass of the Welsh people are inferior to the English in every branch of practical knowledge and skill' (Coupland, 1954: 186). Both external and internal colonisation meant that local languages were denigrated, and 'It is not surprising that the Commissioners should have swept aside the ancient language of Wales as ruthlessly as MacCaulay … had swept aside the ancient languages of India' (Coupland, 1954: 190). Arguments over the use of the Welsh language in politics and education continue to the present day (Cosslett, 2017). The policy of indirect rule was successful in Wales as Welsh local gentry acquired land and influence at the expense of a rural and urban working class, but the dependence of the Welsh economy on England had similar effects to that of its overseas colonised countries, its production and labour being subject to English demands. Wales acquired its own Welsh Assembly after devolution in 1999, with full control of its own education system.

A further effect of internal colonisation, more apparent initially in Wales and England than in the other two countries, was hostility and racism directed against black settlers.[2] Peter Fryer has documented in some detail the divisive role of racism, especially in Cardiff, where white workers were in economic competition for diminishing work with men from the colonies who had served in the Armed Forces in the First World War or on merchant ships. In 1919, South Wales 'experienced one of the most vicious outbreaks of racial violence that has yet occurred in Britain' (Fryer, 1984: 303). The violence began with the familiar colonial charge that black men were consorting with white women. Settlers from West Africa, Somalia and Arab countries were attacked by white mobs. A former colonial Governor, Sir Ralph Williams, wrote in *The Times* (14 June 1919) 'that sexual relations between white women and coloured men revolt our very nature', and called for repatriation. *The Times*, to its credit, pointed out that 'black girls in the colonies were subject to the "lust" of white seducers', and a measured response was printed from Felix Hercules, one of the leaders of a national liberation movement in the West Indian colonies, that if black men were to be repatriated on sexual grounds, then so should white men in the colonies, and a result would be 'a downfall of the British Empire' (*The Times*, 19 June 1919).

Fighting colonialism in Ireland

Ireland, where 'the denigration of Irish culture has a longer and more distinguished history than the Welsh culture', and where after colonisation in 1169 the English fought continually to 'subdue this barbarous country' (Hechter, 1975: 76), can now be regarded as place where internal colonialism has been contested and to some extent overcome. Kevin Myers, discussing the post-war histories of Irish and Afro-Caribbean people in England, noted the ways in which the histories of subjugated states and peoples have always been marginalised or misrepresented in the national history story (Myers, 2015). Former Education Secretary Michael Gove, for example, told the Conservative Party Conference in October 2010, the 'children are growing up ignorant of one of the most inspiring stories I know – the history of the United Kingdom' (Myers, 2015: 4). But that would be his version of the national story, and certainly did not include the miseries inflicted on the Irish population.

Northern Ireland has been a problem for the Westminster Parliament since 1922, the most recent being the 2017 General Election, after which the 10 votes of the DUP allowed the Conservative government to remain in power. After the vote to leave the EU in 2016, the question of the border between the Irish Republic and Northern Ireland, still in the UK, but with a majority voting to remain in the EU, remained contentious. As journalist Polly Toynbee pointed out, the Irish border question was a roadblock to the fantasies of Brexit supporters in the government, 'reviving the centuries-old deep-dyed contempt for the Irish' who dismissed the question 'with an imperial fly-whisk, as a minor irritant' (Toynbee, 2017).

In the very large literature on Irish history (Connolly, 2007; Myers, 2015; Bourke and MacBride, 2016), historians generally agree that the Norman invasion of 1169 was followed by around 800 years of English rule, with resulting violent conflicts, centred round land and religion surviving to the present day. Henry VIII attempted to make the country Protestant, importing English and Scottish Protestant settlers, and introducing a plantation policy similar to that in overseas colonies. Catholic landowners were displaced, and Oliver Cromwell and his army, victorious in 1649, ensured that religious differences became the dominant cleavage in society, the Anglo-Irish Protestants becoming the ruling class. The Battle of the Boyne in 1690, where Protestant King William of Orange defeated deposed Catholic King James II, ensured Protestant ascendancy in Northern Ireland for generations, and an Orange Order still celebrates the battle on 12 July, usually causing retaliation from Catholics. Thereafter the English attempted to Anglicise the country through language and education, especially holding the Irish language in contempt. An Act of Union with what was described as a United Kingdom in 1801 dissolved the Irish Parliament. Absentee landlords caused much misery among the Irish poor, culminating in the famine of 1845-46, when the potato crop failed and a million starved while 2 million emigrated. Despite famine conditions, the English continued to import food from the island (Woodham-Smith, 1962), and the resulting poverty and anger influenced the Irish Nationalist movement. The English Prime Minister Sir Robert Peel drew his ideas of a police force from the Royal Irish Constabulary, established in 1822 to keep control of Irish dissidents.

It was during the famine that the Cambridge academic the Reverend Charles Kingsley visited Ireland after a visit to Jamaica. He later became a Chaplain to Queen Victoria and tutor to the Prince of Wales. He made his dislike of 'black people, the Irish and Jews' plain in his writings, although, as noted above, he felt that the Irish 'human chimpanzees' were, at least, not black. In his well-known children's book *The water-babies* (1863), he managed to include a dishonest Irish woman as a character. A further example of Victorian contempt for the Irish came from Sir Charles Trevelyan, who helped administer famine relief in Ireland but wrote that 'death by starvation' was a discipline for unruly behaviour. He later served on the board of the Charity Organisation Society in England, working to control 'defective populations' (Tomlinson, 1982: 43).

Prime Minister Gladstone was sympathetic to the idea of Home Rule for Ireland, and eventually in 1914 a Home Rule Act was passed, but almost immediately suspended. Nationalists fought in an Easter Rising in 1916 that was brutally suppressed, but independence for most of Ireland arrived in 1922, when an Irish Free State of 22 Catholic counties became a separate nation and a dominion of the Commonwealth. By 2017 the Taoiseach (Prime Minister) of Ireland was Leo Varadkar, who has an Indian father and Irish mother. The remaining six counties became a Northern Ireland Protestant province within the United Kingdom, sending MPs to Westminster but with an Ulster Unionist Party in government from 1921 to 1972. By 1969 discrimination against Catholics led to conflict that lasted over 30 years and became known as 'The Troubles', and in 1971 the DUP developed from a Protestant Unionist Party, led by the Reverend Ian Paisley, who was totally opposed to any power sharing with Catholics, whom he referred to as 'breeding like rabbits'. Enoch Powell, having stirred up anti-immigrant feeling in England, and who had opposed entry into the EEC, became a Unionist MP in 1974 and devoted himself to defending the province as part of the British nation, as the 'soil of the province is British soil' (quoted in Cooke, 2014: 254).

Ending 'The Troubles'?

The para-military groups linked to nationalist Republican parties and the military groups linked to Unionist parties fought each other over the years, with over 3,000 civilians killed. The Westminster government sent in British troops who, after an incident on 'Bloody Sunday' in January 1972, when 13 unarmed people were killed by the Army, exacerbated the conflicts. The British government took over the province with Direct Rule until 1998, when a Good Friday Agreement (The Belfast Agreement), brokered by the British government under Prime Minister Tony Blair, notionally put an end to open conflict and eventually a handing in of weapons. Blair and his children hold both British and Irish passports as Blair's mother was Irish.

The DUP was opposed to the Belfast Agreement, which they regarded as an 'imperfect peace'. In October 2016 DUP MPs, led by Arlene Foster, attended a champagne party at the Conservative Party Conference, and agreed to support the Conservatives in the Westminster government after any elections. After the June 2017 General Election they were the largest party of the 18 Northern Irish parliamentary places, with 10 seats. The Republican party Sinn Féin took 7 seats, but does not attend the Westminster Parliament. In subsequent votes the DUP mostly voted with the Conservative and Unionist Party, and kept the government in power. The Republic of Ireland, under its Prime Minister Leo Varadkar, and also Northern Ireland, seemed more open to the arrival of migrants, both globally and from the EU, and around 17% of the population of Northern Ireland are migrants, including many from Romania. However, cultural racism knows no borders, as when, in an international football match against Switzerland in November 2017, the Northern Ireland team lost by a penalty awarded by the Romanian referee. This led to racist comments on Twitter insulting Romanians in general.

By the middle of 2018, two years after the vote to leave the EU, the question of a border between Northern Ireland and the Irish Republic still dominated discussions on Brexit in both the Westminster Parliament and the EU negotiators in Brussels. Progress was followed in a series of papers written by the Institute for Peace, Security and Justice at Queen's University Belfast (Hayward and Komarova, 2018). In July 2018 Prime Minister May produced a White Paper (HM Government, 2018) that included plans for a 'soft' border between the two countries. The proposals were welcomed in Ireland by Declan Breathnach, Ireland's Spokesperson on North-South Bodies and Cross-Border Co-operation (Breathnach, 2018). In England the paper was criticised by members from all parties and several ministers resigned from May's government, including Foreign Secretary Johnson. A Customs and Trades Bill, drafted before the White Paper, was passed in the Westminster Parliament on 18 July by just three votes, after four amendments by hardline Tory Brexiteers were accepted (Sabbagh et al, 2018). Moves to challenge the leadership of Prime Minister May were deferred until after the summer recess, and the question of the Irish border after Brexit rumbled on.

Class and the white colonised

English elites in the 19th and 20th centuries treated the overseas and internally colonised, and the English working classes, with the same arrogance and contempt. There were similar fears of insurrection and uprisings among the 'natives' abroad and the lower classes at home. In 1819 at the Peterloo Massacre in Manchester, when English workers were holding a peaceful meeting over workers' voting rights, they were attacked by the military, leaving 16 dead and over 600 injured; Irish workers had joined the meeting. This was not something the authorities could tolerate, and one way of dealing with this was to exacerbate divisions between the English working class and any of the internally colonised. This worked well, especially with the Irish. In the 19th century Irish labour was used to dig canals and build railways. But incursions into the textile industry, especially when the Irish were brought in to break strikes, was not tolerated, as described by Elizabeth Gaskell in her novel *North and South* (Gaskell, 1855). Karl Marx studied the working class in Ireland carefully, noting that Ireland sent its surplus labour to the English labour market, which forced wages down. As a result,

> Every industrial and commercial centre in England now possess a working class divided into two hostile camps, English proletarians and Irish proletarians. The ordinary English worker hates the Irish worker as a competitor who lowers his standard of life ... the Irishman sees in the English worker at once the accomplice and stupid tool of the English domination of Ireland. (Marx, 1870: 220)

Robert Winder documented anti-Irish riots in the 19th and early 20th centuries, and the stigmatising of Irish migrants, particularly if Catholic. In 1923 the General Assembly of the Church of Scotland approved a report on *The menace of the Irish race to our Scottish nationality* that documented fears that the Protestant Church would be swamped by an alien population (Winder, 2004: 203). It is noteworthy that the references to 'aliens' and 'swamping' reoccur in speeches and reports from eminent figures over the decades when referring to black, Asian, Jewish or Irish people. Creating divisions through emotive and negative language has long been a tool of political and military ruling classes. One especially emotive area was that of the notices in landladies' windows requesting 'No Blacks, no Dogs, no Irish', and how widespread these actually were. In 2015 there were letters in *The Guardian* describing the signs as old myths of the 1960s, while others claimed they saw such signs. Summing it up, Niall O'Dowd wrote that, 'The era of no Blacks, dogs or Irish is over but should never be forgotten' (O'Dowd, 2013). A photograph of one such sign is held in the Irish Studies Centre at London Metropolitan University.

But further divisions between social and racial and migrant groups, especially the Irish and Welsh, continued to be provided by eugenic theories supporting claims that the lower classes, colonised and migrant groups have lower cognitive abilities than other groups (Tomlinson, 2017). For well over a hundred years there was been a plethora of writing and research on ability, intelligence, mental measurement and eugenics and their educational implications. Usually dating from Francis Galton, second cousin to Charles Darwin who worked to provide a 'scientific' base for selective breeding to improve the genetic inheritance of the human race (Galton, 1869), there have been attempts to suggest that lower classes and racial groups had supposedly less educable minds. It was no accident that early industrialising countries needed to rationalise the unequal treatment of urban slum and migrant populations by popularising notions of inherited differences between these groups, a situation that has continued into the 21st century (Astbury and Plomin, 2014). A book published by University of London Professor Hans Eysenck in 1971 was notable for conflating the lower class, black ('Negro' in some of the book) and the Irish as likely to have lower IQs, although he blamed historical injustices for this:

> If, as the data suggests, the Negroes show some genetic
> influence on their low IQs, this may very well be due
> to the crimes committed against their ancestors, just
> as the Irish show a similar low IQ on account of the

oppression they suffered for so long at the hands of the English. (Eysenck, 1971: 142)

Eysenck also worried that racial quotas in university admissions might disadvantage whites, and recommended that a small upper segment of blacks could 'share the pursuit of happiness with their fellow whites' (Eysenck, 1971: 149), but only if they escaped the ghetto and the lumpenproletariat, both black and white. He actually recommended the 'abolition of the lumpenproletariat as a whole – both black and white' (Eysenck, 1971: 150), which was astonishing coming from a man who had escaped from Nazi Germany before the Holocaust.

Summary

This chapter has briefly described how both before and during the creation of a British Empire and its overseas colonisation, Scotland, Wales and Ireland were internally colonised by the English, with similar economic consequences and rationalisations. It is intended to inform those who (like myself) did not learn much through schooling about the Empire or the English internal colonisation of Scotland, Wales and Ireland. Some knowledge of this history is important to the Brexit vote, as these three countries had different views about the continued link with an EU, and the DUP of Northern Ireland held a balance of power in the Westminster Parliament including issues relating to leaving the EU. The question of a border between Northern Ireland and the Republic of Ireland became one of main issues for dissent between Westminster government ministers and all the political parties in Brexit debates.

The chapter noted that, despite myths about a proud British heritage, all the rulers (Kings and Queens) for over a thousand years in what became Britain have been of European descent. It particularly indicated similarities in the contemptuous and arrogant views that the colonisers held about both the internally and externally colonised, and their lower classes. These were reinforced by 19th-century eugenic views, which have persisted into the 21st century. The next chapter links the slow ending of the British Empire and the independence of former colonies with post-war education policies and the unequal treatment of migrant and minority children in all four countries, although schools and higher education institutions in England were particularly bad at incorporating minority and lower-class children fairly.

Notes

[1]   Cobain (2017) noted that in 2013 the government disclosed that it had been unlawfully hoarding 1.2 million files on controversial aspects of 20th-century British history in a high-security compound in Milton Keynes. The Foreign Office admitted that they had withheld thousands of colonial era files, including those relating to the detention and torture of Kenyans during the Mau Mau insurgency in the 1950s.

[2]   Glasgow, one of the first cities to give up its slave trade in the 1840s, also experienced race violence in 1919. An English left-wing journalist, E.D. Morel, brought Germany into the race and sex wars, asserting in 1920 in the *Daily Herald* that black soldiers deployed by the French on the Rhine were oversexed rapists spreading venereal disease (Reinders, 1968). Refugees in Germany in the 21st century have been accused of similar behaviour.

3

Ending empire: Education for ignorance, 1945-1960s

> Despite a restructuring of education in post-war Britain there were initially few challenges to its underlying colonial–imperial value base which supported beliefs in the superiority of white people and white social institutions. (Tomlinson, 1990: 44)

In Andrea Levy's novel of a Jamaican man, Gilbert, arriving to join the war-time RAF in what he had assumed to be the 'mother country', an American officer from a segregated USA attempts to make sense of a black man mixing with white troops in England. The insulting language used then and later to Gilbert included 'coloured', 'darkie', 'coon', 'nigger', 'blackie', 'wog'. When Gilbert tells his white friend's husband, 'You know what your trouble is, man? Your white skin. You think it makes you better than me. You want to know what your white skin makes you? It makes you white. That's all. No better, no worse than me' (Levy, 2004: 525), this message is incomprehensible to the man, whose education and war-time service as a lower rank soldier in India had convinced him of the superiority of white over all 'coloureds' and foreigners. In the real world, an English officer serving in India who passionately supported the British Empire, Enoch Powell, later an MP, had already written a paper in 1946 opposing any Indian migration to Britain. But the British Nationality Act in 1948 gave all imperial subjects the right of free entry into Britain, although distinguishing between citizens of independent, mainly white, Commonwealth countries and those in the colonies and dependent territories.[1] The Act was possibly, as Robert Winder has suggested, to demonstrate that the British Empire was still a vibrant entity (Winder, 2004: 332).

The fictional Gilbert had arrived back in England in 1948, on a captured Nazi troopship that had been refitted and called the

Empire Windrush. Some 490 men and women came from the Caribbean on this ship, skilled workers of whom over half already had jobs to go to in England. A British government that had overseen the post-war immigration of 200,000 Polish and other European displaced people was so alarmed at the potential arrival of a few hundred 'coloured' workers, that the Foreign Office was instructed that 'no effort be made to help these people, otherwise it might encourage a further influx', and they were initially housed in an old air-raid shelter in Clapham in South London. There was some opposition to the Polish migration from union leaders, and also from the Communist Party, worrying about the threat to jobs (Smith, 2015), but none from the government. If there had been any political leadership similar to that offered to white migrants at this time, the situation of Black, Asian and other minorities might have been different over the following decades, and an education system preparing all young people for a globalised world might have developed. This did not happen, and the political and public reactions to post-colonial immigrants, their descendants and subsequent migrants can be traced to imperial beliefs in nationalism, racism, exclusion and a culture of empire that was 'built into the very fabric of their (white) lives' (MacKenzie, 2015: 197).

This, and following chapters, links the ignorance of empire to developments in education, as people arrived from former colonies, many skilled but increasingly taking over unskilled jobs that the indigenous population did not want. While under the post-war Labour government a welfare state was coming into existence, education policy was largely based on a social democratic consensus that governments should regulate and resource education to achieve redistributive justice and some kind of equality. But this equality did not encompass the children of migrants, who, from the outset, were regarded as problems to be treated differently, dispersed or incorporated unequally into a system that itself remained unequal. This chapter illustrates the relationship between the British class system and the class structure of empire that had embodied a permanent status barrier between citizens in the 'mother country' and those in the Empire. Whatever class conflicts went on in Britain, all social classes were to some extent united in hostility to the arrival of former colonial subjects and their children. Reaction ranged from attempts to remove the arrivals or to limit their entry, to some liberal and business welcome for their labour. There were mixed reactions from socialists and trade unions fighting for working-class justice but confused when this class incorporated an unwelcome colonial 'underclass'. There was little effort within the education system to explain what was happening and why.

This chapter documents the ending of Empire, as the former colonies gained their independence during the 1950s and 1960s, some by planned handover of power, and some by bloody conflict, and the ignorance of the way in which a 300-year-old Empire disintegrated in some 20 years. The nearest many children came to learning about empire and decolonisation was when they or their relatives did their compulsory military service (which ended in 1962) in the former colonies. Even a Professor of Modern History and Empire admitted that, 'When I was at school and university in the 1950s and 1960s I was taught nothing at all about the British Empire' (Porter, 2015: 397). He did not need to be actually taught, as the presence of Empire was there in all schooling. Former Prime Minister Gordon Brown wrote in his memoirs that in the 1950s and 1960s, 'people could be forgiven for believing the British Empire was going to last forever' (Brown, 2017: 33). Despite attempts to differentiate or remove new arrivals from former colonies, they were British subjects. This was in contrast to the German notion of 'guest worker' (*Gastarbeiter*), where migrants were initially regarded as work units and not expected to settle or to bring their families.

Significant events

The aim of selecting these events is to indicate that while the education systems of the UK were being reorganised with class and racial struggles over the form schooling would take, former British colonies were gaining independence, and people were migrating into mainly urban areas of the 'mother country' in response to labour needs. Schools and teachers were not provided with information about decolonisation and why there were new arrivals. The racial beliefs derived from imperial propaganda, and Social Darwinist writings dominated in political, public and education circles.

1944	Education Act; secondary education for all to the age of 15; selective system of grammar, technical and secondary modern schools; General Certificate of Education (GCE) O- and A-levels established in 1951
1945	Labour government elected; Clement Attlee becomes Prime Minister

1945	United Nations organisation set up
1947	India and Pakistan gain independence
1948	British Nationality Act; Burma and Ceylon gain independence
1948	Israel to be an independent 'homeland'; the rights of Palestinians promised
1948	United Nations Universal Declaration of Human Rights
1951	Conservative government elected
1956	Suez Canal invasion by British troops, then withdrawn
1957	Ghana and Malaya (called Malaysia in 1963) gain independence
1958	Race riots in Nottingham and Notting Hill
1959	Independence for Somaliland (former British Protectorate)
1960	Independence for Nigeria and Cyprus
1960-61	Proposed immigration restrictions lead to more immigration from the Asian subcontinent; Birmingham sets up the first Department for Teaching English as a Second Language; the Birmingham Immigration Control Association and Southall Residents Association are set up to oppose the immigration of 'non-whites'
1961	Independence for Tanganyika (now Tanzania) and Sierra Leone; Enoch Powell makes a speech on English nationhood and a vanishing empire
1962	Immigration Control Act; Minister of Health Enoch Powell encourages the migration of health workers from the Caribbean
1963	Kenya becomes independent; HM inspectors write *English for immigrants*; short courses for teaching English as a Second Language set up; white parents in Southall protest against immigrant children in 'their' schools; Minister Edward Boyle rejects ideas of segregated education; Newsom Report on *Half our future*; Robbins Report on university expansion
1963-65	Singapore (colonised 1819) gains independence
1964	Voucher system restricts immigration; Campaign against Racial Discrimination set up; the Commonwealth Immigrants Advisory Council suggest the dispersal of immigrant children; Labour government elected in October
1964	Malta, Malawi and Zambia become independent
1965	Circular 7/65 from the DES suggests no school should have more than 30% immigrant children; 11 LEAs adopt dispersal by bussing; a North London West Indian Association worries about children referred to ESN schools
1965	First Race Relations Act; Race Relations Board and a National Committee for Commonwealth Immigration set up
1965	Circular 10/65 requests all schools to reorganise on comprehensive principles; Sierra Leone and Gambia gain independence
1966	Labour re-elected and a new MP declares 'we have buried the race issue'; Roy Jenkins envisions a society based on cultural diversity, mutual tolerance and equal opportunity; Botswana, Lesotho, Barbados and Guyana gain independence
1966	Local Government Act to provide rate support grant for school staff in 'high-immigrant' areas; 10% census personal data for England and Wales (unpublished) shows 'coloured population' as 924,000
1967	Plowden Report on *Children and their primary schools* includes a chapter on immigrant children; independence for Aden (South Yemen)

1968	Commonwealth Immigration Act: those 'patrials' with a father or grandfather born in the UK have priority; second Race Relations Act passed, but discrimination in education not mentioned
1968	Enoch Powell makes 'Rivers of blood' speech in Birmingham
1969	Black Paper attacks comprehensive schooling and child-centred education; Mauritius, Swaziland and Nauru gain independence
1970	Second report on public schools; Labour fails to integrate public schools into the state school system
1970	Conservative government elected

Empire and decolonisation

If the education system either failed to include information about the British Empire or did so in a distorted form, there was also little attempt to explain the process of decolonisation or why migrants from former colonial countries were entering Britain during the 1950s and 1960s. Political suggestions that unwanted migrants should 'go home' have formed a permanent background to debate on nation identity and who belongs in a nation-state in a globalised world. A Liberal Party member of the House of Lords, Gladwyn Jebb, declared that 'the process of de-colonisation has left us without any positive and generally accepted notion of our position in the world' (Lord Jebb, 1961). 'Us' did not include the former members of colonies who now lived in Britain. The white British continued to mainly define themselves by who was not regarded as British. There was also, as suggested in Chapter One, a desperate need to maintain a fiction of a benign withdrawal from the colonies. Cobain (2016) has recorded the ways in which hidden caches of documents recording brutalities and injustices during colonial rule were destroyed by burning, or in some cases, taken out in crates and dropped into the sea, with the precaution that they would not be washed up by tides.

In 1945 a post-war Labour government was elected, to the discomfort of Winston Churchill and the Conservative Party. A war-torn Britain did not want to return to pre-war inequalities, and the new Prime Minister Attlee promised a new contract between the state and its citizens. This meant a programme that included the nationalisation of mines, railways, some industry and utilities, a national health service, social security benefits, proper pensions for working people and higher taxes all round.

He had one woman in his Cabinet, Ellen Wilkinson, who was made Education Minister. Winston Churchill, explaining all this to his father Lord Randolph Churchill, said there would be no socialist revolution, and 'only those who have extreme principles wear sweaters to Buckingham Palace parties' (quoted in Bew, 2016: 355). Attlee, a product of Haileybury public school and Oxford, believed that the Empire was a force for good and self-government with a rule of law would prevail in the former colonies, although he was uneasy about the militarism and racial superiority that went along with it all. He was present at a Paris Peace Conference in July 1946 that attempted to settle border issues in Europe and its colonies, and agree to minority rights. The USA was at that time supreme in world affairs, a cold war was developing between it and an expanding USSR, and there was agreement in the British government that 'the British Empire was unsustainable in its current form' (Bew, 2016: 412). Attlee hoped that the newly created United Nations (UN) organisation might be an example for a British Commonwealth that was supposedly a United Nations in miniature. Despite war-time conflicts with India (which included arresting and jailing Gandhi), he agreed to a date for Indian/Pakistani independence on 14 August 1947. This proved a costly and horrific undertaking, and debates continue on who was to blame.

Attlee was not unduly worried by immigration of labour, despite a group of his MPs sending a letter claiming that:

> This country may become an open reception centre for immigrants not selected in respect of health, education, training, character, customs and above all whether assimilation is at all possible … and while the British people are blessed by the absence of a racial problem … an influx of coloured people here is likely to impair the harmony, strength and cohesion in our public life. (Watson, 1996: 157)

The letter suggested immigration control would be 'universally approved by our people', and uncontrolled migration would impair cohesion in public life, a claim that would resurface over the years. In the long term it would appear that politicians of all parties then, as later, gave no leadership to welcoming new potential citizens despite the need for their labour. Meanwhile, over the decade, around 2 million people emigrated from the UK, especially to 'white' Commonwealth countries.

The Conservative Party was elected in 1951 with Churchill again as Prime Minister. Churchill continued his opposition to decolonisation and immigration, and in 1955, proposed that a slogan for another election in 1955 should be 'Keep Britain White'. Following Churchill's retirement, Anthony Eden led Britain into what was regarded as a fiasco over attempts to retain the Suez Canal in Egypt after General Nasser had nationalised it. The affair was widely regarded as signalling the end of much of British military power 'east of Suez', and decolonisation continued apace. In 1959 the British Protectorate of Somaliland was declared independent. As an illustration that colonial countries were used as sources of food, this country in the north of the Horn of Africa was initially used to supply camel, goat and sheep meat to the British colony of Aden, taken by the British in 1839, and gaining independence in 1967 as part of South Yemen. As a further illustration of post-colonial ignorance, few realise that Britain in 2018 was still supplying arms to Saudi Arabia to use in a civil war against their former colony.

By the end of the 1960s, over 30 major colonies had achieved independence, welcomed by Harold Macmillan, then Conservative leader, who, in 1964, spoke in South Africa about the 'winds of change' blowing through the continent. By 1960 17 new African States had joined the UN. The Colonial Office, founded in 1768, merged with a Commonwealth Office in 1966, and in 1968 became the Foreign and Commonwealth Office. Between 1945 and 1965 the number of people under British colonial rule reduced from 700 million to 5 million. Those at school during this period were unlikely to have been taught any of this, unless in the occasional special lesson or lecture by visiting dignitaries. Universities took in some students who would later go back to rule in their decolonised countries, but the large increase in overseas students was yet to begin.

Of the several bloody conflicts preceding independence, which were usually reported in the British press along the lines of 'ungrateful natives fighting our troops', major examples were in Malaysia, Ceylon (Sri Lanka), Rhodesia, the Central African Federation and Kenya. African opposition to colonial rule in Kenya centred round the expropriation of land by white settlers and militant action by Africans. A state of emergency during the Mau Mau insurgency uprising led to many atrocities. Ian Cobain's view is that the truth about 1950s Kenya is still unknown (Cobain, 2016: 107), but the British government has only recently paid reparations to elderly Kenyan men tortured during the war. By the end of the 1950s some land was released to Africans, but the state of emergency was still in place. Piers Brendon wrote that while club members at the Meru Club in Nairobi were worried about admitting black men to the club as they might dance with the officials' (white) wives, 11 men were beaten to death in Hola Camp by British troops (Brendon, 2007: 563). In response to this, Enoch Powell MP made a speech in the House of Commons naming Hola as a great administrative disaster, which could be rectified by more responsible British administration (Powell, 1959).

A more peaceful but arrogant example of decolonisation that also involved black–white relationships was illustrated in the British Protectorate of Bechuanaland (named Botswana in 1966). The story was documented by Susan Williams (2006), and a film, *A United Kingdom*, was released in 2016. Seretse Khama, heir to the Kingship of the Protectorate, while studying law in London, married a white woman. Both Labour and then Conservative governments were determined to keep Khama from returning to the country with his wife as it bordered South Africa, where apartheid had been enforced from 1948 and intermarriage was forbidden. They did not want to upset South Africa, as the country supplied Britain with uranium and other minerals that were urgently needed. The Labour government's Colonial Secretary who circulated a memo in the Cabinet advising banishment for Seretse was Patrick Gordon-Walker. Ironically, when a Labour government was finally returned to power in 1964, Gordon-Walker lost his Smethwick (West Midlands) seat to a Conservative who had campaigned with the slogan 'If you want a nigger neighbour, vote Labour'. Sir and Lady Seretse Khama and their descendants went on to rule in Botswana.

A further example of the assumption that imperial governments could move their colonial people around as they pleased came in the later 1960s, when the people in the Chagos Archipelago in the Indian Ocean were forced to leave their islands. The islands had been taken from the French in 1814 and used as a slave trading post. In 1967 the British government bought most of the plantations, which deprived the Islanders of their income, and at the request of the USA, forced them to leave. The largest military base in the world (so far) was then constructed by the American military on Diego Garcia. The takeover of the islands and compensation continue to be a matter for legal debate (Vine, 2011).

Political hypocrisies

In England, anti-immigrant antagonism towards post-war colonial immigrants found support in all social classes and surfaced in all subsequent elections. Later hostility to European migration was increased (evident in the vote to leave the EU). While racism against Black and Asian migration was developing, anti-Irish and anti-Semitic racism continued, although in 1948 there were only some 400,000 Jewish and 600,000 Irish people in England (Kynaston, 2007: 270). All political parties colluded with the hypocrisy of recognising that labour migration was needed while passing immigration control measures. There were outbreaks of violence against immigrants throughout the 1950s and 1960s, and two Bills in the 1950s attempting to outlaw discrimination failed. It appeared that liberal beliefs in equality before the law were sustained when white youths were jailed for attacking Caribbean migrants in Nottingham and Notting Hill in 1958, but this did not last.

Ideological self-images of a tolerant Britain came under strain in the 1960s as more migrants arrived, including those invited to work in transport and in the hospitals, and after a period of intense hostility to immigration, the Conservative government passed an Act in 1962 that limited Commonwealth immigration by the introduction of vouchers. This was initially opposed by Labour Leader Hugh Gaitskell, who pointed out that economic conditions were already slowing down migration, but the Act led to a 'beat the ban' surge in migration from families from the Indian subcontinent just before it was passed. After Gaitskell's early death at the age of 57 in 1963, the new Labour Prime Minister, Harold Wilson, endorsed the voucher system in 1965 and went on to introduce an Immigration Act in 1968. This was designed mainly to limit the entry of Kenyan Asians by distinguishing between 'patrials' – those with a father or grandfather born in the UK – and others. The Act led E.J.B. Rose and Associates, tasked with a five-year study of 'race relations' in England, to assert that:

> A Rubicon was crossed in the spring of 1968. This was when the British Government decided, on grounds of expediency rather than principle, that it could no longer accept responsibility for certain of its citizens because of the colour of their skin. (Rose and Associates, 1969: 11)[2]

Kynaston also noted that 1968 seemed to be the time when black immigrants became the prime 'other' to be attacked and vilified. Shirley Bassey, seventh child of a Nigerian family growing up in the 1940s in Cardiff's Tiger Bay, managed a brilliant stage-singing career, unlike many of her contemporaries, who continued to experience racism that affected their job possibilities.

The Labour government attempted to retain a liberal stance on race and migration with Acts in 1965 and 1968 notionally outlawing discrimination; education was not mentioned until a 1976 Act. Labour also set up a Race Relations Board and a National Committee for Commonwealth Immigration. But the reality was that all political parties were nervous about 'coloured immigration'. Richard Crossman MP wrote in his diary that, 'Since the 1964 Smethwick by-election it is clear that immigration can be a potential vote-loser for the Labour Party if we are seen to allow a flood of immigrants to come in and blight the areas of our inner cities' (Crossman, 1975). A rhetoric of floods, blights and blaming immigrants for inner-city decline had taken hold early. In the relatively affluent city of Birmingham, with a million people and some 50,000 Caribbean and Asian workers, in 1959 local councillors objected to immigrants doing the unskilled work local people didn't want, and complained about their housing in multi-occupied lodgings. John Rex and Robert Moore (1967) documented the actual poor housing and work conditions of migrants in a book that was reviewed by Enoch Powell. His review was mainly a polemic against 'coloured immigration' and suggestions of repatriation. Powell appeared to have forgotten that, as Minister of Health in 1962, he had encouraged migration from the Caribbean for hospital workers. He was a controversial figure who articulated a populist xenophobia that would eventually be taken over by both extremist parties and mainstream politics. In 2018 some of the nurses recruited by Powell reminisced in a BBC television programme about their reception. A common experience was of patients telling them to 'keep your black hands off me' (quoted in BBC Four, 2018).

It has been noted a number of times that in the 1960s England was searching for a new post-imperial identity. As American Secretary of State Dean Acheson famously put it, 'Britain has lost an Empire but has not yet found a role'. Powell's tribalism and outright nationalism provided this (Rich, 1986: 207). His speeches continued to articulate a romantic view of the Empire, and promised a 'lyrical, indeed sublime way forward for a bemused and resentful people conscious of having lost their place in history' (quoted in Roberts, 2014: 128). In a speech on 'nationhood' to the St Georges Society in 1961 he had depicted a vanishing empire from where 'a generation had come home from years of distant wanderings' and were now 'a united people in its island home' (Powell, 1961). His romanticism was not extended to the former colonised people. In speeches in the West Midlands in 1968 and 1969 he deplored the immigration of those he described as 'coloured, Negro and piccaninnies', used the well-known 'Rivers of blood' allusion to the writings of the Latin poet Virgil, and quoted one of his constituents as saying that 'soon the black man will have the whip hand over the white man' (Powell, 1968). He claimed without evidence that the white working class could not obtain houses, hospital beds or school places, and that employers favoured migrant workers, and 'the sense of being a persecuted minority is growing among ordinary English people' (Powell, 1968). All these assertions have resurfaced over the years, up to and beyond the more recent Brexit vote (Tomlinson, 2018).

The main issue in the 1960s was whether immigrant minorities could be incorporated into a working class, which as, British sociologist T.H. Marshall suggested, had only partially achieved legal, political and social citizen rights (Marshall, 1951). Assimilation and absorption of migrants dominated political debate. A government White Paper in 1965 demanded 'control of the entry of immigrants so that it does not outrun Britain's capacity to absorb them' (Home Office, 1965: 2). In one response to the White Paper, Labour MP Robert Mellish told Parliament that there would be racial violence if his white voters in Lambeth thought that 'coloured people' would be given housing in preference to them (Rex and Tomlinson, 1979: 60). Roy Jenkins, while Home Secretary in 1966, thought that there could be an integration of minorities, which was 'not a flattening process of uniformity, but cultural diversity coupled with equal opportunity in an atmosphere of mutual tolerance' (Jenkins, 1966). But evidence of white tolerance of black immigrants or their British-born children was hard to detect.

Although Powell was sacked from the Conservative Cabinet for his anti-immigrant speeches, this was followed by dock workers and market traders in London marching in his defence and claiming support for a white nation-state. In fact, these supposedly spontaneous marches were, according to a memo sent to Harold Wilson by the Security Service, organised by extreme right-wing groups, including remaining members of Oswald Mosley's National Union of Fascists (Norton-Taylor and Milne, 1999). Writer Sarfraz Manzoor recalls the effect Powell's speeches had on him as a boy of Pakistani origin for whom 'Repatriation was the most terrifying word … and who feared what might happen if Powell and his supporters ever gained power' (Manzoor, 2008). It was by no means only racist working-class people who supported these views. By 1969, 327 out of 413 Conservative Associations, mainly in middle-class areas with few minorities, had voted to stop all 'coloured immigration'.

Race policies in the later 1960s were influenced by the civil rights movement and fear of city riots as in the USA, and a language of assimilation was superseded by a government language of cultural pluralism and equal opportunity, while at the same time further immigration control legislation was passed. Subsequent debates have centred round whether assimilation had been a long-term government policy, but even the most obtuse policy-makers would have been aware that globally, minorities in nation-states generally do keep their own languages, religions and customs, providing they do not conflict with the law. The issue in Britain as elsewhere was whether majority and minority could adhere to an over-arching set of values and laws that respected human rights and could be agreed by all. This has not yet happened in Britain. Farzana Shain has made out a persuasive case that policy responses to minorities have been more to do with managing and containing 'problem populations' than any assimilation or pluralism (Shain, 2013).

Education policies[3]

The post–Second World War education system was intended to be central to a welfare state that would distribute resources more fairly and encourage economic growth. The reconstruction of the country required large amounts of labour. This labour shortage was partly due to women who had worked during the war and who then had to give up their jobs. Class antagonisms were as strong as ever. In 1945, one woman was recorded as complaining about food shortages while seeing the Queen pass by in a Royal visit to Birmingham, who 'considering the rationing looked well fed' (quoted in Kynaston, 2007: 105). David Kynaston also noted that the middle classes felt a greater sense of deprivation in the austerity years into the 1950s, and a sense of losing privileges, especially servants and golf!

But education policies were to continue to favour the middle and upper classes. Before the Education Act 1944, some 88% of pupils had left school by the age of 14, only 10% passed public examinations and only 5% went into higher education. The Education Act introduced secondary education for all to the age of 15, but children were to be separated at age 11 on the basis of 'age, aptitude and ability' into grammar, secondary modern and technical schools, the latter remaining undeveloped. It soon became apparent that the Act benefited middle-class children, with some 80% of mainly working-class children going into secondary modern schools and the middle classes dominating grammar schools, with some concessions to the 'bright' working-class child. The practice of streaming in primary schools worked as a form of social selection, and the middle class and the aspirational lower middle classes did their best, as they have always done, to ensure that their children were more successful in competitive examinations for the best state schools. The few working-class children who made it to grammar schools soon disowned their backgrounds and were pleased that they were separated from 'the dim ones' (Jackson and Marsden, 1962: 192). Brian Jackson had previously observed that in the 'A' streams the children were taller and better fed than in the 'C' streams.

The post-war Labour governments actually increased inequalities in the school structure by reducing grammar school places, preventing secondary modern pupils from entering for public examinations, and openly stating that these schools were 'for children whose future employment will not demand any measure of technical skills or knowledge' (Ministry of Education, 1946: 13). It was not until 1963 and the introduction of the Certificate of Secondary Education (CSE) that secondary modern schools were allowed a public examination. Brian Simon noted that 'even under a Labour Government elected with a massive majority the mediation of class relations was still a major function of the education system' (Simon, 1991: 115). But the post-war government was concerned to get as many young people as possible through schools by the age of 15 into jobs needed for economic reconstruction.

The rich and influential, including most members of the government, continued to send their children to private schools, especially members of the prestigious Headmasters' and Headmistresses' Conference (HMC). The intention was to ensure their children could access positions of power and influence. Although the public schools were initially concerned that a Labour government might interfere with their status, this did not happen, and they continued to inculcate beliefs in their superiority over the working classes, people from the colonies and other immigrants, as the testimony of the numbers of ex-public school boys can verify (Gaythorne-Hardy, 1977). A report in 1944 had considered the integration of these schools into the state system, but this was quietly forgotten, and a commission set up in 1965 to examine this possibility produced two reports that were also ignored. Although 90% of pupils (mainly boys) in these fee-paying schools had professional and managerial parents, the chair of the HMC declared in 1964 that 'there is no institution more effective than a boarding school for revealing the irrelevance of class' (Simon, 1991: 322). Both Prime Minister Attlee and future Labour Leader Hugh Gaitskell, educated at public schools, had little interest in the issue, and Tony Benn recorded in his diary in October 1953 that, 'Gaitskell still wants an elite learning Latin verse' (Benn, 1994: 172). Future public school-educated ministers perhaps showed that Latin verse was not the best preparation for government; the Brexit negotiations after 2016 demonstrated that it was mainly men educated at public schools, notably Boris Johnson and Jacob Rees-Mogg (both educated at Eton), arguing for a 'hard Brexit' and failing to support their Prime Minister in her negotiations.

The idea that children should be separated on the basis of testing for 'assumed' intelligence or ability was soon challenged by research, but enduring genetic beliefs and assumptions that social and racial groups could be differentiated as 'more or less intelligent' cast a long and pernicious shadow into the 21st century. Even the report by Lady Plowden in 1967 referred to the difficulty of deciding whether an immigrant child 'lacks intelligence, or is suffering from culture shock or an inability to communicate' (The Plowden Report, 1967: 70). Two reports in 1963 on the education of 13- to 16-year-olds (The Newsom Report, 1963) and higher education (The Robbins Report, 1963) had actually rejected deterministic theories of intelligence. The Newsom Report, which recommended raising the school leaving age to 16 (which happened 10 years later), argued against notions of fixed ability and intelligence, of which the working classes always appeared to have less! Although comprehensive schooling had been supported by some in the Labour Party since the 1920s, and adopted as policy in 1952, the restriction of educational opportunities and access to professional and managerial employment suited those supporting a hierarchical class structure, and also paralleled economic needs for skilled and unskilled labour in post-war reconstruction.

By the 1960s governments around the world were recognising the need for expanded education systems, and by the mid-1960s a broad consensus emerged that non-selective comprehensive schooling be established. The middle classes were also realising that working-class children might enter grammar schools in larger numbers and displace their children, a view that has persisted over the years. Even before Labour won the election in 1964, 90 out of 163 local authorities had submitted plans to become non-selective, although this was only requested, not required, in a 1965 Circular (DES, 1965). This allowed some authorities to procrastinate, and 15 LEAs retained selective schools. The bandwagon for grammar school retention and expansion has continued to roll on into the 21st century.

Optimistic beliefs that a democratic society should educate all its young people to high levels rather than just selected elites was always under attack from a right wing dedicated to preserving a traditional hierarchical society. Both during the 1960s and afterwards, the decade was presented as a period of liberalism when traditions were destroyed and education standards lowered. A series of Black Papers published by right-wing academics and policy groups between 1969 and 1977 resurrected deterministic theories of intelligence, and presented in lurid and inaccurate detail the lowering of standards and the feckless behaviour by the working classes that hindered their school achievements. The national media demonised some urban schools as 'blackboard jungles', a term redolent with the supposed primitive behaviour of 'natives' depicted in 19th- and 20th-century imperial literature. While the Black Papers blamed the poor for their failings, more liberal policies advocated compensatory education along the lines of the Head Start programmes in the USA. In Britain remedial education for children falling behind was intended to alleviate what were described as cycles of deprivation and cultures of poverty (Rutter and Madge, 1976). There was little discussion then, as now, of economic conditions that create poverty.

Education for ignorance

Ignorance about colonial immigrants and where they came from was widespread, and the education system was not about to enlighten children. A survey of 2,000 people in 1948 reported that 67% thought those living in the colonies had a lower standard of living than in Britain, 62% thought they were mainly 'coloured', but only 49% could name one colony (Kynaston, 2007: 272). While the report noted that housewives, the unskilled and those over 60 were the least well informed, even managerial groups were not well informed, especially on knowing the difference between a colony, a dominion and a protectorate. On this last, a history textbook, published by an association of assistant masters in secondary schools, thought that this was something to be clarified for grammar school boys. History was to be taught chronologically, but seemingly giving more attention to medieval monks than the British Empire. By the time the post-war period was reached, it was suggested that there should be some teaching to boys of developments in the Empire, and 'possibly a lesson or two on the peculiar problems of India' and its 'recent crisis', presumably the partition and subsequent massacres (IAAM, 1950: 49). David Cannadine and his colleagues, who recorded the teaching of history through the 20th century, noted the White Paper of 1943 that mentioned that history, geography and modern languages should be taught to give pupils more interest in 'the responsibilities of citizenship in this country, the Empire and the world', but that it remained only an aspiration. By the end of the 1960s they asked 'how did the national narrative which had previously culminated in the 19th century era of global greatness, now look when these supremacies seemed to have vanished?' (Cannadine et al, 2011: 141).

Press reporting at the time of the partition of India blamed sectarian violence, with 'gangs of Muslims assaulting Hindus' as the responsibility of the people, and with the British blamed only for a hasty departure (Rodrigues, 2017). The standard textbook, as previously noted, was Stembridge's *New world geographies* which, in Volume 1, recorded that 'mankind is usually divided into three races: (1) the Caucasian or White Race, (2) The Mongoloid or Yellow Race, (3) The Negro Race' (Stembridge,

1951: 1). This book was based on the 19th-century Social Darwinist classifications; it was still used in the 1970s when Prime Minister Theresa May and her Foreign Secretary Boris Johnson were at school. Colonial historians in other countries with disappearing empires have also recorded that 'Geography text books remind us of the most simplistic and over-determined classification system of them all, that of skin colour' (Fremeaux and Maas, 2015: 386). This referred to the French Empire, whose Minister for their colonies continued to refer to 'races' by colour.

In Britain teachers from former colonies, even when fully qualified, found difficulty in getting work. One, Eustace Braithwaite, with a Physics degree from Cambridge, eventually found a job teaching science in a London school and, as the only black teacher in London, suffered abuse. He eventually wrote a book about his experiences, which was made into the successful film, *To Sir, With Love*. There was little evidence that primary or secondary modern school pupils were learning anything other than the pre-war imperial stories, supplemented by comics and films. Films by this time were mainly focusing on the defeat of Germany, and the Nazis had taken over as despicable enemies. But Tarzan was as popular as ever. Parents brought up on an imperial curriculum were not in a position to enlighten their children. One older man recalled that in his time at school the whole primary school would sit in a big circle in the hall and listen to tales of big game hunters who would display animal skins and assorted African spears and drums (personal communication with the author).

Although the Festival of Britain, organised in 1951 under the Labour government to promote British trade with a post-imperial world, was a great success with the public, Churchill regarded it as socialist propaganda, and ordered the site demolished when he came to power. Business was more enlightened, and many schools continued to receive a book called the *British trades alphabet*, which gave information about companies and their trade around the world and offered competitions and prizes. Cadburys Ltd was especially remembered for free samples of chocolate and even pop-up cardboard cocoa pods to demonstrate how chocolate was made. One science teacher recalled that the *British trades alphabet* series was an important initiative that linked education, industry, technology and trade (personal communication with the author). But the series seldom mentioned the effects of unequal trade on the colonial populations (*British trades alphabet*, 1955).

Education policy-makers in the 1950s and 1960s were more concerned with developing new school and local authority structures and a rising birth rate to worry about changing views and attitudes concerning the British Empire and its aftermath. A post-war teacher shortage led to ex-servicemen being offered a nine-month training programme and sent into schools. Many of these (mainly men) had similar experiences of 'the natives' overseas as had the character in Levy's novel, and had no experience of treating black or other minorities as equals. Public schools often took graduates with no teacher training, and continued with their own traditional curriculum. Civil servants who drafted Education Acts and guidance were, like their political masters in all parties, mainly educated at public schools. The experiences of one National Service recruit, educated at a public school and given a National Service commission, and who subsequently became a teacher, illustrated the incomprehension of some young men sent out to the colonies to oversee independence. Working in West Africa (Ghana), among his duties was distributing condoms to 'the men on their visits to black prostitutes', and he was shocked when older African politicians, who had worked in collaboration with the British, were rejected by young Ghanaians. He had been brought up on patriotic tales and was surprised to find 'British good-will' was not reciprocated. (Hawkes, 2012: 229). But at least he was more understanding than the officers encountered by another National Service recruit sent out to Singapore before Malaya fought for independence. He recorded that, 'We had eight Malays on our fire crew and we were told they were not our equals. Officers told us we must be firm but fair with them but they were not our equal. I thought that some of the officers, if they had not been to public school, wouldn't have made lance corporal in charge of the toilets' (Perry, 2012: 33).

By the 1960s it was clear that teachers in both private and state schools had little idea of their importance in helping along what was a developing multiracial and multicultural society. This was not surprising, given that most had been educated in the ethnocentric curriculum, with the pink maps on classroom walls and a curriculum that combined elements of nationalism and racial arrogance with beliefs in superior moral and Christian benevolence towards imperial subjects. In the literature on the education of immigrant children in the 1960s, assimilationist approaches were dominant. Jenny Williams, studying schools in Birmingham, wrote that 'teachers see their role as putting over a set of values (Christian), a code of behaviour (middle class) and a set of aspirations in which white collar jobs have higher prestige than manual' (Williams, 1967). One head teacher, responding to a survey in the 1960s, replied that, 'I do not consider it the responsibility of an English state school to cater for the culture and customs of a foreign nature' (quoted in Townsend and Brittan, 1973: 13).

Historians of empire, whether champions or critics, appear to agree that the spread of modern ideas and institutions, democracy, the rule of law, secularism, rationalism, technology, capitalism and human rights, along with football shirts, came from Western nations (Porter, 2015). The idea that these noble ideas were spread peacefully to former colonies lingered on, without any mention of force or guns. Beliefs that colonial populations were inferior in their culture and lifestyles were expressed openly. Chigozie Obioma eventually concluded that colonialism in Africa was so thorough and the civilisations, tradition and cultures so eroded that the only way of viewing modern life was through a Western lens (Obioma, 2017). It was not surprising that some head teachers thought that 'customs of a foreign nature' would not be appreciated in English schools in the 1960s.

Education and minorities

Britain was not alone in its contradictory responses to migration and the incorporation of migrants and their children. Post-war migration had led to world-wide debates, especially in Western countries, about the merits of assimilation versus pluralistic co-existence. Assimilation required that a nation-state should have one majority culture with minorities abandoning their own cultures and languages to become effective citizens. This view was initially espoused by both liberals and traditionalists, and education was to bring this about. The second report from the

Commonwealth Immigrants Advisory Council (CIAC) asserted somewhat pompously that:

> A national system of education must aim at producing citizens who can take their place in a society properly equipped to exercise rights and perform duties the same as other citizens ... a national system cannot be expected to perpetuate the values of immigrant groups. (CIAC, 1964)

Assimilationist ideologies were soon challenged as civil rights protest movements emerged during the 1960s. Within these movements racial discrimination had emerged as a major factor to be challenged. In Britain a first generation of settlers had incentives to move towards some kind of absorption into a society promising social and economic equality, but they soon realised that hostile assumptions about race and culture prevented equal educational and employment opportunities for them and for their children. Black and Asian movements against injustice quickly developed. A West Indian Standing Conference, which brought together various groups, was established after the Notting Hill riots. The Indian Workers Association, with a history from the 1930s, continued to defend workers' rights in and out of trade union movements (Rex and Tomlinson, 1979: 267), a Campaign Against Racial Discrimination was set up in 1964 following a visit to Britain by Martin Luther King, and a North London West Indian Parents Association was active in voicing concerns over the education of black children. There was initially no central policy or planning to meet the incorporation of immigrant children; the DES defended this on the grounds that 'Neither the scale of future immigration or the patterns of settlement could be seen until the early 1960s' (DES, 1971: 14). This was nonsense, as it was clear that settlement was where labour was needed in inner cities, but these were places where schools serving the working classes were already neglected and ill resourced. Government papers continued to refer to undesirable concentrations of Commonwealth immigrants that should be broken up, and a Birmingham Association of Schoolmasters lamented that racial enclaves were here to stay.

White parents in Southall complained about the numbers of immigrant children in 'their' schools, and it was suggested that no school should have more than 30% of minority children. In 1964 the CIAC recommended the dispersal of children on the grounds that they affected the progress of other children and hindered their assimilation into 'normal' school life. Dispersal by bussing became official policy, although only 11 local authorities adopted this, and the policy was ruled illegal in 1975. In 2017, Joe Henderson, a researcher in Huddersfield, made a video to put on YouTube interviewing adults who had been bussed as children to an all-white school. There was never any suggestion that white children be bussed (Henderson, 2017). Despite confusion over the numbers of immigrant children, one specific policy was from the Home Office, not the Education Department, to distribute money, via Section 11 of a Local Government Grant, to areas where immigrants from the Commonwealth had languages and customs different from their local communities. The then respected school inspectors (Her Majesty's Inspectorate, HMI) focused on teaching English to immigrants and brought together specialist language teachers. Policies aimed at all deprived communities included Educational Priority Areas, and an Urban Aid programme, set up by the Labour government in 1968, partly as a response to Enoch Powell's inflammatory speeches (Tomlinson, 2008).

Blaming minority children

As policy-makers and schools could not admit to, or were not aware of, their own ignorance of colonialism and subsequent migration, they were not in a position to consider changes that were needed to educate all children in a society where, literally, the Empire had come home. So the default position was to blame migrant children and their parents for deficiencies. Black, Asian and other minority children had barely arrived before psychologists and educational researchers began to conduct psychometric tests to measure 'intelligence' and ability, and used tests of attainment standardised on white populations to declare the children were of low ability or under-achieving. The issue of the over-placement of black children in what were then schools for the 'educationally subnormal' (ESN, a category not abolished until 1981), caused much anxiety for Caribbean parents, and in 1969 the North West London West Indian Association complained to the Race Relations Board that it was racial discrimination (Tomlinson, 1981). Bernard Coard published his classic paper *How the West Indian child is made ESN in the British school system* in 1971 (Coard, 1971).

Parents from Caribbean countries, where there had been no general secondary education until 1953, had assumed that even if they took low-paid work, their children would have educational and job opportunities, and were shocked and angry at the levels of discrimination they and their children faced. Even well-qualified parents found their qualifications did not lead to equal treatment by schools – a situation continuing over 40 years later (Rollock et al, 2015). Supplementary schools became popular with parents, both to supplement poor school teaching and to give a fairer historical account of colonialism and Caribbean and African development. Any course labelled 'Black Studies' was regarded as a dangerous activity, and in 1972 the Chief Education Officer in Birmingham visited a school where a Black Studies course was incorporated into a Community Studies course and closed it down (Rex and Tomlinson, 1979: 186). But by 1981 the DES were lamenting that 'minority parents appear to be losing confidence in what schools are teaching their children (DES, 1981: 41).

Debates on the racial politics and the morality of IQ and other forms of testing had been in progress for some time, both in the USA and Europe, as test results were used to denigrate immigrants and minorities. But this was largely ignored, and much of the research in England continued over the years to be politically naive and damaging. Explanations for any lower educational performance of minority children over the years ran along the lines of lack of English, interference from Caribbean dialects, migration shock, family disorganisation, male dominance, male absence, female dominance, cultural difference, child-minding, low self-esteem, identity problems and low socioeconomic status. School difficulties, low teacher expectations, stereotyping of children and experience of racial hostility were also explanations, but overall assumptions remained that black and Irish children had a lower intellectual capacity for learning. Arthur Jensen (1969), in an article in the *Harvard Educational Review*, concluded that compensatory education for black children was misplaced due to their inferior intelligence, and, as noted in Chapter Two, his former student, Hans Eysenck, later a London University professor, as previously noted, demonstrated a peculiar historical view when he concluded in his 1971 book that, 'Negroes and the Irish' had lower mental capacities due to crimes committed against their ancestors (Eysenck, 1971: 142).

Positive practice

There was, however, a growing awareness in urban schools that blaming immigrant children for their deficiencies was not good enough, and teachers had been left to solve the problems of educating for a multiracial society, in which all people would live together harmoniously. The first collection of essays by practising teachers in the 1960s was *The multiracial school* (1971), edited by Julia McNeal and Margaret Rogers, Julia McNeal being the daughter of former Labour Leader Hugh Gaitskell. This collection showed that some teachers were taking seriously the need for resources and a changed curriculum for all children, and were aware that white children needed an education to 'combat the indifference and hostility that exists between different national and racial groups' (McNeal and Rogers, 1971: 15). They were also aware that the children grouped themselves along ethnic lines, a recurring issue not just in the majority but also in the minority groups. Teachers' willingness to deal with these issues depended on their training, and as teachers came through their own schooling with an acceptance of the British Empire and an ignorance of its consequences, training was desperately needed. It was not until 1969 that there was recognition that 'all teachers should be equipped to prepare children for life in a multicultural society' (Select Committee on Race Relations and Immigration, 1969: para 214). But the cultural values filtering down through all social classes still encouraged beliefs in the economic social and racial superiority of white Europeans. It was unlikely that attempts to absorb the children of the former colonies into an education system in denial and embedded in public hostility towards immigrants would be easy. As Gilbert, in Andrea Levy's novel, found, even after finding a job, his white workmates were still asking, 'When are you going back to the jungle, oi darkie, you ain't answered me, when are you going back where you belong?' (Levy, 2004: 317).

Summary

This chapter has linked the dissolution of the British Empire in the 1950s and 1960s with education policies in England, as former colonies gained their independence. It suggests that imperial beliefs and images were still engrained in public understanding and educational structures, and policy-makers and schools were not able to, or interested in, changing this. The arrival of former colonial immigrants was met with hostility and incomprehension, and education did little to enlighten people about the reasons for migration or to combat the nationalistic sentiments spread by prominent politicians. There was considerable hypocrisy from politicians of all parties over migration. Post-war education was based on a social democratic consensus that governments should regulate and resource the whole system fairly, and improve schooling for all children. Although, to a certain extent, this happened, the middle classes continued to benefit the most. It did not happen for the children of migrants, who, from the outset, were regarded as 'problems' to be dispersed, or who were treated unequally in poorly resourced urban schools. Positive treatment eventually came from HMI and money for teaching English, and from some teachers who realised that there was a need for what, in a later report, became an 'education for all' (Lord Swann and Committee of Inquiry into the Education of Children from Ethnic Minority Groups, 1985). From the 1970s political antagonisms ensured that educational ignorance about empire and migration continued.

Notes

[1] Canada and its various territories gained independence as a (white) dominion in 1847-71, Australia 1852-90, New Zealand 1852 and South Africa 1872-1910. By the 1960s these countries were referred to as the

old (White) Commonwealth. More recent decolonised countries were the 'New Commonwealth'.

2   The study was the largest carried out by the Institute of Race Relations, an organisation founded in 1958. From 1971, conflict in the Institute and a 'revolution' among the staff led to funding being withdrawn and the Institute becoming a smaller Marxist organisation headed by Ambalavaner Sivanandan. The Institute's journal *Race* became *Race & Class*, edited by Darcus Howe, later a TV producer and documentary maker.

3   The policies here refer to England and Wales. Scotland had some control of its education system from 1945 and Northern Ireland had partial control. After devolution in 1997/99, Wales and Northern Ireland controlled their own education systems.

4

Post-imperial anxieties and conflicts, 1970-90

> We all thought the empire was a marvellous thing. It was a force for good throughout the world. When Britain chose to give her empire away we were rather saddened – the colonial people had all the blessing of colonial rule and look how casually they dismissed them. (National Service cadet officer, quoted in Shindler, 2012: 92)

> If we went on as we are, by the end of the century there would be four million people of the New Commonwealth or Pakistan here. Now that is an awful lot and I think it means people are rather afraid this country might be swamped by people with a different culture. (Thatcher, 1978)

An empire mindset never really died. For some, colonial rule was a blessing given up by ungrateful people, and for many, including a prime minister, the arrival of former colonial subjects into the colonising country was regretted. By 1978, some politicians claimed that just 1.5 million black and Asian people, a third actually born in Britain, might swamp the other 55 million. National servicemen who had served overseas were, as Colin Shindler has noted, among many who regretted the ending of the British Empire. From the 1970s all political parties were in agreement that immigration from the former colonies, euphemistically termed 'New Commonwealth' countries, should be limited. Whereas in the 19th and earlier 20th centuries politicians, adventurers, academics and others were openly racist over colonial conquests of supposedly inferior peoples, by the mid-century, an ideology of conservative imperialism had developed to try to smooth moral dilemmas. *Civis Britannicus sum* ('I am a British citizen') and accompanying legal rights was a claim all people in the Empire could make, but it assumed colonial people would stay put in their countries. Conservative imperialism, liberal ideologies concerned with human rights and socialist notions of the brotherhood of all workers disappeared with the invited arrival of colonial workers and their families. By the 1970s notions that might earlier have been dismissed as morally unacceptable became the unspoken assumptions of all political parties.

This chapter documents the continuation of an anti-immigrant ideology and its linkage with the idea of an exclusive British identity, and the developing reactions of a younger generation becoming more race conscious. By the 1980s conflicts surrounding the acceptance of black and other minorities into what was becoming a multiracial and multicultural society and their equal participation as citizens became the major contested issue. The old British Empire had been transformed into a Commonwealth of former colonies, dependencies and British overseas territories.[1] This was not a process without conflict, as the issue of Grenada, independent in 1974, and the Falkland Islands (Las Malvinas), acquired in 1833 and still an overseas territory, indicated. Closer links with Europe were becoming a reality, with a referendum in 1975 cementing entry into a European Economic Community (EEC), and Prime Minister Thatcher signing up to a Single European Act in 1986. In 2018, when papers were released after 30 years, her 1988 speech in Bruges, Belgium, suggested that she was in favour of developing a Single Market and 'Our destiny is in Europe, part of the Community' (quoted in Roy and Bowcott, 2018). What was described as globalisation and a global economy was developing, which was causing further migrations of people and their labour world-wide. In Britain, questions of identity became crucial, with much antagonism to minorities based on whether differences of colour, culture and religion were at odds with notions of a British national identity. In the 1980s, a radical restructuring of public welfare provision began to take shape with the introduction of market forces into education, health and other social services, and an extended market in housing, which resulted in more inequalities and disadvantages for working-class and minority groups. A working class openly at war with the government was subject to a defeat when the miners' strike of 1984-85 ended in capitulation. A racism based on culture and religion as well as colour encouraged Powellite views of an exclusive national identity, and provided more rationalisation for xenophobia and hostility towards minorities.

Education policies were moving towards non-selective schooling and some curriculum change, accompanied by what was to become a familiar charge that educational standards were too low and failing to produce a literate and skilled workforce. A need to play down any special arrangements for immigrant (black and Asian) children to placate a hostile white population underpinned policies, and minority children were subsumed under the label of 'disadvantage': 'Immigrant children share with indigenous children the disadvantages associated with an impoverished environment' (DES, 1974, 2). Despite more Race Relations legislation, the terminology of race or racism was avoided in education policy documents. In 1984, a paper produced by the Council for National Academic Awards (CNAA) on including multicultural understanding in teacher training courses had any references to anti-racism deleted by DES officials (Tomlinson, 2008: 86). Despite all this, the 1980s was actually a period of some educational advance for minorities, and there was more focus on the needs of a society by then being described as multicultural or multi-ethnic. The Swann report (Lord Swann and Committee of Inquiry into the Education of Children from Ethnic Minority Groups, 1985) was regarded as 'the boldest, most comprehensive statement on multicultural education so far produced in Britain' (Williams, 1988), with the resulting right-wing backlash from nationalists seeking to preserve imperial notions of a national identity free from the contamination of 'alien cultures'.

Significant events

1970	Conservative government elected; Circular 7/70 cancels expectations that secondary schools need become comprehensive schools
1971	Immigration Act limits right of abode to patrials with a father or grandfather born in the UK – others to obtain work permits and register with the police; Home Office sets up a Race Relations Research Unit
1971	McNeal and Rogers publish *The multiracial school*; Eysenck publishes

	Race, intelligence and education, suggesting black and Irish people have lower IQs than other groups
1971	DES produces two surveys on *The education of immigrants*
1972	Expulsion of Ugandan Asians by Idi Amin – 27,000 arrive and many go to Leicester despite the City Council claiming that 'Leicester is full'; DES discontinues collection of statistics on immigrant pupils
1973	School leaving age raised to 16; Select Committee on Race Relations and Immigration publishes a report on education, making 24 recommendations; Trevor McDonald becomes ITV's first black news reader (he retired in 2005 and was given a Knighthood)
1973	War in the Asian subcontinent; Pakistan secedes from the Commonwealth; Bangladesh becomes a separate country
1973	Recession as price of oil increases; collapse of the youth labour market
1974	Labour forms a minority government; Roy Jenkins announces an amnesty for illegal immigrants; abolition of direct grant schools; DES publishes *Educational disadvantage and the needs of immigrants* (1974); a Centre for Disadvantage was set up in Manchester but closed in 1980
1974	Grenada, claimed by the British in 1763, gets independence
1975	(February) Nation-wide vote to join the European Economic Community (EEC); 17,300,000 voted to join, 8,400,000 were against
1975	Home Office report on *Racial discrimination* and Bullock Report on *A language for life* published; Sex Discrimination Act passed; Margaret Thatcher becomes Conservative Party Leader
1976	Gurdip Singh Chaggar is murdered at a Southall bus stop – police say it is not a racial crime; Enoch Powell says 'mugging' is a racial crime; Shadow Home Secretary William Whitelaw says 'The British Empire has paid its debts' and calls for inner-city programmes to defuse racial tension; third Race Relations Act and Commission for Racial Equality (CRE) set up; James Callaghan makes Ruskin College speech
1977	Select Committee on Race Relations and Immigration reports on *The West Indian community* and claims, 'We are a multiracial, multicultural country' (Select Committee, 1977); the Black Papers (Cox and Boyson, 1977) attack comprehensive education and 'Marxist infiltration' in education
1977	In by-elections in Stechford and Ladywood in Birmingham, the National Front come third, with the Liberals fourth
1978	Warnock Committee reports on *Special educational needs* (DES, 1978) with no mention of Caribbean parents' anxiety about their children; Viv Anderson becomes the first black footballer to play for England
1979	Conservatives win the general election; Mrs Thatcher becomes the first female prime minister
1979	Rampton Committee set up to enquire into the education of children from minority groups; during confrontations with the National Front in Southall, Blair Peach, a teacher, is killed
1980	Education Act
1980	Rhodesia finally becomes an independent country called Zimbabwe
1981	Race riots in Brixton, Toxteth and other cities; Home Office reports on *Racial disadvantage*; also Rampton Report on *West Indian children in our schools*; Special Education Act abolishes 'categories of handicap'
1982	(April) Falkland Islands (Malvinas) War against Argentina

1982   Scarman Report on the Brixton disorders; Schools Council for the
         Curriculum abolished; Lower Attaining Pupils Project (LAPP) for
         bottom 40% of pupils; 20 LEAs have multicultural education policies;
         new guidelines for Section 11 funding; some 40 black supplementary
         schools in operation
1983   Conservatives re-elected; the USA invades the British Caribbean island
         of Grenada
1984   Honeyford affair in Bradford; Council for the Accreditation of Teacher
         Education (CATE) set up
1985   Lord Swann's Committee reports on *Education for all* (1985); Archbishop
         of Canterbury's report *Faith in the city* is called a Marxist document;
         riots in Toxteth and Handsworth; national Anti-racist Movement
         in Education set up; DES publishes a White Paper on *Better schools*
         (1985), stressing all pupils should understand the traditions and values
         of British society; Oliver Letwin advises Margaret Thatcher that 'race
         riots were caused by individual bad character and attitudes'
1986   Parliament ratifies the Single European Act that sets up a Single Market
         and allows free movement of labour; DES offers Education Support
         Grants for multicultural projects in white schools (120 funded by
         1988); O-levels replaced by GCSEs; corporal punishment outlawed in
         state schools; national priority in-service courses for teachers; Ahmed
         Ullah is stabbed to death in Burnage School, Manchester
1987   Conservatives win a third general election (four black MPs elected); DES
         creates a post for inner-city education and education for a multicultural
         society; white parents in Dewsbury set up a school in a pub for their
         children; a Campaign for Real Education is set up to support British
         culture and the Christian religion; Black History Month introduced in
         schools
1988   Commission for Racial Equality (CRE) publishes *Learning in terror*; St
         George's Medical School admits their selection procedures discriminate
         against minority ethnic groups and women; Immigration Act removes
         right for New Commonwealth citizens to bring in marriage partners;
         Section 28 of a Local Government Act forbids the 'promotion' of
         homosexuality in education
1988   Education Reform Act; National Curriculum; Key Stage assessments;
         parental right to 'choose' a school continues; schools are able to opt
         out of LEA control and be 'grant-maintained'; inner London Education
         Authority abolished; National Curriculum Council (NCC) set up
1989   Schools in Birmingham with largely Muslim intakes vote to become
         grant-maintained; copies of Salman Rushdie's book *The Satanic verses*
         are burned in Bradford; Secretary of State for Education requests the
         NCC take account of the multicultural nature of society and sets up
         a working group, their subsequent report being censored; the Labour
         Party produces *Multicultural education: Labour's policy for schools*
1990   Education Secretary rules that a parent in Cleveland has a right to
         remove her child from a multiracial school as parental 'choice' takes
         precedence over Race Relations legislation; Norman Tebbit MP argues
         that Asian loyalty to Britain can be judged by whether they cheer for
         an English cricket team

Politics and ideologies in the 1970s

By the 1970s there was a general consensus among politicians, their advisers, the public and academics of various theoretical persuasions that 'race' was a problem and a likely cause for conflict and violence. John Rex and Sally Tomlinson undertook an empirical study, and concluded that by the 1970s 'crucial decisions had already been taken, and the status of black and brown men [sic] in Britain, had already been declared different from and inferior to, that of the native-born British citizen' (Rex and Tomlinson, 1979: 47). Researchers at the Birmingham Centre for Contemporary Cultural Studies, under the direction of Stuart Hall, further concluded that a 'siege mentality shaped the 70s', and political class struggles incorporated a racism that linked a black presence, illegal migration, young unemployed people and white people who identified with 'alien cultures' as enemies (Centre for Contemporary Cultural Studies, 1982: 27-9; Hall, 1978).[2] Sir Alfred Sherman, a former Communist Party member turned right wing, and a political adviser to Mrs Thatcher, declared that 'The imposition of mass immigration from backward alien cultures is just one symptom of this self destructive urge reflected in the assault on patriotism, the family … the Christian religion, in public lives and schools … and all that is English and wholesome' (Sherman, 1979).

Although in 1970 Conservative Prime Minister Edward Heath told his local party that 'There is no reason why cultural diversity should not be combined with loyalty to this country' (Heath, 1970), both local and national parties were asserting ideas of patriotism and a national homogeneity that excluded minorities. There was much opposition to the arrival in 1972 of some 27,000 Asians with British passports, mainly educated people with entrepreneurial skills, expelled by Idi Amin from Uganda. Despite hostility, many settled in Leicester and rejuvenated businesses there. There was similar hostility to the arrival of Asians expelled from Malawi and Vietnamese boat people taken in as refugees, both the results of British and French imperialism. The Conservative Monday Club in Parliament campaigned for the repatriation of Caribbean and Asian people, and took exception to what they called a 'race industry'. This comprised the various commissions and groups supporting legislation against discrimination, especially the Race Relations Act 1976, which included education for the first time, and created a Commission for Racial Equality (CRE). In June 1976 a teenager, Gurdip Singh Chaggar, was murdered in Southall by white youths, but the police decided it was not a 'racial crime'. Over the following years there were many more racial murders. In 1976, in a speech in Leicester, Shadow Home Secretary William Whitelaw, referring to immigration, announced that 'the British Empire has paid its debts' (Lord Whitelaw, 1976) by allowing the entry of the former colonised into Britain.

The Immigration Act 1971 had gone some way to satisfying the anti-immigrant lobby, by distinguishing between 'patrials' and non-patrials', and subsequent Acts controlled the entry of wives and children. Former imperial subjects, from rural and urban backgrounds, had settled where their labour was needed, and white flight and discriminatory housing policies had ensured spatial segregation. Minorities, especially with different languages, religions and cultural traditions, were openly regarded as a threat to a British national identity. Trade unions were not much help, despite industrial disputes being led by Asian workers.[3] One trade union leader, William Carron, referred to people not born in the country who 'dip their fingers' into the National Health Service (NHS) and other benefits to which they had not contributed (Rex, 1973). This was as untrue then as it has continued to be over the years, as migrant workers' tax contributions have always been more than any benefits claimed.

Enoch Powell's role was important as he had moved from being an advocate of imperialism to being an arch advocate of a nationalism that excluded New Commonwealth immigrants. His concern with immigration control could be linked to his own political advancement (Foot, 1969), but other political parties were also playing to popular antagonisms. Through the 1970s the neo-Nazi National Front, developed from fascist anti-Semitic movements in the 1930s, made electoral gains, particularly in the West Midlands.[4] Although Powell had been dropped from the Conservative Shadow Cabinet by Heath when he made his anti-immigrant speeches, he turned his attention to opposing the 1972 European Communities Bill, bringing Britain into the

EEC, a forerunner of the EU. He gave a speech in Lyon telling the French that 'the British people are profoundly opposed to the Community' (Powell, 1971), although most of the Conservative Party were in favour (and most of the Labour Party opposed). It was Prime Minister Harold Wilson who held a referendum in 1975 whereby a majority of the British people voted to stay in the EEC. Powell went to Northern Ireland where he became an Ulster Unionist MP from 1974 until 1987. His major ambition there was to keep the province as part of the 'British Nation'.

A major political issue in the 1970s was the reaction of a younger second generation of immigrant descent, mainly schooled in Britain, who were aware of their own disadvantages in failing to obtain equal rights to education and jobs. With increasing youth unemployment, despite the variety of youth training schemes developing, Caribbean and Asian groups faced discrimination (Troyna and Smith, 1982). Between 1973 and 1979 the unemployment of black youth increased at twice the rate as that for white youth. Influenced by the civil rights movement in the USA, the Pan-African National Congress and the anti-apartheid African National Congress, many young Caribbeans asserted a militant black identity, and relations with the police deteriorated, with 'SUS' laws (questioning on suspicion of crimes) and a tabloid media asserting fears of black crime. The police were reluctant to bring a prosecution when a white teacher, Blair Peach, died from injuries in 1979 sustained during a march opposing a National Front rally in Southall. By the 1980s, what the media described as race riots and the government termed racial disturbances took place in Bristol, Brixton, Southall, Toxteth and Birmingham. The Home Affairs Select Committee noted a deteriorating state of race relations and the 'grim realities' of young people and their parents whose expectations of life in Britain had not turned out well (Home Affairs Committee, 1981: vii).

Politics and ideologies in the 1980s

By the 1980s, the old British Empire had been transformed into a Commonwealth of former Colonies and Protectorates, still leaving the government responsible for a few overseas territories, including several that were havens for tax avoidance by rich individuals and multinational companies. Rhodesia, having been subject to white rule for longer than most colonies, became Zimbabwe in 1980. Prime Minister Thatcher, in power from 1979 until 1990, made much of the nationalist sentiment created during the Falklands War, declaring at a Victory parade, 'The war had dissolved secret fears that Britain was no longer the nation that had built an empire and ruled a quarter of the world' (Brendon, 2007: 635). She wrote tetchily about how uncooperative the Commonwealth Heads of Government were, especially when they wanted her to support sanctions against the apartheid regime in South Africa. During a Special Conference of Commonwealth Heads of Governments in London in 1986, she noted that, 'Kenneth Kaunda [Zambian President] was in a thoroughly self-righteous and uncooperative frame of mind when I dropped in to see him' (Thatcher, 1993: 521). She also found it 'intensely irritating' when Kaunda told her that Africa was not her area. She made a visit to Kenya in 1988, but it confirmed her worst fears of the backwardness of African countries. She wrote, 'At the government guest house Denis [Thatcher's husband] tried to run a bath but found there was no water and it had to be brought up in dustbins from the cellar' (Thatcher, 1993: 524). Despite her apparent support, she was no fan of the EEC, and wrote much in her memoirs of her dealings with EEC politicians, most of whom she appeared to despise. But she did believe that closer trading links were necessary, and in signing up to the Single Market in 1986, wrote that, 'We must have a European Single Market with the minimum of regulations – a Europe of Enterprise' (Thatcher, 1993: 745).

A global economy was developing that encouraged the movement and migration of people, bringing about both cultural convergences and more hostile resistance to migrants. Challenges to the old Empire continued. In 1982, Argentina occupied the Falkland Islands off the Argentinean coast in the South Atlantic, which they had always claimed were their Islas Malvinas (Argentinean people had been moved off the island when the British had moved in). A war resulted, in which, as noted in Chapter One, David Tinker, a naval officer, wrote to his father that his fellow shipmates regarded the Argentineans as only 'wogs' and assumed that they could easily be defeated. David's father was Hugh Tinker, a Professor of Politics, who had spent his career writing against imperialism. It was a supreme irony that David was killed, aged 26, by a French Exocet missile supplied to the Argentineans (Tinker, 1982). An editorial in *The Sunday Telegraph* managed to link the war with a denigration of citizens in the UK, asserting that, 'If the Falkland Islanders were British citizens with black or brown skins, spoke with strange accents or worshipped strange Gods, it is doubtful whether the Royal Navy would fighting for their liberation' (Worsthorne, 1982). A further challenge to Britain was in 1983, when the USA invaded Grenada, a former British colony in the Caribbean, without informing the British government. Bernard Coard, whose book on the miseducation of Caribbean children galvanised several generations of practitioners and activists (Richardson, 2005), had returned to the island as Deputy Prime Minister.[5]

Whose identity?

During the 1980s there was a grudging acceptance of the reality that colonial immigrants and their children were 'here to stay', and conflicts surrounded the acceptance of black, Asian and other minority people into a multiracial and multicultural society. Their equal participation as citizens became a major, contested issue. Questions of national identity continued to be raised, and antagonism to minorities centred on whether differences of colour, culture and religion were permanently at odds with a British identity. Young people responded with open conflict. In 1980 there was rioting in the St Paul's area in Bristol. The local National Union of Teachers (NUT) reported that black frustration over discrimination in schooling and employment, and police harassment, was the cause (Avon NUT, 1980). By June 1980, some 40 minority organisations had established a National Council for Black Organisations, and criticised the policing of minority people. In January 1981 a fire broke out in a house in New Cross, London, in which 13 young black people died. After the police had discounted a racial motive, 15,000 people marched from New Cross to Westminster demanding an end to racial murders. In response, the police launched 'Operation

Swamp' to check on black people in Brixton, where rioting broke out in April 1981, followed by riots in Toxteth, Liverpool, Manchester, Birmingham, Coventry, Leeds and other towns. Home Secretary Whitelaw appointed Lord Scarman to hold an inquiry, and his report blamed negative police practices, poor education and youth services, and discrimination in employment and housing (Lord Scarman, 1982).

Papers released 30 years later showed that Oliver Letwin, then a young adviser to Margaret Thatcher, later an MP and chief adviser to former Prime Minister David Cameron, wrote that as 'lower class unemployed white people had been living for years in appalling slums without a breakdown in order', riots and criminality by black people was the result of 'bad moral attitudes' and if given money, they would use it for Rastafarian arts and crafts and a disco and drug trade (Travis, 2015: 3). In 2000, Letwin, educated at Eton and the University of Cambridge, became well known for declaring that he would rather go out and beg on the streets than allow his children to go to a local comprehensive school. Appointed by Cameron in 2015 to develop Cabinet policy, in 2018 he was still an MP. But urban rioting in the 1980s forced the government to pay more attention to racial disadvantages. Michael Heseltine was appointed as Minister for Merseyside to coordinate ameliorative policies with an urban programme and Youth Training schemes. In 1983, a Conservative election poster featured a young black man with the slogan, 'Labour says he's black. Tories say he's British'. After the Conservatives were elected again, there were riots in Handsworth, Birmingham and Tottenham, London, and in other areas in 1985.

Paul Gilroy pointed out that the idea of national belonging used military and patriotic metaphors of war to describe minorities after conflicts. Some descriptions included 'the enemy within', 'unarmed invasion', 'alien encampments' and 'New Commonwealth occupation', which were all used to describe the black and minority presence in cities. He wrote that by the 1980s there was a 'racial nationalist portrait of Blacks as fundamentally alien' (Gilroy, 1987: 153). But while the majority society was attempting to define itself by who was 'not British', business leaders working in a global economy noticed that discrimination was bad for business. Free market supporters and a racist nationalism were in competition, although they had in common 19th-century beliefs that the state should not interfere or regulate markets or worry about inequalities in wealth or low wages. The governments during the 1980s encouraged privatisation and market forces in the public as well as the private sphere, with consequent inequalities and insecurities, including in education. In 1988 an Action for Cities programme was initiated to make inner-city areas more attractive to business, but over the following decade, around one-and-a-half million jobs were lost in inner cities.

By the 1980s religion had been added to race as a source of white hostility, as Muslim communities began to request funding for Muslim schools on a par with the existing religious schools – Anglican, Catholic and Jewish schools. Salman Rushdie's book *The Satanic verses*, regarded as insulting Islam, was burned in Bradford in January 1989 and a death threat (*fatwā*) issued by Iran's Supreme Leader against Rushdie. As Robert Winder pointed out, the notion of tolerance was now debatable; the idea of a 'benign elite graciously tolerating the outlandish habits of its inferiors' was now challenged (Winder, 2004: 415).

Norman Tebbit's cricket test, by which he claimed that loyalty to the country was judged by whether people cheered for an English team, was put into practice when Caribbean and Asian cricketers played in the English team. Although Labour lost the 1987 General Election, four black MPs were elected – one being Diane Abbott, who, by 2018, was the longest serving black (and female) MP; and an Asian councillor, Mohammed Ajeeb, became the first Muslim Lord Mayor in the city of Bradford. Labour ended the decade by producing a paper that claimed that, 'Britain is manifestly a multicultural society with a plurality of cultures. We believe that any education system ... must ensure that all children develop an understanding of and sensitivity too, this plurality of cultures and traditions' (Labour Party, 1989), something which, as Shakespeare might have said, 'Is a thing devoutly to be wished'!

Education policies in the 1970s

The Education Act 1944 emerged out of a consensus between a coalition government, the churches and the education system at all levels. Secondary education was compulsory to the age of 15, and children were to be separated on the basis of 'age, ability and aptitude', although as Brian Simon later noted, 'Even under a Labour Government elected (in 1945) with a massive majority, the mediation of class relations was still seen as a major function of education' (Simon, 1991: 115). In the 1970s Labour encouraged comprehensive schooling, improved education for children with special needs, and although they failed to address divisions created by a private school sector, education seemed ready to break with the past. What happened was a determination to hold on to a past of selection and division. After the Conservatives were elected in 1979, Mrs Thatcher became Education Secretary and her first Act was to cancel free school milk – those little bottles of milk at break time that had seemed as permanent as the British Empire. Her next was to announce that local authorities need not develop comprehensive schools. The ideological battles over education in these decades have been documented by, among others, Benn and Chitty (1996), Lawton (2005) and Tomlinson (2005). The 1970s brought a retrenchment of egalitarian and innovative policies. Global economic events put schooling under stress, as the effects of a rise in oil prices led to a recession and resulting youth unemployment This was partly solved by raising the school leaving age to 16 in 1973 and setting up a series of Youth Training Schemes run by the Manpower Services Commission.

Ironically, Labour Prime Minister James Callaghan made a speech at Ruskin College, Oxford, in 1976, claiming that what he called – and subsequent ministers have delighted in quoting – the 'education establishment', was not adequately preparing children for the world of work, and he called for a great debate on education. The speech and resulting publicity pleased the Conservatives and those opposed to comprehensive schooling, demoralised teachers, and was regarded as an own goal by Labour. Despite accusations of lowered standards, Shirley Williams, Labour Education Secretary, produced a 1977 Green Paper *Education in schools* (DES, 1977) which made it clear that more children were now in schools for longer and improvements in education were continuing. This did not prevent education becoming a permanent scapegoat for a troubled economy, with consistent attacks on schools, teachers and later on colleges and universities. Reactionary views of education were encapsulated in a series of Black Papers mainly produced in the later 1970s (Lawton, 2005: 85).

Education policies in the 1980s

The focus of education policy during the 1980s was on free markets and privatisation. The ideology underpinning reforms was that of a 19th-century liberal individualism in which consumers of education (children, young people and their parents) embraced the laws of markets and the values of self-interest and family profit. Mrs Thatcher had attended a direct grant grammar school, direct funding from the DES having been abolished by Labour in 1975, and was determined to bring this back, which she did through grant-maintained schools 'free' from local authority control. There was also money to encourage assisted places for supposedly brighter pupils to attend private schools, a scheme that benefited middle-class children more than minority children (Whitty et al, 1998).

Most of Thatcher's ministers had been privately educated, especially at Eton. Her vision incorporated an appeal to moral authoritarianism and a nostalgic imperialism in which individuals were to have a hierarchical understanding of their class, gender and racial position. As she wrote, 'I never felt uneasy about praising Victorian values ... because they summed up what we are now discovering – they distinguished between the deserving and the undeserving poor' (Thatcher, 1993: 627). By the 1980s she may have softened her stance on the very Victorian practice of beating children, as corporal punishment was outlawed in state schools in 1987, but not in private schools until the 1990s – in 1961 she had voted in favour of birching young people. Education from the 1980s was to be a commodity, with parents notionally free to choose schools, which was, in effect, an invitation for the middle classes to compete to take over the best state schools. The curriculum was also to be centrally controlled and LEAs eventually disappeared. The 'left-dominated' Inner London Education Authority was the first to go (Thatcher, 1993: 590). The idea for a Black History Month, originating in the USA, was taken up in 1987 by a Ghanaian teacher, Akyaaba Addai-Sebo, who coordinated projects for the Greater London Council. This was a particular irritation to Mrs Thatcher.

Ten Education Acts were passed between 1979 and 1988, and eventually every area of education was subject to reforming zeal. The relationship between central and local government, funding, school structures and governance, curriculum, assessment, pedagogy, teacher autonomy and training, inspection, Early Years and post-16 training, relations with parents, vocational and higher education, these were all subject to scrutiny, criticism and legislation. Although many more comprehensive secondary schools came into operation during the 1980s – by 1990 some 90% of children attended these schools – there was continued pressure to retain forms of selection and ration education. It was a decade when the realisation by government that all children and young people were capable of being educated was a cause for anxiety. As one civil servant told a researcher, 'We are beginning to create aspirations we cannot match. In some ways this points to the success of education in contrast to the public mythology that has been created … we have to select, to ration educational opportunities, people must be educated once more to know their place' (Ranson, 1984: 241). This sentiment appeared to be implicit in most subsequent education policies, especially with persistent Conservative support for selective grammar schools.

Having led the Conservative Party to a third election victory, Mrs Thatcher claimed that raising the quality of education was a major aim of her government. Teachers and LEAs, especially those attempting to come to terms with a multiracial society, were the enemy apparently opposing this. Even the Church was regarded as an enemy. A report by a committee led by the Archbishop of Canterbury (1985) criticising conditions in inner cities was condemned as Marxist-inspired. Thatcher told the Party Conference in October 1987 that, 'The chances of youngsters getting a decent education … was often snatched from them by hard-left education authorities and extremist teachers … children who need to be able to count and multiply are learning anti-racist mathematics – whatever that may be' (Thatcher, reported in Hughill, 1987). For good measure, children were not being taught to respect traditional moral values and were apparently being taught that they had an inalienable right to be gay! A section in the Local Government Act 1988 put a stop to local authorities supposedly promoting homosexuality, a measure only repealed in 2003.

The Education Reform Act of 1988, introduced by Education Secretary Kenneth Baker, contained 238 sections and 13 schedules, and gave the Secretary of State 451 new powers. It was concerned to increase the influence of the central state on education and reduce local powers and teacher influence. Major features of the Act were the introduction of a subject-centred National Curriculum assessed at four Key Stages (KS), KS 4 being the GCSE (formerly the O-level), school admissions changed, and through local management schools were to receive their own budgets. Control of education in London passed to 12 boroughs. Mrs Thatcher was not happy with the National Curriculum proposals and the subject working groups Baker had set up. Teachers and task groups on assessment became the opposition, and she was particularly concerned with the English and History proposals. Indeed, when the History working group produced a suggested curriculum in 1989, 'I was appalled … there was insufficient weight given to British history … not enough emphasis on history as a chronological study' (Thatcher, 1993: 596). Right-wing beliefs, fears of left-wing influence and of any developing multicultural schooling dominated this 1988 reform. As a Cambridge professor recorded, 'the 1988 Act should have looked forward with confidence to a better multicultural, multilingual and multifaith Britain entering a new relationship with itself and the rest of the world … but it did not' (Hargreaves, 1993).

Miseducating minorities

It was not surprising that the education of the children of post-colonial immigration to Britain should be a problem for educators. Policy-makers, civil servants and teachers at all levels had themselves been educated through an imperial curriculum, and had no training and little understanding of how to incorporate the children into a system that was itself unequal and hierarchical. There was eventually more pressure on the government to produce policies and funding for what the House of Commons Select Committee, in a report on *Education*, described as immigrant children with an ethnic background. The report made 24 recommendations for improved education, criticised the DES for not being well informed of what was being done locally or nationally, and 'was frequently struck by the haphazard was a crucial part of human race relations has been dealt with' (Select Committee, 1973: 55). With imperial hindsight, it now appears inevitable that the denigration, slurs and stereotyping of black and minority people over the past 200 or so years would continue. Poet Benjamin Zephaniah summed up nicely the attempt by his head teacher to fit him into the stereotype of black sportsman, insisting he should be good at cricket and boxing. Eventually 'trying not to look Afro-Caribbean', he replied, 'I am very good at formation flying, Sir' (Zephaniah, 2005: 157).

Although the NUT took the view that, 'The curriculum should have a wide international outlook and the future must lie in an education directed at the needs of a multiracial society and not the specific question of educating children from immigrant families' (Tomlinson, 2008: 53), the DES preferred to lump all minority children, whether immigrant or not, into a category of 'disadvantage' – a euphemism for 'poor' that has endured over the years. Thus the DES asserted that minority children shared with the indigenous children in urban areas 'the educational disadvantages associated with an impoverished environment' (DES, 1974: 2), and the Home Office concurred. Basically, black and minority people should not complain, as poor whites shared their neglected urban environment of poor housing, schools and health services. American scholar David Kirp noted that governments use the language of disadvantage, deprivation or non-English-speaking and prefer almost any label to a racial one (Kirp, 1979). And as noted, whites took flight from these areas if they could.

It was astonishing that the Warnock committee set up in 1973 to look into *Special educational needs* (DES, 1978) ignored the over-representation of black and other minority children in special schooling of all kinds, and the anxiety black parents had demonstrated over the years about this issue. A study carried out during the 1970s on the way black and working-class children were regarded as candidates for the then schools for the educationally subnormal (ESN), recorded much ignorance among the professionals – head teachers, psychologists, social workers and medical officers – about minority children, and much racism, covert or overt, was evident. Some of their comments were noted in the book *Educational subnormality: A study in decision-making* (Tomlinson, 1981), and some were not included as the personnel were still in work. Thirty head teachers were interviewed and tended to operate within a framework of stereotypes about black children. There was an assumption that the children would be slow learners, create disciplinary problems and come from disorganised or violent homes. Some comments were:

'They [West Indian children] are bound to be slower. It's their personalities, they lack concentration....'

'The temperament of the West Indian child is more volatile, disruptive, easily stirred....'

'They are violent – a lot of none of you whites are going to tell me what to do.'

One female head of a girls' school commented that, 'Enoch Powell is right. He has an avid love of his country as many people have. There are enough immigrants and there is going to be trouble' (quoted in Tomlinson, 1981: 145–7). In notes not published at the time, this head also said, 'Some of the girls are not fit to clean Enoch Powell's shoes.'

The educational attainments of minority children and young people continued to be a focus for anxieties, especially for Caribbean parents. A black–white gap in achievements turned into a 40-year farce, with researchers initially using tests standardised on white children in a climate of assumptions of the inferior 'intelligence' of black children (Eysenck, 1971; Herrnstein and

Murray, 1994). This was reinforced by comparisons between black and other minority achievements, Chinese and Indian pupils eventually becoming 'model minorities' as their school achievements improved. Caribbean and Pakistani (Muslim) pupils usually lagged behind, with explanations focusing on families and culture. As David Gillborn and his colleagues eventually pointed out, the goal posts were consistently moved to redefine achievement, which had the effect of restoring historic levels of race inequity (Gillborn et al, 2017).

A major issue in the 1970s was the use of Creole and dialect speech by Caribbean children, which many teachers regarded a sloppy and lazy, despite the Bullock Report (1975) pointing out that Jamaican and French Creoles had their own linguistic grammars and structures. The Rampton Committee inquiring into 'West Indian' achievement, set up by the Labour government before the 1979 election, and almost closed down by Mrs Thatcher, also repudiated language issues as causing under-achievement (DES, 1981). In the 1980s, young black people were developing the dialect speech as part of a cultural identity linked to the Rastafarian movement and Reggae music, which, together with the 1980s riots, created more fear and hostility from the police and public.

Multicultural policy

A combination of riots and reports persuaded the government that education for an ethnically diverse society was important if only to promote public order, and the Rampton Committee was allowed to continue its work, chaired now by the Liberal Party's Lord Swann. Their 807-page report, complete with evidence and consultation, constituted a high point in positive recommendations for all pupils living in a multiracial, multicultural society, and briefly commented on the education of Chinese, Vietnamese, Ukrainian, Cypriot, Italian and Traveller children as well as the children of established black and Asian communities. The report thought it necessary to include a chapter on research into IQ testing and 'intelligence' as a sop to the persistent assertions of a lower black IQ (Lord Swann and Committee of Inquiry into the Education of Children from Ethnic Minority

Groups, 1985). During the 1980s a number of LEAs began to produce multicultural education policy documents. Bradford LEA, with a large Asian population, published a memorandum suggesting ways of improving education for all young people and countering racial hostility and discrimination. The head teacher of one local school did not share these aspirations and wrote an article in the *Times Educational Supplement* suggesting that, 'The responsibility for the adaptions and adjustments involved in settling in a new country lies entirely with those who have come to settle' (Honeyford, 1982). After a further article complaining about multicultural bigots and the hysterical political temperament of the Indian subcontinent, a campaign was launched against him and he took early retirement. Bradford and the Honeyford affair led to an open polarisation of views on the education of minorities in a system designed for white children. In Dewsbury in 1987, a group of white parents insisted that their children should not be taught in a school with Asian children and opened a school above a pub, and in Cleveland a parent won a case for her daughter to be transferred to a predominantly white school as she was 'learning Pakistani' (Tomlinson, 2008). In 1989, copies of Salman Rushdie's book *The Satanic verses* were burned in Bradford by clerics who considered that the book insulted Islam. Rushdie had to go into hiding after the *fatwā* (death threat) was issued against him by Iran. He survived to write much more, but the incident ignited fears of Muslim assertion, and Muslim schools requesting admission to the state system were refused. A similar incident had occurred in 1960 when a Catholic priest in Ireland had publicly burned copies of a novel by an Irish female writer. The incident went unremarked by politicians, with much of the media castigating the writer for criticising Irish life (O'Brien, 1960).

Manufacturing ignorance

The 1970s and 1980s set the stage for the manufacturing of ignorance about the nature of a post-imperial society. On the whole, the white population were aghast that former colonial people from the Empire had now come to live, work and remain in Britain. Demands from minorities, most now confirmed as

British citizens, that they be accorded equal rights, accompanied by angry conflicts, were taken as proof that they should never have been allowed into the country. Immigrant settlement, as noted, was mainly in urban areas where there was work but housing and schooling was poor. A white working class were united with other social classes against black and other minorities. Successive governments understood that racial discrimination and hostility was a source of potential conflict, but it was always understood that overt action in support of minorities or offering leadership in a post-imperial world was not something any government could do if it wished to be elected. But governments also understood that the nature of British society was changing in a global context, and joint ventures with Commonwealth countries were making it uneconomic to hold hostile attitudes towards former colonial settlers.

The antagonisms towards attempts by teachers, LEAs, the HMI, black parents and organisations attempting to develop education for a multiracial, multicultural society suggested an educational nationalism that was not just a white backlash against ideas of democratic pluralism and equality (Tomlinson, 1990). It supported a myth that black and other minorities in Britain had full opportunities to assimilate into a British way of life. Educational nationalism denied that there were barriers placed in the way of minorities achieving in education and employment other than obstacles they created for themselves. It also depended on a mythologised British heritage, culture and values, assumed to be shared by all white individuals regardless of class or gender. Roger Scruton, who has made numerous contributions over the decades to political and educational nationalism, especially when he edited the Conservative journal *Salisbury Review*, wrote that, 'a child brought up in the British way of doing things is encouraged to question and criticise … a child brought up in such a culture does not need "alternatives" which so many educationalists wish to foist on him [sic]' (Scruton, 1986: 132). The previous year, Education Minister Keith Joseph, in a retirement speech, acknowledged that Britain was now an ethnically mixed society, but reiterated the view that, 'a tradition of tolerance was one of Britain's most precious virtues and British history and cultural traditions are, or will become, part of the common heritage of all who live in this country' (Joseph, 1986).

The problem with this was, as has been noted, that imperialism largely took the form of military conquest, the taking over of land and labour, slavery and the denial of human rights, and migrants from colonial countries had always been subject to discrimination and a conspicuous lack of tolerance. The working groups preparing the content of subjects for the new National Curriculum from 1988 were all subject to central government scrutiny and omissions. The Mathematics working group report, overseen by the DES, included the comment that, 'It is sometimes suggested that the multicultural complexion of society demands a "multicultural" approach to mathematics with children being introduced to different number systems, foreign currencies and non-European measuring and counting devices. But this would confuse children and we have therefore not included any multi-cultural aspects in our attainment targets' (Bishop, 1993: 34). Even that classical mathematician and engineer Archimedes was given short shrift.

It was not surprising that research into white children's views of minorities in the 1970s and 1980s mainly showed racism, stereotyping and rejection. Many schools in all-white areas thought that notions of a multicultural society did not apply to them. Rob Jeffcoate's work for a Schools Council project found that 11-year-old pupils held views of exclusion, repatriation and stereotyping. Some comments were that, 'England is meant for whites, blacks should be thrown out', 'Whites invented telly so only white people should go on telly' and 'It is not right for black people to come and take our shops and things, they are trying to take over our economy' (Jeffcoate, 1979: 98). One girl of 11 thought that 'once we owned the whole world' and there were 'too many coloureds in our country' (Jeffcoate, 1979: 99). Things had not improved in the 1980s when researchers for Lord Swann's report interviewed children in white schools. A typical comment was, 'There are too many Pakys and foreigners in our country', and at one school the researcher was told by older pupils that, 'We've got to talk to you about niggers and wogs and things' (Lord Swann and Committee of Inquiry into the Education of Children from Ethnic Minority Groups, 1985: 292).

Teachers found it difficult to come to terms with the racial antagonisms and cultural ignorance displayed by pupils. There was evidence of longstanding white parental antipathy to their children being educated alongside minority children. Parents, in their turn, had been through an imperial education. Various organisations opposing any multicultural, anti-racist or multifaith educational efforts were set up, supporting an English and Christian curriculum. A Campaign for Real Education had some political support, and the Parental Alliance for Choice in Education supported the Dewsbury parents, who also supported the demands of Muslim parents for separate state-funded Muslim schools, as this would separate Muslim children from 'the rest' (Naylor, 1988). In 1986, a disturbed white boy stabbed fellow pupil Ahmed Ullah in the playground of a Manchester school. As the school had an anti-racist policy, sensational media coverage followed the murder, giving the impression that the policy was to blame (MacDonald et al, 1989). LEAs and schools with multicultural anti-racist policies were presented by right-wing politicians and media as the 'looney left'.

Curriculum possibilities

After James Callaghan's intervention in education in a speech at Ruskin College in 1976, bureaucratic control of the curriculum was strengthened, with more questioning of the acceptability of curriculum content. A Green Paper produced by Education Secretary Shirley Williams in 1977 noted that:

> Ours is now a multiracial and multicultural country and one in which traditional social patterns are breaking down.... The curriculum appropriate to our imperial past cannot meet the requirements of modern Britain. (DES, 1977: 10)

After she made this claim, no national policies resulted. But a large literature followed, advocating and suggesting varieties of multicultural education and an equally large literature critiquing those suggestions. Claims that black pupils were diverted into a different curriculum rather than the formal subject-centred one were hard to demonstrate. They were just taught badly by teachers who had no training in how to teach all children. Black Studies, World Studies, Peace Studies and changes in subject areas were all attacked, although supplementary schools did their best to supplement teaching and learning outside formal schooling. The report by Lord Swann's Committee suggesting that a plural democratic society might require a re-thinking of national identity was regarded by the Conservative MPs in the Monday Club as a 'profoundly dangerous document aimed at re-shaping British society' (Pearce, 1986).

But by the later 1980s there was some agreement that the curriculum in all schools, not just those with minority children, needed changing. Teachers began to write about their practices, and publishers and writers of textbooks began to think more carefully about the incorporation of multicultural and global information in all curriculum subjects. Kenneth Baker, as Education Secretary, encouraged Education Support Grants for 'Educational needs in a multicultural society', and 23 projects in 'white' areas from North Tyneside to the Scilly Isles were set up between 1985 and 1988. These good intentions did not last long. Baker approved the setting up of a Multicultural Task Group in 1989, to produce 'Guidelines on multicultural education in the National Curriculum'. The Group comprising head teachers, advisers, professors and the HMI (six of whom were from minorities) duly did this, but their report was never published. The most that was conceded was one page in a National Curriculum Council Newsletter (Tomlinson, 1993).

By the end of the decade, an editorial in the *Times Educational Supplement* noted that, 'Unspoken anxieties about ethnic differences underlie several bits of educational policy ... there seems to be a definite though unformulated attempt to starve multicultural education of resources and let it wither on the vine' (TES, 1990).

Summary

This chapter has covered post-colonial politics and ideologies, and education developments over two decades to 1990. Nostalgia for a lost Empire was accompanied by continued hostility to the former imperial subjects who were invited to bring their labour into the country. While a British Empire had been transformed into a Commonwealth of former Colonies, closer links with Europe were developing, with Parliament agreeing to a Single Market in which trade barriers and tariffs would be agreed among EU countries. The welfare state was being dismantled, privatisation and markets in public services encouraged, and New Commonwealth citizens excluded from a narrowing concept of a national identity. At the same time, what would now become a continuing debate over immigration in the coming decades – the need for labour – was developing. Politicians of all parties continued to believe that policies directed at immigrants and their children were bad for their electoral chances, and the children were lumped together with that intractable group, 'the disadvantaged'. Race riots galvanised the government into some action, and there was a slow realisation that the country really was multiracial and multicultural. Suggested curriculum and other changes in the education system were met with much hostility, especially on the grounds that British cultural traditions and sense of identity were being attacked or contaminated. Into the 1990s, things did not get much better.

Notes

[1] A list of former British colonies, dependencies and overseas territories gaining their independence in the 1970s and 1980s is included in the Appendix at the end of this chapter. By 2017 there were three dependencies and 14 small overseas territories (several of them tax havens) left over from the British Empire (see Dorling and Tomlinson, 2019).

[2] A white boy with two adopted black brothers remembers how he and his brothers were subjected to racial taunts and abuse at school in Oxford in the 1970s and 1980s. Danny Dorling is now Professor of Human Geography at the University of Oxford.

[3] In 1973 Asian female workers at Imperial Typewriters in Leicester led a strike over pay, and in 1977 a strike by Asian workers at the Grunwick Laboratories in North London led to fights between police and pickets.

[4] The National Front became the British National Party (BNP) a forerunner of the United Kingdom Independence Party (UKIP) and other far-right parties, for example, Britain First.

[5] As the government in Grenada was Marxist-orientated, the USA was determined to end this and so invaded the island. Bernard Coard was later accused of involvement in the killing of Prime Minister Maurice Bishop.

He spent 19 years in prison and is still fighting to clear his name (John, 2010).

Appendix

Independence was acquired by the following British Colonies and Protectorates in the 1970s and 1980s:

1970   Fiji, Tonga, Western Samoa
1974   Grenada (invaded by the USA in 1983)
1975   Papua New Guinea
1976   The Seychelles
1978   Solomon Islands, Tuvalu (Ellice Islands), Dominica
1979   St Lucia, St Vincent and Grenadines, Kiribati
1980   Rhodesia (Zimbabwe), Vanuatu (New Hebrides)
1983   Brunei
1997   Hong Kong

5

Inequalities, a European Union and education markets, 1990-97

> Historians may probably decide that not much of lasting significance happened in Britain during John Major's seven years. (Hastings, 2007)

> Since my son Stephen was killed with such arrogance and contempt, I've had a different life … it was as if I had to put on armour every day in order to survive. (Lawrence, 2007: ix)

The comment from historian and author Max Hastings for once got it wrong. A great deal happened during the seven years of John Major's premiership. He took over as Prime Minister in November 1990 after excusing himself with toothache in hospital while his colleagues removed Margaret Thatcher from her post. Despite being regarded as a 'grey man' of politics, with cartoonists depicting him as wearing his underpants outside his trousers, global conflicts, financial mistakes, the European Union, immigration and asylum-seeking, race and religious issues all marked his time in office. Another view of the period was that 'sleaze built up slowly through the 1990s' (Tiratsoo, 1997: 208), and Major became a prisoner of a strident and undisciplined Eurosceptic right. What was to be a most contentious policy, the signing up before the 1992 General Election to the Maastricht Treaty that created a European Union, did not figure much in this election, which Major won against all expectations. He inherited from Thatcher support for a Single Market to replace the old rules of a Common Market, where separate countries had their own trade rules, and this boosted trade, employment and investment over the decade. But in signing the Treaty he argued for an 'opt out' from a single euro currency and a Social Chapter that included workers' rights. He also pushed the

Thatcher privatisation of public utilities even further, selling off the railways to private companies, and replacing an unpopular 'Poll Tax' with a Council Tax on households.

The education policies of Major's years in office helped to dismantle the influence of local authorities on education, created education markets and school privatisation, and set the stage for a break-up of a state education system.

A further crucial event during the period was the murder in 1993 of 18-year-old black student Stephen Lawrence by five white youths. This led to the 25-year search for justice against the police and judicial racism led by his mother, now Baroness Doreen Lawrence. This chapter documents the issues and tensions arising from the signing of the Maastricht Treaty creating the European Union in 1992, and the surge in the numbers of asylum-seekers and refugees escaping wars and conflicts, often in countries once colonised by Britain. It notes that more popular racism was directed at Islam, and the murder of Stephen Lawrence became a catalyst for understanding the way in which post-imperial racism permeated the whole society. While education policies were turning education into a competitive market, with the 'naming and shaming' of schools and government taking control of curriculum and assessment, there was a concerted effort to dismiss any multicultural dimensions and any attempts to educate all young people in the art of living together.

Policy preview

While Major was acquiescent if not enthusiastic over the EU, he did find determined opposition from those who became known as Eurosceptics. Prominent among these was a young *Daily Telegraph* journalist, Boris Johnson. Johnson produced ludicrous stories about European regulations demanding straight bananas and cucumbers, and other anti-European newspapers and their owners and editors were also keen to produce myths and lies about the Union (Smith, 2017). In dealing with the parliamentary Eurosceptics Major did what Prime Minister Theresa May was to do some 26 years later – he appointed them to his government, although he had, in an interview, described them as 'bastards' (Castle, 1993).[1] James Goldsmith, a rich businessman and father of MP Zac Goldsmith, set up and funded the Referendum Party in 1994, which gained 2.6% of votes in the 1997 General Election. Eventually this Party merged with UKIP. By 1996 the Eurosceptics were demanding a referendum on staying in the EU, and several of them were still around and agitating for a referendum in the Cameron government from 2010.

During this period the arrival of workers from EU countries, asylum-seekers and refugees from global conflicts – notably after 1992 from the collapsed Yugoslavia – raised more tensions about immigration. Economic migrants from former Eastern European communist countries arrived after the collapse of the Berlin Wall in 1989. Issues of race, culture, religion, spatial segregation and discrimination were downplayed, although after the first Gulf War in 1990, popular racism began to be directed against Islam as a world religion. There was, as Stuart Hall noted, more understanding among the public that the tea and sugar in their 'cuppa' came from post-imperial India and the Caribbean (Hall, 1991), but this probably owed more to developing global communication and advertising than to education in schools. While world migrations, cultural convergences and the effects of wars became more obvious, policy-makers continued along familiar lines of regarding minorities as problems, and politicians continued to deride multicultural education as a left-wing activity. Although between 1988 and 1996 one or more Education Acts were passed each year and the Secretary of State for Education was handed some 1,000 new powers, a new National Curriculum was more a vehicle for testing and assessment than any new content to help along an understanding of a post-imperial world. John Major, who had left grammar school with O-levels, left office in 1997 after his election manifesto had promised a 'grammar school in every town', a policy still urged by the Conservatives over 20 years later.

Significant events

| 1990 | (November) Saddam Hussein attacks Kuwait in the first Gulf war; John Major takes over from Margaret Thatcher as Conservative Leader; Poll Tax becomes a Council Tax |
| 1990 | Nine EU countries signed the Schengen Agreement allowing free movement of people and attempts to create more equitable immigration policies |

1990	Education Secretary turns down a request for a private Muslim school in Brent to become state-funded; over 500 children in Tower Hamlets have no school place – the Court absolves the local authority of blame
1991	Census in Britain includes an ethnic question for the first time
1991-99	Break-up of former Yugoslavia; ethnic conflicts result in some 2-4 million refugees in European countries; Serbs, Kosovans, Albanians and others seek asylum in Britain; Civil War in Somaliland, a former British Protectorate granted independence in 1991, brings Somali refugees
1991	Culloden Primary School in Tower Hamlets is attacked in the tabloid press for giving too much attention to speakers of English as a Second Language
1991	(September) Rioting by white youths in Newcastle and North Shields; economic deprivation and policing blamed; also riots in Oxford on the Blackbird Leys estate
1992	Conservatives win the General Election; John Smith takes over from Neil Kinnock as Labour Leader; John Major signs the Maastricht Treaty but with an opt-out from the Social Chapter and the euro currency; 'Black Wednesday' on 16 September; Sterling currency left the European exchange rate mechanism (ERM); Conservative economic policy in crisis; Scott Inquiry into arms sales to Iraq published
1992	White Paper *Choice and diversity* (DfE, 1992) published and an Education (Schools) Act creating an Office for Standards in Education (Ofsted); DES becomes the Department for Education (DfE); Higher Education Act allows polytechnics to become universities; further education colleges to be independent of local authorities
1992	NUT publishes anti-racist guidelines for schools; at the October Conservative Conference Major says teachers should teach children how to read and 'not waste their time on the politics of gender, race and class'; an inquiry by the Commission for Racial Equality notes that the assignment of minority pupils to lower ability sets and bands is unlawful
1993	Asylum and Immigration Act; more controls on asylum-seekers
1993	(April) Stephen Lawrence murdered in Lewisham by white youths – no arrests and government refuses an inquiry; first chair of NCC confirms that it was made clear to him by ministers that any multicultural anti-racist education was a 'no-go' area; Mrs Thatcher's memoirs make clear her distaste for multicultural education and changes in the History syllabus
1994	John Smith dies; Tony Blair is elected Labour Leader; Teacher Training Agency created; no special training for teaching in a multiethnic society; new syllabus for Religious Education approved; Herrnstein and Murray publish *The bell curve* claiming people in a black underclass have lower IQs
1995	Hackney Downs School becomes the only school closed down by an Education Association that included Michael Barber. In 2017, Barber was appointed Head of an Office for Students which has the power to close universities
1995	Riots in Bradford between young Asians and whites; Major resigns as Conservative Leader and is re-appointed; volcanic eruption on the island

	of Montserrat, acquired by Britain in 1632, brings half its population to Britain
1996	Two Education Acts repealed and consolidated much previous legislation; a clause reiterates that religious education should reflect Christian traditions; a further Act controlling immigration is passed
1997	Fourth Policy Studies Institute report notes differences in education and vocational qualifications and life chances between ethnic groups (Modood et al, 1997)
1997	General Election; Major promises a 'grammar school in every town' and leaves office, asserting that 'education policies must be colour blind, they must just tackle disadvantage'; New Labour elected and Tony Blair becomes Prime Minister

The politics of wars and immigration

Wars and migration in the early 1990s had crucial consequences for issues of race and religion in Britain over the next few decades. A month before John Major took office in November 1990, Saddam Hussein, President of Iraq, invaded Kuwait. Iraq had become a British Mandate in 1920. Although becoming notionally independent in 1933, it had, for most of the 1980s, fought a war with Iran over territory and religion, which had killed over half a million young men. A British arms firm, Matrix Churchill, had, during this period, exported weapons, claiming they were 'machine tools', to the Iraq military. In January 1991, a coalition, led by the USA and the UK, attacked Iraqi troops and forced their withdrawal from Kuwait. This war was supported by both Conservative and Labour politicians. Hussein continued in power until the second Iraq war in 2003; the consequences of this conflict are still terribly apparent in the Middle East and also in Britain today.

During the first Gulf War, Hussein attempted to represent the war as a *jihad* (holy war) against the West, and some Muslims in Britain felt that their communities and religion were under attack again, after the Honeyford and Salman Rushdie affairs. The Bradford Council of Mosques sent a letter to the Queen and to John Major asking for troops to be withdrawn from Iraq. In East London, especially centred round the East London Mosque, young Muslims were joining radical Islamic groups.[2] Mutual fears surrounding the presence of Muslims in European countries had escalated over the years, and as John Rex (1996: 8) noted, 'Islam as a focus for racist hostilities was at least as important as colour.' The label 'Islamophobia' to describe this situation had been popularised in other European countries (Karakasoglu and Luchtenberg 2002), although it had been present since Queen Victoria's reign, when her friendship with the Muslim Indian, 'the Munshi' (noted in Chapter One), was derided by her court.

The 1991 British Census was the first to ask about ethnicity, and 94% of the population described themselves as White British or White Irish, with 5.9% claiming to belong to one of the ethnic groups specified.[3] In 1994, a fourth survey by the Policy Studies Institute demonstrated that a 'black–white divide' that had provided a political label up to the 1980s was now more complex (Modood et al, 1997). Tariq Modood noted that the differences between minorities had become as important and significant to the life chances of minorities as the similarities. Some young Asians found difficulty in alternating between Western individualism and an 'ethnic assertion', while still responding to parental traditional appeals. The more open identification of a Muslim identity created a situation where popular racism began to be directed at Islam as a world religion. In Britain, as in France and other countries, Muslim women's dress became a permanent focus for hostility. In 1990 a school in Altrincham, Cheshire, banned two Muslim girls from wearing the hijab (headscarf) in school. Young black people, demonised as an 'enemy within' during the 1980s, were overtaken by a spiralling demonisation of Muslims.

Political attention in the early 1990s focused on immigration from various countries. After 1989, when the Berlin Wall came down, economic migrants from former communist countries began to arrive in Britain. In 1992, the Maastricht Treaty created a European Union out of the European Economic Community (EEC), with 15 member countries at that time. The Treaty was intended to 'promote economic and social progress which is balanced and sustainable, in particular the creation of an area without internal frontiers' (Maastricht, 1992). Article B:3 of the Treaty guaranteed an internal Single Market with an elimination of customs duties and the free movement of goods, persons, services and capital. Movement of people was initially not excessive. European Roma, who had long suffered rejection and persecution, was one group who then arrived in

Britain, and Home Secretary Kenneth Clarke recorded in his memoirs that, 'We managed to keep things reasonably under control and immigration was not in my time the crisis ridden and poisonous subject of public debate it became in later years' (K. Clarke, 2016: 285). He had earlier recorded that he objected to 'nostalgic nationalistic protectionism in which people indulged … the British economy benefits from the fact we are open and welcoming to inward (and outward) investment' (K. Clarke, 2016: 176). By September 1992, benefits to the economy disappeared when on 'Black Wednesday' the sterling currency was 'ejected' from the European exchange rate mechanism (ERM), interest rates increased and mortgage holders were threatened with repossession of their homes (Geddes, 2013).

It was war and conflict around the world, often proxy wars actually fought between the 'Great Powers', that brought asylum-seekers[4] from civil wars that included people from the first Iraq War, and groups from Somaliland, Southern Sudan, Sierra Leone and Zimbabwe (all former British territories), Kurds of Turkish origin, Somalis from the former Italian colony, and during the Balkan wars, people from Bosnia, Kosova and Albania. The pre-EU member states, excluding Britain, had signed the Schengen Agreement in 1990, allowing passport-free movement between countries but with increased border policing and a data base on criminals, asylum-seekers and visitors. All countries were anxious to limit the numbers of people from outside Europe, and in England an Asylum and Immigration Act in 1993 and a further Act in 1996 restricted numbers of immigrants from outside the EU, and brought in 'fast-track' detention and removal of those refused asylum. The Major government also had to deal with the consequences of the Northern Irish 'Troubles', as the Irish Republican Army (IRA) took its war to mainland Britain, attacking Warrington in Cheshire and Downing Street in 1992, a bomb exploding in the City of London in 1993.

There was considerable debate over the possibility of citizens from the colony of Hong Kong, due to be returned to China in 1997, coming into the UK, and the government ensured that only a limited number arrived. In the event, many went to Vancouver in Canada and helped create a booming economy there. Similar negative treatment was handed out to the British overseas citizens of Montserrat, a Caribbean island that suffered a volcanic eruption in 1995 and people had to leave. Half of the population came to Britain where they were treated as homeless and offered little help. A study of the experiences of the children arriving in London schools found teachers denigrating their language and some asking the children where Montserrat was (Shotte, 2002).

The politics of sleaze

While all governments have their share of corrupt and questionable activities, the Major government was either unlucky or more questionable in that over the seven years, a number of senior politicians were found to have indulged in financial and/ or sexual peccadilloes. In 1995 journalists from *The Independent* collected enough stories about parliamentarians to compile a 'Sleaze List' (*The Independent*, 1995). This included MP David Mellor, Secretary of State in the Department of National Heritage, who resigned in 1992 after tabloid revelations of an extra-marital affair that involved toe sucking, closely followed by MP Stephen Norris, apparently conducting numerous extramarital affairs (Sylvester, 2000). In 1994 Tim Yeo, Minister in the Department for the Environment, resigned having fathered a child out of wedlock. More important were the financial scandals, journalists from *The Sunday Times* having asked MPs to submit questions in Parliament in return for money. The 'cash for questions' became a lasting scandal, especially when MPs Neil Hamilton, a Trade and Industry Minister, and MP Tim Smith were paid £2,000 each to ask questions on behalf of Mohamed Al-Fayed, the owner of Harrods. More scandal ensued when MP Jonathan Aitken, former Chief Secretary to the Treasury, sued *The Guardian* over allegations that he had taken money from Saudi businessmen for a stay at the Ritz in Paris, and had procured prostitutes for them in England. He was found guilty of perjury and imprisoned, on his release studying theology and being ordained. An article in *The Daily Telegraph* in 2013 concluded that 'cash for questions' was a scandal that should have changed the face of British politics, but it did not (Watt, 2013). It was also unfortunate for the government that an inquiry into selling what were described as 'machine tools' to Saddam Hussein in the 1980s was published in 1996 (Scott Inquiry, 1996). The inquiry showed that government departments and ministers had been lying about the sales.

The lies published in tabloid newspapers about EU regulations over the period could also be classed as sleaze. Mikey Smith (2017) documented some of the Euro-myths put forward that included the EU banning corgi dogs, prawn cocktail crisps, mushy peas, requiring standard-sized condoms and Christmas trees, curved bananas and cucumbers, and even banning saucy postcards and double-decker buses. Some of this nonsense, as noted, was published by Boris Johnson, later British Foreign Secretary, until resigning in July 2018. It was unfortunate that at the Conservative Party Conference in October 1993 Major had made a speech that urged the country to go 'back to basics' and learn more honest self-discipline, respect the rule of law and take responsibility for one's own actions rather than relying on the state, and he set up the Nolan Committee to report on standards in public life. His own reputation was later called into question when former MP Edwina Currie revealed in her diaries (Currie, 2002) that in the 1980s she had enjoyed a four-year extra-marital affair with him. When the activities of former MPs who were leaving government and joining companies they had helped privatise became public, it was not surprising that historian Nick Tiratsoo described the period as characterised by 'Sleaze which damaged the Tories to their core' (Tiratsoo, 1997: 209), and helped a Labour victory in 1997.

Education did not escape questionable activity on the part of those in charge. John Haggitt Charles Patten, Education Secretary from 1992 to 1994, a former lecturer in Geography at the University of Oxford, who had taught geography to future Prime Minister Theresa May, was in charge of implementing major Education Acts. He described Tim Brighouse, Chief Education Officer in Oxfordshire and then Birmingham, as a 'nutter' and 'a madman walking the streets frightening the children' (Pyke, 1994). Brighouse sued him and won £25,000 in damages, which he gave to schools, and he went on to improve London's schools in the 'London Challenge'. Patten went on to enter the House of Lords and to write a book, *Things to come: The Tories in the*

21st century (Patten, 1995). The book did not sell well. Chris Woodhead, appointed as Chief Inspector of Schools in 1993, was also reported to have a dubious past – a questionable relationship with a young pupil at a school where he had previously taught (Bright, 1999). The early 1990s was certainly a period that illustrated the hypocrisy of politicians criticising schools and teachers for 'lowered standards' and 'failing pupils' when those in government had acted so irresponsibly.

Class and deprivation

Eminent historian, Tony Judt, wrote in his *Postwar: A history of Europe since 1945* that under Margaret Thatcher, Britain's privatising economy had become more efficient with an expanded market for goods, services and labour. When John Major signed the Maastricht Treaty in 1992, Jacques Delors, President of the European Commission, accused him of making Britain a 'paradise for foreign investors', 'a charge to which Thatcherites could happily plead guilty' (Judt, 2005: 543), with everything from bus companies to electricity supplies having been sold to competing private companies, and citizens now being consumers and 'stakeholders'. But 'as a society Britain suffered a meltdown, with catastrophic long-term consequences ... for Thatcher, class warfare, suitably updated, was the very stuff of politics' (Judt, 2005: 545). Class war, of a kind unknown since the 1930s and harking back to Victorian views of the dangerous poor, certainly reappeared in the 1990s. Inequality and poverty took on new dimensions after a decade when bankers and investors enjoyed increased wealth, but many working-class people were 'Caught in permanent poverty. Private affluence was accompanied by public squalor' (Judt, 2005: 544).

The default position was, as usual, to blame the victims. American Charles Murray, fresh from bemoaning the rise of an underclass in the USA, wrote in 1990 about *The emerging British underclass* (Murray, 1990). According to him the ways to identify an underclass were mainly by babies born to single mothers, criminals and drop-outs from the labour force, with poor people especially defined by their 'deplorable behaviour' in not taking jobs. He likened the spread of an underclass to a contagious disease (Murray, 1990: 68). Murray continued to be an important influence on Conservative policies, writing again in *The Sunday Times* in 1994 that well-educated people would become New Victorians, returning to traditional morality, while a 'new rabble' of a low-skilled working class, especially those single parents, would continue to be a drain on society (Murray, 1994). Murray was presumably not well informed about the sleaze in the political class, documented above, at this time.

Murray's views on an American underclass, apparently mainly black single parents, was elaborated further in his book with Richard Herrnstein, which purported to demonstrate the lower intelligence of black Americans, who are likely to create social problems, especially crime (Herrnstein and Murray, 1994). Labour politician Frank Field, who had already written about an underclass, contributed a piece to Murray's 1990 book, with suggestions on how to counter the growth of underclass groups, which he at least noted might have structural underpinnings. He also wrote that, 'there is no racial basis to Britain's underclass', although 'many blacks are to be found in its ranks' (Field, 1990: 38). David Willetts, Director of the Centre for Policy Studies set up by Prime Minister Thatcher, supported Murray's notion of genetic determinism in producing a lower class during a Policy Studies seminar in 1990 (James, 1990). Willetts, an MP from 1992 to 2015 when he moved to the House of Lords, became a crucial figure in higher education. He was appointed Minister of State for Universities and Science in David Cameron's coalition government from 2010 to 2014, and introduced the rise in tuition fees from £3,225 to £9,000 in 2010, later selling the Student Loans Company to a debt-collecting agency, thereby removing £160 million from the public debt. He also managed to infuriate women by suggesting that social mobility for men had stalled because of the increased entry of educated women into the workforce.

Although in August 1991 Michael Heseltine, Environment Secretary, had set up a bidding process for Urban Aid Grants for deprived areas (a sort of game show in which 21 authorities bid but only 11 won), the following month it was the white socially and economically deprived who came to political and public attention as an 'underclass' that made its presence felt. In

September there were riots on white housing estates in Newcastle upon Tyne (Meadow Well), North Shields (Rye Lane) and in Oxford on the Blackbird Leys estate (and also in many other towns and cities that were less well recorded nationally). As many riots began with young men stealing cars and inviting police retaliation, the then Education Secretary Kenneth Clarke came up with a novel explanation – he blamed the Society of Motor Manufacturers and Traders for enabling easy car thefts (MacIntyre, 1991). What was needed were more car alarms and more police! Murray returned to his theme of family collapse and community disintegration in 1994, returning to Newcastle's Meadow Well and those single mothers, and forecast the scenario of *New Victorians and the new rabble* (Murray, 1994).

What was actually happening was a widening gap between rich and poor families. The Thatcher government had encouraged income inequality and reduced Social Security as a supposed incentive to work, despite much work disappearing. On the European Community definition, the proportion of people in poverty in Britain rose from 8% in 1979 to 19% in 1993. Low-income families were concentrated in certain geographical areas, especially council estates and inner cities, while other urban and suburban areas became more prosperous. A report by the still respected, old HMI, concluded that, 'Schools in disadvantaged areas do not have the capacity for sustainable renewal, beyond the school gates are underlying social issues of poverty, unemployment, poor health, and inadequate housing' (Ofsted, 1993: 45).

At least in the media discussions following white riots there were no suggestions that however feckless the underclass might be, they were not intellectually deficient; they were merely undeveloped due to poor education. This was in contrast to the rise of a 'new IQism' (Mirza, 1998), which again covertly connected black children's ability with lower intelligence, which affected teacher perceptions. In 1995 race was a feature in riots among white, Indian and Pakistani young men in Bradford. Asian community leaders blamed problems of unemployment, poor housing and low school expectations as alienating a younger generation, and noted that Asian young people were not prepared to put up with the racism their parents had suffered (Donegan,

1995). Future 'riots' as Britain became more multiracial and multicultural were a mix of white versus minorities, minority groups fighting each other, and minority groups plus whites fighting racist groups. All this was linked to poverty, deprivation, alienation and racial injustice. Even as a black and Asian middle class developed, and professional people from overseas were fast-tracked into the country, the default position remained that 'for people of colour, race is in everything we do, because the universal experience is white' (Shukla, 2016).

Race and harassment

One consequence of European policies on immigration was a resurgence of fascist neo-Nazi parties, especially in Germany, Austria, Holland and France. In Britain the British National Front, now the British National Party (BNP), continued its recruitment of young white racists, and racial violence and attacks on minorities and immigrants continued. Much of the press, especially some of the papers owned by Rupert Murdoch, kept up a stream of denigration of asylum-seekers as 'bogus welfare scroungers, 'stealing British jobs' and 'swamping' Britain all over again, and the BNP exploited fears of both legal and illegal immigration. The number of refugee children had always been difficult to establish, but by 1997 there were estimates of around 40,000, living mainly in London, with schools receiving no extra assistance for them. Political interest in racial harassment and violence was minimal during the early 1990s, although evidence mounted as to its extent. The Runnymede Trust, established to study issues of racial justice and equality, published a report in 1993 on *Racist attacks and harassment: The epidemic of the 1990s* (The Runnymede Trust, 1993).

The views of white parents had never been well researched, but evidence had mounted that white parental antagonism to those regarded as racially or culturally different was the norm. Elinor Kelly, researching racism in schools for the Macdonald Inquiry (Macdonald, 1989), produced a list of a hundred derogatory insults aimed at minority children, and suggested that white parents followed politicians in ignoring or condoning racist behaviour. In June 1992 the House of Commons held its first debate on racial equality for six years, led by the then Shadow Home Affairs Secretary Roy Hattersley. The government response was that, 'we have forceful policies to tackle racial discrimination and disadvantage' (*Hansard*, 1992). In September a black Chelsea football player was attacked with an iron bar by a white youth and the chair of the CRE asked for new legislation on racial violence, but it was refused. Then in April 1993, the 18-year-old black A-level student Stephen Lawrence was attacked and killed at a bus stop in Lewisham by five white youths. The Macpherson Inquiry into his murder became a defining moment in the history of race and racism in the country.

Stephen's mother, Doreen Lawrence, described the shocking way she and her family were treated by the police. Even in the hospital she was treated badly and was initially prevented from seeing her son's body. It was not until, at a press conference arranged several days later, she heard that five white youths had approached Stephen and his friend Dwayne Brooks shouting, 'What, what nigger', before Stephen was stabbed (Lawrence, 2007: 73). She later heard that the Crown Prosecution Service had dropped charges against the accused youths. The Major government refused an inquiry into the murder and it was left to Doreen and Neville Lawrence to pursue a private prosecution. It was not until 1997 that the Labour government agreed to an inquiry and a report was finally published in 1999 (Macpherson, 1999). In 2012, almost 18 years after the murder, two of the youths were convicted of the murder, and it was 20 years before it was confirmed that one of the police actions was to spy on the Lawrence family. A police officer, who had posed as an anti-racist campaigner from 1993 to 1997, and who was a member of a special unit charged with spying on political groups, confirmed a mission to spy on the Lawrence family and friends and to smear the campaign for racial justice that became a national concern through the 1990s (Evans and Lewis, 2013). The Macpherson Report introduced the notion of institutional racism, another way of describing the underpinning of police and other public institutions with beliefs in the inferiority of black and minority people. Nothing much had changed since the 19th century. The concept was much derided, then and later, the favoured explanation continuing that it is just a few 'bad apples' or hostile individuals who are racist rather than whole social structures. In 1994, pupils at a school in East London were moved to other schools as racial harassment increased after the election of a BNP councillor in the area, and police reported a rise of 33% in racial violence in London. Racial hostility and harassment was not confined to cities; a study in rural Norfolk interviewing minority residents – which included black, mixed race, Asian, Japanese, Cypriot, Irish, Traveller and Jewish people – found that all had experienced some form of racism and harassment (Derbyshire, 1994).

Education policy

The Major government was characterised by what seemed to be a frenzy of education legislation, but was actually part of a long-term strategy to change the whole education system from a national system democratically run to a semi-privatised, centrally controlled system. There were four Education Secretaries during the seven years: John Macgregor took over from Kenneth Baker from 1989 to 1990 but was thought to be too nice to teachers. Kenneth Clarke took over until mid-1992, later boasting in his memoirs that he had introduced the league tables showing winners and losers in school testing. But he regretted this when he decided that polytechnics should become universities, some of them opened what he considered to be second-rate arts faculties, to gain a greater veneer of respectability. John Patten, despite the Brighouse incident reported above, was appointed to implement the policies set out in the White Paper *Choice and diversity* (DfE, 1992). He commented that 'Good schools that attract most pupils will get more money. Poor schools that cannot attract pupils must improve standards or wither and perish' (Patten, in DfE, 1992: Introduction). He was rapidly replaced and Gillian Shepherd took over from 1994 to 1997. She made an example of those 'failing schools'.

The aims of legislation included strengthening a market ideology to be achieved by parental 'choice' of school, government control of the curriculum and assessment, further eroding of the powers and responsibilities of local government, teachers and their trainers, and demands for accountability from individuals and institutions. This applied to universities, increasing in number by 1992 when a Further and Higher Education Act allowed polytechnics to become universities and further education colleges became independent of local authorities. Further education colleges had long been a destination for black and minority students to gain vocational and academic qualifications, but Clarke decided that the colleges 'did not matter to their local councils' (Clarke, 2016: 277). Universities were to be funded by a Higher Education Funding Council (HEFC), and a group of vice-chancellors of research-dominated universities, calling themselves the Russell Group after the hotel they met in, claimed to be the top universities. It was jokingly suggested that similar meetings of other Vice-Chancellors could be held in McDonald's restaurants which would their demonstrate their second class status.

Teachers and their training were a particular target for the Major government, with teachers gradually stripped of their professional status and becoming more a technical workforce delivering a National Curriculum. Much publicity was given to beliefs that university education departments and the remaining higher education colleges were hot-beds of left-wing theory, multicultural education and 'progressive' child-centred methods. A Teacher Training Agency (TTA) was created by the 1994 Act. Schools were to be inspected by the new Office for Standards in Education (Ofsted). There were widespread objections to the TTA, including those from the NUT. The Union's then Assistant Education Secretary, Michael Barber, wrote that the TTA would lack independence and would be subject to political interference (NUT, 1993), although his views changed when he became a government adviser.[5] Ofsted, superseding the old HMI that had conducted independent inspections of schools and given schools and government helpful advice, now employed private teams of inspectors. The first Chief Inspector, appointed by the government and retained by Labour after 1997, was Chris Woodhead, whose willingness to criticise schools and teachers proved useful to succeeding governments and initiated a climate of pointless fear in schools that persisted into the 21st century. When Woodhead was accused of amending an Ofsted report on reading, carried out in three boroughs, deleting sections referring to poverty and bilingualism, a chair of one of the boroughs observed that 'Mr Woodhead is as much use in the battle for higher standards as a chocolate teapot' (quoted in MacCleod, 1996: 2). Mr Woodhead was also credited with referring to anyone with a professional interest in education as 'The Blob', a phrase used later by Michael Gove when Education Secretary.

Following the Education Act 1988, open enrolment and local management of schools, whereby funds followed pupils, was the mechanism that made some schools richer and some poorer. It also led to a diversion of funds into marketing and public relations, and encouraged parents to become vigilantes and complainers rather than partners. A long Education Act in 1993 made further attempts to make schools grant-maintained (GM), including the notion that failing schools could be made to 'go GM' just as in later years under-performing schools were to be forced into becoming 'academies'.

The operation of market choice of school was quickly shown to be a crude method of social selection. This escalated over the years as house prices near 'good' schools shot up. GM schools were funded directly from the Education Department, as had been the direct grant grammar schools that Labour had abolished. Business-funded city technology colleges (CTCs), schools specialising in different subjects, and Anglican, Catholic and Jewish schools, educating some 23% of pupils at that time, were encouraged to opt out of local authority control, all this claiming to demonstrate' diversity'. Even the Conservative Education Association worried that 'if schools do opt for GM status an even larger part of the £14.5 billion spent annually on schools will be spent by bodies that are not democratically accountable' (CEA, 1992). This was a foretaste of the large amount to be spent in the future by undemocratic Academy Trusts that came to control large numbers of schools and their funding. The main result of 'choice' of school was that road traffic increased by 20% in cities as parents drove their children to school. The publication of league tables comparing schools' test results became an annual media event and a political weapon for subsequent claims that effective and poor schools could be easily identified. American scholar Michael Apple later commented that, 'While race talk may be absent in the discourse of markets, it remains an absent presence that I believe is fully implicated in the goals and concerns surrounding support for the marketisation of education' (Apple, 1999: 12).

Failing schools

By the 1990s a new educational phenomenon appeared in Britain; this was the 'failing school', a demonised institution whose teachers and governors were deemed to be responsible for the under-performance of the pupils.[6] They were also blamed for failing local communities and, that ever-present category of citizen, 'the disadvantaged'. Press coverage of failing schools was negative and insulting, as journalists competed to discover the 'worst school in Britain' (Brace, 1994). Politicians also competed to demonstrate their 'zero tolerance of failure'. Tony Blair, as the 1997 General Election approached, attempted to outdo the Tories in stressing 'no tolerance for under-performing schools' in a lecture in Oxford (Blair, 1996). The notion of failure was not new, but had previously been mainly associated with individual pupil failure. In England and Wales from 1945 the secondary education system was premised on the assumption that 80% of pupils at age 11 would fail to demonstrate potential for academic learning. The increasing number of comprehensive schools expanded access to examination courses during the 1960s, and changed attitudes to girls' education, improved teaching and had allowed larger numbers of pupils to enter public examinations. Thus the 1940s figures were reversed. By the 1990s over 80% of young people were achieving passes in academic courses, numbers gaining vocational qualifications increased and by 1993, around 33% of 18- to 19-year-olds were attending university – many at the 'new' universities. A public consciousness was developing that recognised the importance of qualifications, and a decline in the deferential attitude that 'education is not for the likes of us'.

This success was of little interest to politicians or the media, and persistent propaganda claiming low standards and incompetent teachers was used to establish an increasing hierarchy of schools and centralised control of education. Margaret Thatcher, always supporting selection for secondary level, expressed 'deep personal dissatisfaction with schooling', and continued to blame teachers who were 'less competent and more ideological than their predecessors' (Thatcher, 1993: 598). LEAs, especially if Labour-controlled, were also blamed for low standards, with migration, English as a Second Language and families that did not value education also coming under attack. Less attention was paid to lack of resources, crumbling buildings, under-paid teachers and the spread of poverty and unemployment. Neither was there much interest in the situation that had developed in Tower Hamlets in London where, by 1990, some 500 Bangladeshi children were without a school place, the local authority, short of money to build more schools, blaming parents who would not travel out of the area for fear of racial attacks. The local Law Centre took the case to a judicial review and Lord Justice Woolf gave the curious judgment that the duty of an LEA to provide school places was 'not absolute' (Tomlinson, 1992: 444).

Pillorying individual schools became a policy, with initially around 200 secondary schools targeted as failing and in need of 'special measures'. Unsurprisingly, these schools were in predominantly urban areas attended by minority children, English as a Second Language speakers and those with special educational needs. Culloden Primary School in Tower Hamlets was criticised in the tabloid media for giving too much attention to English as a Second Language learners and to children with special needs. While national education systems had become a key focus for the incorporation of racial and minority ethnic groups into the economy and civil society, the educational policies of the early 1990s contributed to disadvantages by race and class. Minority students had to bear additional market burdens, as they were likely to be regarded as undesirable, attend 'failing schools' and those with reduced budgets. Black students fared particularly badly in the marketisation of schooling (Tomlinson, 1998).

The classic example of the failing schools policy was Hackney Downs School in London, which became a by-word for a failing school. This former grammar school became a comprehensive in 1974, with boys achieving public examination passes on a par with similar London schools, and by the 1980s it was taking in large numbers of minority and migrant pupils and those expelled from other schools. The intake included pupils with African, Caribbean, Indian, Pakistani, Bangladeshi, Kurdish and Turkish backgrounds and other groups. In the 1990s there had been four head teachers in six years, and the buildings were in severe disrepair. The chair of Hackney Education Council from 1988 to 1990 was Michael Barber, who was not initially critical of the school. Arguments between the local authority, the Chief Education Officer (Gus John, one of the first black Chief Education Officers of an education authority to be appointed), parents, governors and the DES ensued over the next five years as to whether the school should be closed (Barber, 1995, 1996; Tomlinson, 1995, 2005; O'Connor et al, 1999).

The failing schools legislation allowed for the setting up of an Education Association to inspect schools and take over their running if necessary. In July 1995, when Hackney Council had decided to keep the school open, and a week after the Secretary of State Gillian Shepherd had decided not to intervene in Hackney Downs School, she changed her mind and appointed the one and only Education Association to investigate the school. Members included a businessman with interests in GM schools and CTCs, the former head of a private school, a former Chief Executive Officer of a Conservative-controlled London borough, a chartered accountant and Michael Barber, who (before this Association had decided the school needed to be closed) had written that it was 'the school that had to die' (Barber, 1995). Despite parents challenging the closure decision in a judicial review, the school was closed with precipitate haste, and the boys transferred to a neighbouring school, where the examination performance in the following year was no better than at Hackney Downs.

Eventually the school was demolished and a new school was built on the site, costing some £35 million of taxpayers' money, with Michael Wilshaw, a future head of Ofsted, as head teacher. With a selected intake − the school would later be accused of taking too few pupils with special needs − but claiming 'traditional' teaching, the school initially had good examination results and became a favourite for visits from Tony Blair when he became Prime Minister. Michael Barber, employed by Labour to lead a Literacy Task Force in 1996, and later heading Blair's Standards and Effectiveness Unit, claimed in an interview in 2011 that 'The stand we took on Hackney Downs became a foundation of New Labour's education policy' (Wilby, 2011). The Labour government under Blair continued the policy of naming and shaming schools, which, as 'choice' policies developed, ensured that these failing schools were largely attended by pupils from poor, minority, refugee, special needs and English as a Second Language backgrounds. It eventually became clear that it was easier to blame schools than to restructure education or plan the economy to ensure all young people had an educated future.

Whose National Curriculum?

With wars, migration, the EU and privatising public utilities, it was not surprising that the Major government had little time to examine in detail the content of the school curriculum or debate existential questions such as what kinds of knowledge young people would need as the 21st century approached. The main interest was in developing tests that would demonstrate winners and losers in the educational market. The National Curriculum, the pride of Baker's Education Reform Act 1988, was developed over several years, and much of the work was left to civil servants and advisers, who had themselves largely been educated at private schools that were exempt from the National Curriculum.[7] There was certainly no enthusiasm for examining Britain's place in relationship to her former Empire, or her new European partners. Instead, there was a growing and determined attack on any changes by the educational nationalists, the right-wing groups around Mrs Thatcher and John Major who demanded a return to what they termed a 'traditional' curriculum. They labelled any of the 1980s activities that went under the name of 'multicultural', 'anti-racist education', 'global' or 'world studies' as subversive of British culture, likely to be associated with left-wing egalitarianism and leading to lowered standards (Palmer, 1986). Empire as a topic was an 'absent presence', and although Royalty was still touring Commonwealth countries, the inclusion of former colonial subjects as citizens was still a matter for regret, and the school curriculum was not about to provide the *Education for all* Lord Swann's committee had envisaged.

It has already been noted that an 'English' national identity had been in crisis since the Second World War, as the nation lost its Empire. It has also been noted that the idea of an exclusive national identity cannot be understood without understanding British imperialism, colonial expansion and the way imperial ideologies entered the school curriculum. Despite efforts made by educators from the 1970s to develop a curriculum more meaningful in a multicultural society and to develop anti-racist strategies, those influencing a National Curriculum were still clinging to notions of the cultural, linguistic and political superiority of the English nation, and wished the curriculum to define the boundaries of a national identity and assert a 'traditional' (Victorian) culture and heritage. While a National Curriculum with recognised standards in state schools was generally agreed by the later 1980s to be necessary, it was a relatively small group of politicians and lobbyists who determined that it should be a 'British' (English) curriculum, and certainly not an international curriculum. Political attack on any content suggesting equal opportunities, anti-racism or multiculturalism was ever present during the creation of the National Curriculum, and these areas were banished from discussion, as the work of the Mathematics working group, documented in the previous chapter, demonstrated.

> As regards multicultural education ... what must be said was that it was made starkly clear to the National Curriculum Council that whatever influence it might have would be rapidly dissipated by entering what was widely seen as a no-go area. (Graham, 1993: 132)

Duncan Graham, appointed as the first chair of the National Curriculum Council (NCC) by Kenneth Baker in 1988 – who welcomed him with a malt whisky – wrote, 'The right-wing of the Conservative Party was listening to lobbyists who were continually saying how terrible it was that none of the country's children – apart from their own – could read or write' (Graham, 1993: 6). He noted that the educational traditionalists were the same people who talked of a return to Victorian values, and pointed out two junior ministers who saw the NCC as dominated by professionals, educationalists and teachers who attempted to block much of the NCC's activities. He named one of these as Michael Fallon, who 'believed the NCC was dangerously left-wing' (Graham, 1993: 99). Fallon subsequently had a long career in Conservative governments, culminating in the post as Defence Secretary, before resigning in 2017 over 'inappropriate conduct' (Castle, 2017).

Secretary of State, Kenneth Baker, had determined a broad, 10-subject National Curriculum, with working groups of teachers, producing detailed suggestions on what each subject should contain with cross-curricular themes, a recipe, as Graham noted, for interference and argument. He soon realised that civil servants rightly saw this as their first chance of having real power over the education system, and 'junior officials would come to NCC meetings to tell a group of teachers, for example, how geography should be taught' (Graham, 1993: 13). Geography, History and English were always the most contentious subjects. Geography, as noted previously, was, up to the 1960s, frankly imperialist, and had moved slowly towards internationalism, but even in the 1980s taught material that was highly questionable. Dawn Gill, Head of Geography in a London school, and an intrepid anti-racist campaigner, pointed out, for example, that worksheets on a 'Geography for Young School Leavers' project taught into the later 1980s contained a worksheet on Dallas USA, juxtaposing information that 'Dallas is a visual mess, its crime rate is a disgrace, and 19% of its population is Negro' (King and Reiss, 1993: 94). But the National Curriculum Geography working group made a valiant attempt not to duck the issues, and the final report of their group included a section on 'Geography for a multicultural society'. They were to be disappointed when the DES draft orders for National Curriculum Geography concluded that, 'The Secretary of State recognises that geography lessons will sometimes deal with conflicting points of view…. However, he considers that the main emphasis should be on teaching knowledge and understanding of geography rather than on people's attitudes and opinions' (DES, 1991a).

History in the National Curriculum aroused fierce debates, especially over the History working group's wish to produce a curriculum for a multicultural society. Governments around the world, especially dictatorships, have often attempted to reinvent their national histories, recognising that what is taught as history is crucial to the creation of a national identity. Rob Phillips (1998) discussed in some detail the battle for control of which historical stories should comprise the National Curriculum and the political interference that ensued. As he noted, the struggle for the 'big prize' of the nation's story led to thousands of articles, letters and editorials in the quality and tabloid press, and demonstrated the influence of those who wished to link history teaching to what they considered to be a patriotic, nationalistic, cultural identity. The final report of the National Curriculum History working group claimed that one of the purposes of school history was 'to contribute to pupil's knowledge and understanding of other countries and other cultures' (Booth, 1993), but this was not acceptable to the traditionalists. Kenneth Baker was sympathetic to right-wing views that school history paid to little attention to a British heritage and had become anti-patriotic (Graham, 1993: 63). The final study units, and the statutory orders for history, came across as largely about 'white indigenous people'. For example, a unit on 'Expansion, trade and industry 1750-1900' omitted much that was negative about empire. The group's chair was Commander Michael Saunders Watson, owner of Rockingham Castle in Nottingham. He did not toe the expected line, and clashed with Margaret Thatcher, who interfered considerably with the proposals from the History working group. He also objected to Kenneth Clarke's proposal that history should end in 1945.

Graham's conclusion regarding the History and Geography interference by politicians raised serious questions about the role of ministers in the school curriculum and the dilemmas when politics clashes with educational views. The English working group suffered similar interference. This group, headed by Professor Brian Cox, included several members who were concerned about bilingualism and multicultural education. Cox wrote later: 'Conservative politicians were over-confident they knew the right policies and to a large extent were contemptuous towards the professional teacher.' Mr Baker, for example, ' ... wanted a short report with an emphasis on grammar, punctuation and spelling ... whereas the Group assumed that the curriculum for all pupils should include informed discussion of the multicultural nature of British society, whether or not the school is culturally mixed' (Cox, 1991: 11, 19).

But the negative influence of politicians was most clearly indicated by the open repudiation of the report of a Multicultural Task Group set up by the NCC in response to a letter from the Secretary of State that the NCC was 'to take account of ethnic and cultural diversity and the importance of the curriculum in promoting equal opportunity for all pupils regardless of ethnic origin or gender' (Tomlinson, 1993: 21).[8] The NCC had noted that multicultural education was a controversial area, and the Task Group was well aware that any debates prefaced by 'multi' or 'anti' were anathema to influential people with the ear of government. The group set about suggesting ways in which schools could incorporate multicultural issues into all subjects and the implications for LEAs, school, teachers, governors and parents. The report of five chapters presented by the Task Group was never published. The only reference to it was in one page of an NCC newsletter, which noted, 'The NCC does not see multicultural education as a subject, but as a dimension which permeates the whole curriculum and the Council would draw on the work of the Multicultural Task Group to see that this would happen.' There was little subsequent evidence that permeation occurred (see Tomlinson, 1993).

Summary

This chapter has attempted to demonstrate that a great deal happened during the government headed by John Major, which had negative consequences for future dealings with the EU, with immigration issues, and with the education of all young people for a multiracial and multicultural society, all of which affected the later Brexit vote. While the first Gulf War set the stage for future conflicts in the Middle East and retaliations that affected the British population, politics was dominated by persistent Euroscepticism, and by the untruths and sleaze that came to be associated with some politicians. The period consolidated the education policies that enhanced market ideologies, competitive individualism and privatisation, that were to dominate the development and eventual possible break–up of a state education system. It initiated a school inspection system that superseded a helpful and respected inspectorate, and introduced cruel and pointless policies of naming and shaming schools that did not do well in constantly updated tests and examinations. Markets and choice policies created new disadvantages for minority young people, as they were most likely to be attending urban schools regarded as 'undesirable' and to be labelled as 'failing'. These policies were embraced by an incoming Labour government and its advisers. The period and preceding two years also saw the development of a determinedly 'National' Curriculum, interfered with by the views of right-wing politicians and their advisers. It was not a curriculum for all children and young people, and certainly not one with which racial and minority ethnic groups could identify. It did grave disservice to an indigenous population who, as the British empire was disappearing, needed some truthful accounts of the past and present realities about living in a multiracial and multicultural global world.

Notes

[1] The Europsceptics at that time, although not named in his interview, but recorded in Stephen Castle's article, were Michael Howard (Home Secretary), Peter Lilley (Social Security), Michael Portillo (Chief Secretary to the Treasury) and John Redwood (Secretary of State for Wales).

[2] The East London Mosque was eventually recognised as a centre for radicalising young Muslim men, influenced by the cleric Omar Bakri Muhammad, who was eventually deported from Britain.

[3] The 1991 Census categories were: White, White Irish, Black Caribbean, Black African, Black Other, Indian, Pakistani, Bangladeshi, Chinese, and Other Groups. Birthplace was also requested.

[4] Asylum-seekers become refugees when they are given the right to remain in a country.

[5] Michael Barber had an extraordinary career as by 2018 he was chair of an Office for Students (OfS) with great power over universities.

[6] The failing schools legislation was set out in DfE Circular 17/93.

[7] The National Curriculum was intended to 'promote the spiritual, moral, mental and physical development of pupils at school and in society: and prepare pupils for the opportunities, responsibilities and experiences of adult life' (Education Act 1988, Section 1.2).

[8] Sally Tomlinson was a member of this Task Group.

6

New Labour: Wars, race and education, 1997-2005

Miss, why is your skin like this? (Five-year-old white girl to Ghanaian teacher in London in 2005, quoted in Akomaning, 2018)

After 18 years of Conservative rule, the British people were apparently ready for a new Prime Minister and a revamped Labour Party now known as 'New Labour'. They got this on 1 May 1997, when public school-educated Anthony Charles Lynton Blair became Prime Minister at the age of 43. Much was made of the notion that there was a 'new dawn' in politics. His close adviser, Alastair Campbell, wrote in his diaries describing the Blair election win, 'as we got to the Festival Hall … TB worked the crowd, then up to the lectern and a "new dawn" and they cheered every word' (Campbell and Stott, 2007: 187). A number of books were hastily written to celebrate this accomplishment, some celebrating and looking forward to his premiership (Mandelson and Liddle, 1996), some more cautious (Rawnsley, 2000), and later some frankly hostile, accusing him of turning the country into *Fantasy island* (Elliot and Atkinson, 2007). The Campbell diaries and Blair's own memoir (Blair, 2010]) gave their exhaustive account of the years after Blair took over as Leader of the Labour Party, after the untimely death of John Smith in 1994. In his speech to the Labour Party Conference in October 1997 Blair affirmed a commitment to social justice and to education as a means to a socially just society (Blair, 1997a). Then, in 1998, Blair referred to the equal worth of all individuals, claiming that 'The attack on racial discrimination now commands general support, as does the value of a multicultural society' (Blair, 1998: 3), and in a later speech celebrated as his 21st-century message, asserted that 'nations that succeed will be tolerant, respectful of diversity, multiracial, multicultural societies' (Blair, 1999). So, it may be asked, what went wrong? It might have gone wrong from the start of Blair's government – although he claimed beliefs in social and racial justice, by the end of his tenure, Blair was blaming black gangs and parents for racial violence, and supporting selective education policies for 'high flyers' (Gillborn, 2007).

This chapter notes that the New Labour government initially embraced an ideology of a 'third way', joining capitalist market competition with social democracy and a reformed welfare state with education as a means to help create a socially just society. It claimed education as a priority and continued the avalanche of market-driven education legislation and policy initiatives that had characterised 18 years of Conservative rule. Initially it attempted to take on a number of social and racial grievances and inequities. This included setting up a Social Exclusion Unit in the Cabinet Office, ordering an inquiry into the Stephen Lawrence murder, offering Muslim schools the same state funding as other voluntary-aided schools and creating an Ethnic Minority Achievement Grant. Race returned as a presence rather than an 'absent' presence.

New Labour seemed eager to affirm Britain as embracing a national identity that valued cultural diversity and recognised the rights of minorities, although Blair had never expressed much support for this previously. By Labour's second term in office from 2001, it was clear that the government had not grasped the scale of the problems in creating a multicultural society. More conflicts in northern English towns in 2001 ushered in another examination of what constituted a British 'national identity', and there was agonising over what constituted multiculturalism and how to create 'community cohesion'. This was not helped by further immigration control acts, and a luke-warm view of the EU, with some dithering over whether to hold a referendum on joining a single euro currency. Echoes of empire returned after terrorist attacks in New York on the World Trade Centre in September 2001 led to joint Allied invasions of Afghanistan in 2001 and the former British territory of Iraq in 2003. It was *Blair's wars* (Kampfner, 2003) that were to be the main legacy of his premiership, and at his handover as Prime Minister to Gordon

Brown in 2007, notions of a progressive, inclusive Britain were giving way to xenophobia and disunity.

Significant events

1997	(May) New Labour wins the General Election; European Year Against Racism; David Blunkett becomes Education Secretary
1997	Social Exclusion Unit (SEU) set up with a brief to inquire into school exclusions and truancy with special reference to black pupils; a Qualifications and Curriculum Authority (QCA) set up; William Macpherson asked to chair an inquiry into the murder of Stephen Lawrence; Muslim faith schools to be offered state funding
1998	Bernard Crick (tutor of Blunkett during his degree course at the University of Sheffield) reports on citizenship and the teaching of democracy in schools (with two paragraphs on multicultural education); Education Action Zones (EAZs) set up to improve education in inner-cities areas, later part of an Excellence in Cities programme
1998	Human Rights Act brings European Convention on Human Rights into UK law; Crime and Disorder Act brings more penalties for racial crimes
1998	School Standards and Framework Act ends GM schools but schools can become foundation, voluntary aided or community schools (the first two controlling their own admissions); Teaching and Higher Education Act
1998	Enoch Powell dies and there are many obituaries and tributes to his patriotism
1999	Final devolution of governing powers to a Scottish Parliament and a Welsh Assembly; the Belfast Agreement (Good Friday Agreement) devolved government to a Northern Irish Parliament, although the DUP voted against this Agreement
1999	Excellence in Cities programme includes Gifted and Talented programme; Sure Start Centres set up, focusing on disadvantaged children aged 0-3
1999	Macpherson Report on the murder of Stephen Lawrence suggests there is institutional racism in the police force; NUT passes a resolution against racism at its annual conference
1999	Asylum and Immigration Act introduces vouchers instead of cash for asylum-seekers, enforced dispersal and detention on arrival
2000	Race Relations Amendment Act requires local authorities and schools to have race equality policies, with Ofsted to review these; TTA produced online guidelines for teachers in place of courses that were taught in universities and colleges on teaching for a multiethnic society; Woodhead resigns as head of Ofsted
2001	Census records 4.5 million (8%) of the UK population identifying as minority ethnic, with a younger age structure for those of Pakistani and Bangladeshi origin; David Blunkett becomes Home Secretary
2001	(June) New Labour elected again with nine black and Asian MPs; Department for Education and Employment becomes the Department for Education and Skills (DfES); (July) riots in the northern towns of Oldham, Bolton, Bradford and Burnley; (9 September) Ted Cantle sent

	to visit and report; destruction of World Trade Towers in New York by men of Saudi Arabian origin; more hostility to Muslims as Blair joins the USA in the war in Afghanistan
2002	White Paper presents new policies on nationality and citizenship, English language and citizenship tests; proposal that children of asylum-seekers should have separate schooling, as Blunkett claims the children are 'swamping' some schools
2002	Nationality and Immigration Asylum Act; more border controls and an increase in detention facilities and deportation orders; citizenship courses to be mandatory in all schools; first academy schools set up
2003	(March) Invasion and war in Iraq
2003	Victoria Climbié report by Lord Laming; White Paper *Every Child Matters* (Department of Education/Home Office)
2004	Higher Education Act allows for fees of up to £3,000 in universities and sets up Office for Fair Access (OFFA); Mike Tomlinson's report suggesting an overarching diploma at 18 is repudiated; David Blunkett resigns as Home Secretary
2005	Trevor Phillips, head of CRE and designate head of a new Equalities and Human Rights Commission (EHRC), claims that the UK is 'sleepwalking into segregation'; (June) New Labour elected for a third term; the Conservatives under Michael Howard run a losing campaign vilifying immigrants; Education Act increases school inspections and schools are 'causing concern' if they fail to achieve set targets for pupils; the term 'local education authority' is abolished but continues to be used
2005	(July) Four young Muslim men, educated in English schools, suicide bomb London Underground trains and a bus; (August) 18-year-old black student Anthony Walker is axed to death in Liverpool; (October) conflicts in Birmingham between black and Asian young men

Politics, ideologies and war

A month after New Labour's election, Prime Minister Tony Blair spoke at a European Socialists Conference in Sweden, telling fellow socialists that 'our task is not to fight old battles but to show there is a third way, of marrying an open competitive economy with a just, decent and humane society' (Blair, 1997b). The 'third way', an ideology borrowed from Bill Clinton in the USA, was intended to marry market competition and the deregulation of business with social democracy and a reformed welfare state. The European Socialists were not convinced and continued to support social democracy and regulated capitalism. They were right to do so, as what was going wrong in Britain since the 1980s was the growth in inequality of wages, wealth and life chances, and this was exacerbated under the Blair years (Wilkinson and Pickett, 2009; Dorling, 2010). Labour's historic ideological commitment to state intervention to achieve equality and social justice rapidly gave way to a continuation of neoliberal policies from the right. This included privatisation, flexible labour markets and a competitive individualism, with people supposedly lifting themselves out of poverty with the help of state authoritarian policies. While this worked for some families from overseas – 11 of the top 12 families in the 2017 Sunday Times Rich List were from India, Russia, Canada, Sweden and Italy – it did not do much to help the working classes and many minorities. Policies increasingly left the middle classes fearful for their children's futures. Inequality led to more blaming of immigrants and minorities as the cause of social problems.

But New Labour accepted that those living in countries internally colonised by England should be given a measure of independence, and powers were devolved to the Scottish Parliament, a Welsh Assembly and a partial resolution of the conflicts in Northern Ireland through the Belfast Agreement in 1999. There was more open recognition that the country now incorporated large numbers of minority ethnic groups with different migration histories, economic positions and religions, whose claims to be part of the society could not be ignored. The European Convention on Human Rights was incorporated into UK law in 1998, and as noted in Chapter Five, a defining moment in British race relations came after an inquiry into the murder of Stephen Lawrence was set up and the report in 1999 brought the concept of institutionalised racism and problems in the police force to public attention (Macpherson, 1999).

Home Secretary Jack Straw set up a Commission on the Future of Multiethnic Britain in 1998 (Parekh, 2000), but this proved to be a disaster, with its report condemned by the media for attacking 'Britishness'; Straw and Blair hastily disassociated themselves from it. The report had actually suggested in one chapter that, 'There has been no collective working through the Imperial experience. The absence from the National Curriculum of a rewritten history of Britain as an Imperial force, involving dominance in Ireland as well as Africa, the Caribbean and Asia, is proving an unmitigated disaster' (Parekh, 2000: 25). It suggested better ways of supporting community diversity while fostering a shared national identity, a theme repeated in subsequent academic and political literature, but at the time even *The Times* criticised the findings of the Commission (the author was a member), asking 'who do these worthy idiots think they are?' (Kaletsky, 2000). It was instructive that in 1998 Enoch Powell had died and his obituaries praised his patriotism and support for an exclusive sovereign national identity. In a later book evaluating Powell's life and work, Iain Duncan Smith, a notable voice in the campaign to leave the EU, wrote praising Powell's opposition to the Maastricht Treaty and his view that 'we have traded away Parliament's supremacy to others, whether to foreign institutions or the British judiciary' (Duncan Smith, 2014: xvii).[1]

While Blair had not demonstrated much interest in foreign policy, he was keen to demonstrate patriotism. One election poster for the 1997 election included a British bulldog, but led to arguments as to whether the dog's testicles were too big on the poster. He subsequently led the country to war five times in six years, four of which were in Muslim countries. He supported Bill Clinton and the USA bombing in Iraq in 1998,[2] sent troops to defend the government in Sierra Leone (a British colony until 1961), sent troops to Kosova in the Balkans, and supported President Bush and the USA in invading Afghanistan in 2001 and Iraq in 2003 (Kampfner, 2003). As noted, Blair considered invading Zimbabwe again in 2007. Blair's wars did not endear him to EU members or to Muslim and other Asian minorities in Britain, and the wars in Afghanistan and Iraq subsequently encouraged some young people into terrorist activities.

Multicultural fears

After the Second World War, global migration encouraged the development of a large literature on multiculturalism, recognising that there are now few or no monocultural societies in the world. In England, while the country was becoming more multicultural as more people from former imperial colonies arrived and, in due course, became citizens and others arrived as economic or refugee migrants, social institutions were slow to catch up. Attempts in education to bring in multicultural and anti-racist perspectives in education continued to be met with hostility. But despite supporters being attacked as 'left-wing loonies', a political discourse had developed recognising the reality of multiculturalism that was later incorporated into the language of 'diversity'. But the issue of what was traditionally in the private domain of families – languages, religion, marriages – and what was in the public domain of state institutions, was always contentious (Rex, 2004). Despite New Labour's stated commitment to ending racial discrimination and creating a socially just society, any philosophies of the common good continued to be utopian in a society structured along class, gender, race and ethnic lines, with groups in competition for scarce resources. A shared identity seemed conspicuously lacking, as the BNP continued to gain influence in high minority areas, gaining three council seats in Burnley in 2002 and 18 overall in England in 2003. Two weeks after the Parekh Report (2000) was published, a young Asian prisoner was killed in his cell by a white youth who resented being in prison 'with someone whose race and origin he despised' (Kelso, 2000). Hostility to European migrants began to be documented in education. In 2004, a school in Stoke-on-Trent found that five newly arrived Czech Roma children had dropped out. When asked, the other minority children in the school told staff that racism was so routine they did not really identify it. The BNP had distributed leaflets in the town claiming that English was not the first language taught in the school (Wallace, 2004: 8-10).

Despite New Labour's 2001 electoral commitment to a multicultural inclusive society, any policies or ideologies defining a multicultural society reverted back to simplistic assertions that minorities had failed to 'integrate' after riots in the northern towns of Bradford, Bolton, Oldham, Burnley and others in July 2001. The destruction of the World Trade Center in New York in September 2001 by educated men originally from Saudi Arabia signalled a more general hostility to Muslims, and commitment to multiculturalism was weakened with more pressure on minorities to embrace what were claimed to be the responsibilities of British citizenship. Meanwhile, British companies continued to buy oil from Saudi Arabia. A Ministerial Group on Public Order and Community Cohesion, led by Ted Cantle (Cantle, 2001), was set up to visit northern towns and other cities. The Group expressed surprise at the 'parallel lives' people lived, and made recommendations about education that virtually repeated those made in the Education Support Grants (ESG) for projects supported by Baker in the 1980s (Tomlinson, 1990). There were also reports on the disturbances from Lords Clarke, Ritchie and Ousley, the latter a former chair of the CRE, and the final report consolidated the findings (Ministerial Working Group, 2001). In reality, despite talk of ethnic groups deciding to live parallel lives on the basis of ethnicity, the major factor was economic – where can you afford to live and where the jobs are. A later study in London demonstrated that people were becoming more mixed in areas by ethnicity, but less mixed by income (Dorling and Thomas, 2016).

David Blunkett, Home Secretary in 2001 after his years in education, commissioned a White Paper that outlined new politics for citizenship and nationality, requiring future citizens to learn English and pass a citizenship test, despite funding for teaching English as an Additional Language (EAL) being cut. A Nationality, Citizenship and Asylum Act followed, which proposed separate schooling for asylum-seekers' children – a move that was hastily dropped. In April 2002 Blunkett had claimed in a radio broadcast that these children were 'swamping some British schools' (BBC News, 2002). His remark was defended by the government and he never apologised. Policies of dispersal of asylum-seeking and refugees meant that families were often housed in areas hostile to their presence, and there was an increase in racist abuse and hostility, especially from young white people. Blunkett managed to conflate the presence of long-established citizens with newer arrivals when he asserted that there were norms of acceptability, and 'those who come into our home ... should accept these norms' (quoted in Tomlinson, 2008: 135); Oliver Letwin, then Shadow Home Secretary, told the Conservative Party Conference in 2003 that asylum-seekers should be deported to a far-off processing island, although he never specified which one. Blunkett had to resign his post in 2004 when it transpired that he had fast-tracked a visa for the foreign nanny of a former lover.

Centralising education

The New Labour government under Blair had three years to prepare for power, and three pages in his 40-page election manifesto promised smaller classes, demanded higher standards and setting (placing children in ability groups) in schools, and zero tolerance of under-performance. Increased funding was promised but compromised when the newly elected government announced it would stick to Tory spending and no raised taxes. Despite hyping the priority of education, spending on education as a proportion of GDP actually declined, from 4.8% in 1996 to 4.7% in 1998. A raft of education policy initiatives and Acts followed between 1998 and 2005. Michael Barber, who, as noted in the previous chapter, had announced that the closure of Hackney Downs school as 'failing' influenced future Labour policy, was made head of a Standards and Effectiveness Unit. Literacy and numeracy task forces were set up plus a plethora of other groups on adult learning, special needs, university for industry and a New Deal advisory group and others. There was even a Red Tape Reduction Working Group. In 2001 Barber became head of a Delivery Unit in the Cabinet Office, checking how targets set in education, health and other institutions were being met – Liberal Leader Charles Kennedy worked out that the government had set up some 4,585 targets for schools, colleges and LEAs to achieve (Kennedy, 2000).

A major Education Act in 1998 abolished GM schools, but secondary schools could become foundation, aided or community schools. The Conservative policy of 'specialist schools' was extended, with more business sponsorship, and beacon schools were to become examples of good practice. Estate agents reported that house prices rose near beacon schools. LEAs were to promote high standards, but with reduced powers. The selection of 10% of pupils by 'aptitude' for secondary schools was permitted, a distinct broken promise (see Lawton, 2005). Market forces were helping to create 'failing' schools, with Blunkett declaring that persistent failure would not be tolerated and a macho language of zero tolerance, tough policy and pressure continued. It was not until October 1998 that the public humiliation of urban schools and their teachers was largely abandoned, with the head of one inner-city school serving a poor, black intake, noting bitterly that, 'We have had a Herculean task to improve in a climate of hostility' (Gardiner, 1997).

But as school exclusions had reached over 10,000 a year, a Social Exclusion Unit (SEU) set up in the Cabinet Office aimed to reduce this, although setting no targets! A majority of exclusions, truants and those placed in schools for the emotionally and behaviourally disturbed (EBD) were young black males. An Ethnic Minority Achievement Grant replaced previous funding for minority education. There was much discussion about investing in human capital, competing in a global economy and the need for more privatisation and business interests in state education. There was also a focus on Early Years and childcare facilities for all mothers to help them return to the workforce, and in 1998 a national Child Care Strategy was launched promising more childcare places paid for by public, private and voluntary sectors. Childcare was treated more urgently after the torture and death of an eight-year-old child of West African origin, Victoria Climbié. This led to a public inquiry and a Children Act requiring education, health and social services to work more closely together. Sure Start Centres, the idea of Treasury official Norman Glass, were set up from 1999 bringing together professionals from all services for children aged 0-3, and these expanded into Children's Centres, although a review of the project in 2007 claimed it had failed to address the question of ethnicity with rigour or sensitivity. In one area white parents told Bangladeshi parents they could not use the centres (Craig, 2007).

Privatising education

Under New Labour education was to become less of a democratically state-funded system and more of a commodity to be bought and sold. Private companies were brought in to run national programmes from inspections to school dinners, schools were built with the Private Finance Initiative (PFI), and from 2002, schools could form themselves into companies and sell goods and services to each other (see Ball, 2007). A diversity of schools was encouraged, with more faith schools to include

Muslim schools, more Anglican, Catholic, Jewish and other faiths, specialist schools and CTCs.

But the policy that led to the most fragmentation, privatisation and eventual removal of democratic accountability from schooling was the creation of academy schools. Called city academies in the Learning and Skills Act 2000, three academies opened in 2002. Enthusiastically embraced by David Blunkett, Peter Mandelson and adviser Andrew Adonis (all three later to become Lords), these were to be independent state-funded schools set up as limited companies with charitable status. Sponsors from business, sport or other groups would contribute money and appoint a majority of governors. They were outside local authority democratic influence, under central control via the DfES, and controlled their own admissions – an open invitation for covert selection. Blair was enthusiastic, holding 'breakfasts' in Downing Street for sponsors, including American investment bankers, and two of the early academies were under the control of evangelical creationist Christians. Blair, perhaps due to his own private education at the Empire-minded Fettes school (see Chapter One), had never, despite early utterances, really embraced non-selective education or social and racial justice. His slogan 'Education, education, education' was lampooned in a cartoon by Steve Bell in 2001. This depicted Blair shouting into a megaphone, 'Education for everyone of excellence: You thickies can whistle for it!' (reproduced with permission as the frontispiece in Tomlinson, 2017). Local authorities themselves were also claimed to be at risk of 'failing' and could be taken over by private companies. Islington, the London borough home to Blair before the General Election (and to Jeremy Corbyn for many years) became the first LEA to be taken over by a private company, Cambridge Associates. The firm Capita, which has had a chequered career of fraud and failings over the years, was appointed to take over education in Leeds. Capita was also appointed in 2001 to run an Individual Learning Accounts programme for students that eventually closed with accusations of fraud.

Controlling higher education

Following a report in 1997 a Teaching and Higher Education Act brought in a £1,000 fee for university tuition and arrangements for student loans. The success of comprehensive education from the 1970s had resulted in a wider and more diverse body of students qualifying for university entrance, but university staff pay was squeezed. Arguments on whether private schools took a disproportionate number of places at top universities persisted, and a 2003 White Paper made widening access and participation to include more working-class, minority and mature students a priority for a further Act in 2004. Although opposed by 100 Labour MPs and passed by only five votes, this Act raised fees to £3,000 a year and set the scene for further fee increases. An Office for Fair Access (OFFA) was set up to oversee fairness in admissions, and successive governments began boasting that more working-class and minority students were going into higher education, albeit mainly to former polytechnics.

Modernising the teaching profession was a favourite theme of the Blair government, which meant more control of pay, recruitment and conditions of service. Incompetent teachers were blamed for low pupil performance, which unsurprisingly led to recruitment problems. Reports suggesting that more minority teachers might improve pupil attainments and lives were never acted on. The TTA, which had taken over organising teacher preparation, produced guidelines in 2000 on how teachers should prepare for teaching in a culturally diverse society, as face-to-face courses had more or less disappeared. This mainly took the form of ticking boxes, but in 2003, a website was prepared as a resource for teachers covering some information on race, class, religion, in bilingualism, Roma and Travellers. A Race Relations Amendment Act in 2000 had made it obligatory for all educational institutions to produce and monitor race equality policies, but research two years later indicated that only 20% had done this. Muslim dress continued to be an issue. One court case in which a 14-year-old girl wished to wear a *jilbad* (long dress) at school took four years to resolve (Tomlinson, 2008: 153).

The Education Act 2005 increased Ofsted's power, with a semi-privatised inspectorate, increased local authority competition for new secondary schools, and extended the powers of the TTA to support all the 'schools' workforce', including the requirement, as in previous Acts, 'to promote the spiritual, moral, behavioural, social, cultural, mental and physical development of children and young people' (Education Act 2005, Section 75).

There was no requirement for curriculum change to achieve these rather elaborate goals, and evidence continued to accumulate that, like the little girl questioning her teacher's dark skin, white understandings of a black presence was not something schools were teaching.

The madness of testing

Under the Blair then Brown governments, the system was set for a future in which the madness of measurement, target setting, inspection and blame characterised education from Early Years to higher education. One experienced teacher and writer rightly remarked that, if religion was once the opium of the masses, high stakes test results have become the crack cocaine of the education system. It was noted in Chapter Three that children from colonial countries barely had time to sit down in school before psychologists and educational researchers began to measure their intelligence and attainments, as if there had never been over 200 years of denigration of their families in colonised countries that had their own histories, languages and possible development shattered, plus Victorian eugenic beliefs in the innate inabilities of the colonised. A number of coherent theories attempted to explain educational performance by class, race and gender.

Studies of the 'Empire effect' in Britain from historical, sociological and political angles remain overdue. German sociologist Ulrich Beck, contemplating modern societies, wrote that 'the world is unhinged … it has gone mad' (Beck, 2016: 1). The madness of assuming that it was possible to compare the test results of the descendants of those formerly colonised in a hostile, xenophobic society with young white people continued, with no historical understanding as to the different modes of colonisation, or the different ways the education system treated various minorities.

Most migrant parents from former colonies were unsurprisingly concerned about the educational achievements of their children, and ambitious for them, knowing that they would be disadvantaged in employment and life chances unless they achieved the same level as white children in whatever forms of schooling and testing were offered. On the whole they were and continue to be disappointed in what they have been offered, as the school systems changed, exam success became more crucial and racism continued in its various forms, in and out of institutions. Government ambitions to overcome 'achievement gaps' between white and minority students were rendered pointless by 'Moving the goal posts' (Gillborn et al, 2017) – which redefined levels or benchmarks of what constituted success in examinations. The use of data showing differences between the public examination passes of different minority groups led to what had been noted in the USA as the creation of 'model minorities'. In England this led to invidious comparisons between higher attainments of Chinese and Indian-origin pupils as against Caribbean, African, Pakistani and Bangladeshi pupils, and also led to panic if any minority pupils appeared to perform better than any in what was assumed to be the whole of a white working class.

The plethora of research and collection of data on educational achievements of various groups of children and young people at all levels in education developed into a burgeoning industry. Initially research was small-scale and mainly qualitative – interviewing and observing. Later, especially since there were now large amounts of data available from, for example, the 2002 Pupil Level Annual School Census (PLASC) that collects information on individuals by achievement, ethnicity, gender and free school meals (FSM) – the proxy for poverty – large research grants are given to those who use quantitative methods and elaborate statistical analysis to demonstrate which groups are up or down in the high stakes testing.[3] The emergence of a further global industry PISA (Programme for International Student Assessment), instigated by the OECD (Organisation for Economic Co-operation and Development), created panic in governments as the results purported to show which countries were up or down in competitive tables. PISA enthusiasts were supportive of markets, choice and efficiency in schooling, less so for democratic participation by schools, teachers, parents and the young people themselves (Meyer and Benavot, 2013).

The absent curriculum

So why was it, that after several hundred years of Empire, and 60 of Commonwealth, with now around 9 million citizens from former colonial countries in Britain, did a five-year-old have to query her teacher's dark skin in 2005? The answer to the little girl could have been:

> Well, dear, in 1821, your white ancestors took over my rich country, where we have dark skins. They called it the Gold Coast and made the people there slaves or working for hardly any money and they took food and goods out to give to the white people in Britain. It was not until 1957 that the country became Ghana and got its independence from what was the British Empire. My parents and I had the right to come and live in Britain and in the 1960s my father came and qualified as an accountant and I am a teacher. I hope as you go through school you learn more about the British Empire and what happened to all the people in countries that were taken from them for so long, and perhaps why white people still keep asking why we have dark skins.

Thirteen years later, the criminal barrister and legal affairs journalist Afua Hirsch, of Ghanaian, German and English heritage, put it plainly: 'A lot of British people don't fully accept that you can look like me and be British' (Hirsch, quoted in Clark, 2018). She noted that there is still no language to adequately describe 'What corporate-speak such as Black and Minority Ethnic (BAME) and "diversity" try to hide ... that this country has never had a civil rights movement, a moment of national reckoning where we grappled with the end of empire and the disappearance of imperial words like Negro and coloured' (Clark, 2018: 19).

The New Labour government was not short of ambitious targets and visions. Michael Barber, perhaps the nearest the government came to having a theorist or ideas man, published his vision of a 'world class education system' in 2001 (Barber, 2001). The principles laid out to achieve this included a diversity of secondary schools, state and private, and demands for high standards from all, while separating out the gifted and talented. Barber claimed in 1999 that the Numeracy and Literacy Hour had 'changed the face of primary education for ever' (Bower, 2016: 182), with primary schools leaping in two years to be the third best in the world. In fact, the Literacy Hour was a year old and the Numeracy Hour had not started. Lawton later commented that his vision was a managerial, technicist approach to the delivery of a traditional education (Lawton, 2005). While the New Labour government was willing to follow Conservative policies of central control of curriculum and assessment, it was similarly reluctant to encourage curriculum change to prepare all young people for life in a multiethnic society.

There were no ideas on how the traditional curriculum could develop into an education for a multicultural democratic society. It gradually became clear that the New Labour government, although they used a rhetoric of a more inclusive Britain and had the means to direct the school curriculum into one more suitable for the 21st century, had no plans to do this. The work of several generations of teachers, local authorities, academics, parents and communities was disregarded. There was a plea at a conference on history teaching held at the British Empire and Commonwealth Museum in Bristol in July 2004 for more teaching of empire all through schooling, with one teacher claiming that there had been 'public awkwardness and embarrassment about our Imperial past' (Mansell, 2004: 3), and a Schools History project produced a textbook on *The impact of empire*. But the most that was offered to all pupils was a focus on citizenship education, following a report by Bernard Crick, David Blunkett's former tutor (Crick, 1998). Citizen education became mandatory in schools from 2002. Osler and Starkey, major researchers in citizenship education, pointed out that the Crick report) made no mention of racism, and focused mainly on cultural differences (Osler and Starkey, 2005:

90). Nothing that could really inform all pupils about the past and present nature of the society they lived in was contemplated.

Summary

This chapter has suggested that despite New Labour's declared commitment to a socially and racially just society, supporting multiculturalism and anti-discrimination, the reality turned out differently. Journalist Gary Younge suggested that initially the potential existed for the government to support an inclusive 'hybrid sense of Britishness' (Younge, 2007), but positive policies in the first term of office rapidly changed as fears of supposedly segregated minorities and their religions increased. There was a continuation of anti-immigration policies, and following disastrous wars in Afghanistan and Iraq, an increased threat from a small number of young terrorist Muslims that led to claims that multiculturalism had somehow failed. The implications of this was that a supposedly cohesive society was disrupted by the presence and lives of minorities. Sustained antagonism to immigrants and minorities was enhanced by the market policies and inequalities that the Labour government encouraged. Economic inequality increased, and the rich got even richer while the poor got poorer over the New Labour years (see Dorling, 2017). This left low-paid workers feeling threatened by economic migrants and refugees, adding to the continuing hostility to settled former colonial people. Contradictory policies, especially in education, encouraged individual competitiveness and separation, including by faith schooling, Although the educational achievements of all young people continued to rise, as they had been doing since post-war policies actually allowed more to learn and pass public examinations, issues of the lower attainments of black and Muslim pupils continued to be researched as though all things were equal. Politicians found it convenient to side-track the issues by reference to poor white boys and model minorities. The focus on testing and targets left the issue of what was being taught in educational institutions, that might contribute to understanding how the society had been shaped by empire and its consequences, ignored. In his resignation speech in March 2007, as he handed over to Prime Minister Brown, Blair included such lyrical comments as this country is a blessed nation, the British are special and the world knows it.

Enoch Powell (and perhaps later Donald Trump in the USA) could not have put their patriotic sentiments better.

Notes

[1] The British justice system is supposedly independent of Parliament. In 2017, judges were attacked in the media as 'enemies of the people' for supporting the right of MPs to vote on a final Bill to leave the EU.

[2] On 12 November 1998, a paper entitled 'Iraq's weapons of mass destruction' was presented to Parliament. Further developed, this was to be used as justification for the invasion of Iraq in 2003.

[3] Other large data sets include the Longitudinal Study of Young People in England (LSYPE) and the Millennium Study of young people born at the turn of the 21st century.

7

Not so New Labour: Race and education, 2005-10

The flood of illiberal measures unleashed by the Blair-Brown regime since 9/11 shows that beneath the accoutrements of civil society the ancien regime is alive and well … a government that has presided over growing inequality and sustained London's role as a happy hunting ground for the rich. (Marquand, 2009: 34)

The polarising effects of terrorism and war accelerated the regression to atavistic notions of Britishness and race. As Blair leaves office, he has the curious distinction of having realigned the level of public racial discourse with his own – by lowering it. (Younge, 2007)

A respected author, journalist and chronicler of British politics wrote in the early 1990s that the quality of government depends on the talent inside the two Houses of Parliament, and especially in the Cabinet (Sampson, 1992). Since then, over the past years, the British public has been presented with a number of seemingly ineffective, quarrelling and self-interested politicians and an increasing number of equally self-interested advisers and rich lobbyists. The dysfunctional relationship between Prime Minister Tony Blair and Gordon Brown, who, full of grievance that Blair did not depart sooner than June 2007, directed attention away from crucial national issues. These included the inequalities of income and wealth that had, by the early 2000s, reached a high point unknown since the 1930s, the looming global financial crisis that left the Queen wondering 'why did no one notice it coming?' (Pierce, 2008), the relationships with the EU, and an education system that was fragmented and separatist. Racism and xenophobia were, as Younge noted, fed by Blair's wars and their aftermath. It was ironic that after leaving office in 2007, one of Blair's invitations was to stand by the River Jordan while media mogul Rupert Murdoch had his daughters baptised in the holy waters.[1]

This chapter takes the story up to the defeat of the Labour government in 2010, a legacy of wars in Afghanistan and Iraq overshadowing any earlier positive race policies. There were intensified hostilities to Muslims, asylum-seekers, Eastern Europeans, including Roma, black British citizens and others. The Prevent programme, set up after the London bombings in 2005 by young Muslims, fed suspicion and alienation among Muslims and anger from teachers expected to police young people. Discussion about the enlargement of the EU as eight more countries joined in 2004 was not on the school curriculum or debated with the general public, and much of the media remained hostile to enlargement. The inclusion of Bulgarian and Romanian workers in 2006 led to increased antagonism to immigration, despite the needs of employers. Debates about Britishness, national identity and community cohesion rumbled on, and education policy-makers remained reluctant to recognise that market competition and a diversity of schools were exacerbating social and racial divisions. The encouragement of faith schools did not appear likely to diminish segregation, and on the Academies Programme Colin Crouch had commented in 2003 that, 'once public services are treated as commodities … how long will it be possible to defend their being subsidised and not bought or sold in the market like other commodities' (Crouch, 2003: 25). While many young people were aware that they would live their lives in a globalised world, with rapid communication and population movement, the failure to think seriously about a curriculum for a globalised future – which would need an understanding of the past – left schools either trying to ignore tensions or unable to cope with conflicts in and out of school. The continued political stress on immigration control and crude attempts to prevent any radicalisation of young people leading to them attacking their fellow citizens or joining external wars, fed public hostility to long-settled citizens, economic migrants and asylum-seekers.

Significant events

2004	Lord Hutton's inquiry into the Iraq War is published
2005	Education Act; TTA is enlarged; competition to set up new schools could include religious or parental groups
2005	(May) Trevor Phillips, Designate Head of the new Equalities and Human Rights Commission, claims, 'We are becoming more polarised by race and faith and sleepwalking into segregation'
2005	(June) New Labour elected for third time; (July) four young suicide bombers blow up London Underground trains and a bus
2005	Prevention of Terrorism Act; Prevent Strategy initiated, to be overseen by the Home Office; Immigration, Asylum and Nationality Act (the sixth since 1990)
2006	Education and Inspections Bill; controversy over admissions, selection and faith schools; Equality Act establishes a single Commission for all aspects of equality; (May) BNP puts up 357 candidates in local elections; University of Leeds lecturer suspended for claiming white people are more intelligent than black people and describes himself as an 'unrepentant Powellite' (Asthana and Salter, 2006)
2006	(August) Blair tells his Cabinet that terrorism and immigration are two major public concerns; *The Sun* (23 August) pictures a topless page 3 girl, saying she is 'very worried about immigration'; a Commission on Integration and Cohesion is set up; Jack Straw publishes an article criticising the wearing of the *niqab* by Muslim women
2006	(November) MPs demand an enquiry into the Iraq War, which is rejected by Foreign Secretary Margaret Hodge; Ministry of Defence says the war has so far cost £4 billion
2007	(March) Celebration for bi-centenary of abolition of the slave trade; London Mayor Ken Livingstone apologises for London's role in slavery and a legacy of racism; no events organised to celebrate 50 years of the EEC, despite the Union now including 400 million people in 25 countries, and forming a quarter of the world economy; in local elections in May 200 Muslim councillors are elected; Muslim Bashir Ahmed is the first Scottish-Asian member elected to the Scottish Parliament; 56 BNP councillors elected round the country; (June) Siddiqui Report on Islamic studies in higher education
2007	(27 June) Gordon Brown takes over from Tony Blair as Prime Minister; (July) attempted bombings at London and Glasgow airports; worst floods for years and foot-and-mouth disease in livestock; Northern Rock bank in Newcastle collapses; (October) Brown declines to call a General Election; (December) David Miliband, Foreign Secretary, signs the Lisbon Treaty in Portugal with Brown arriving later (a consolidation of previous EU Treaties)
2007	Education Department split into Department for Children, Schools and Families (DCSF) and Department for Innovation, Universities and Skills (DIUS); a Children Plan aims to eradicate child poverty with 10 goals to be archived by 2020
2008	Global banking crisis; Brown is worried that 'the western economy was slowing and faced collapse' (Brown, 2017: 303); 850 British companies

	go bankrupt in three months; Education and Skills Act raises staying-on age in education/training to 18
2009	(April) Brown convenes G20 meeting in London to sort out the world economy; Treaty signed in Lisbon to amend previous European Treaties by member states comes into force; Article 50 allows for countries to leave the EU; (May) parliamentary expenses scandal; DIUS abolished and renamed Department for Business, Innovation and Skills (BIS); Apprenticeship, Skills and Children Act; funding for those aged 16-18 to return to local authorities
2009	(October) Lord Browne's Review of higher education and funding set up; Michael Gove, Shadow Education Minister, lays out plans for education at Conservative Party Conference promising to 'destroy the education establishment' and return schools to a traditional curriculum and traditional British values
2010	(May) Brown calls a general election, resulting in a hung Parliament and eventual coalition between the Conservatives and Liberals; Brown resigns and Ed Miliband is elected leader of the Labour Party; the EU is not a major issue in the election, but UKIP, under leader Nigel Farage, takes 3.2% of the vote; future Lord Chancellor George Osborne claims spending cuts and austerity are required in the country; (November) the Lord Browne Review recommends increases in higher education fees to be paid by students

Dysfunctional politics

For New Labour, politics did not seem to work well when discussed over either Italian spaghetti or British steak and kidney pudding. Political commentators agreed that the antagonistic relationship between Tony Blair and Gordon Brown affected most of the political decisions of the New Labour government, especially from 2004 (Boulton, 2008). Brown claimed in his memoirs that an agreement before the 1997 election that Blair should be Prime Minister and Brown should take over during the second term of the Parliament was made before a much-quoted dinner in an Italian restaurant in Islington. By 2003, the war between the two men seemed to overshadow the war in Iraq earlier in the year. The disastrous consequences of this Iraq War were becoming apparent, despite a report by Lord Hutton appearing to excuse Blair and his team from any responsibility (Hutton, 2004). After Brown had attacked Blair at the 2003 Labour Party Conference over the war and over his privatising of public services, Deputy Prime Minister John Prescott gave a steak and kidney pudding dinner for the two men in his Admiralty House flat to reconcile their differences, but the relationship worsened, and Blair announced his intention to stay on as Prime Minister until after the next election (Rawnsley, 2010; Brown, 2017). One of the contentious issues had been the increase in fees for higher education to £3,000 a year. Brown was very much against this policy, and Rawnsley has described the parliamentary scene when the vote was taken and an increase in fees was agreed by five votes: 'Brown stuck up 5 fingers and thrust them into Blair's face' (Rawnsley, 2010: 236). The 2005 General Election manifesto included a commitment to a place in school, college or training for every 16- to 19-year-old, and a 2008 Act raised the leaving age for all young people to remain in education or training to the age of 18.

Disunity and diversity

Beliefs that Britain had become a disunited kingdom in which immigration and multiculturalism were the enemies became more widespread during the 2000s. Some commentators continued to claim that a once united British society had been fractured by the presence of racial and ethnic groups and the arrival of more economic migrants and refugees. The mythical assumptions of a once cohesive society were actually nonsense in the light of the historical divisions in society by class, wealth, gender and racial lines. It did not need Peter Mandelson's well-reported claim in a speech to computer executives in Los Angeles that New Labour was 'intensely relaxed about people getting filthy rich', adding later, 'as long as they pay their taxes', to underline the disparity in wealth and income that actually characterised the period (quoted in Rawnsley, 2010: 477). Despite claims that New Labour had lifted a million children out of poverty, and a New Deal for Communities had invigorated declining areas, by 2006 the Office for National Statistics (ONS) recorded that the gap between rich and poor was the same as when Mrs Thatcher left office in 1990, and the richest fifth of UK households had incomes 16 times greater than the poorest. These poor households included a disproportionate number of Pakistani and Bangladeshi households, although a few of the richest included some Muslim, Sikh and Hindu households, with wealth often accrued in business in minority communities or transnational businesses.

The early Blair government assertions on respect for diversity and valuing a multiracial, multicultural society rapidly gave way in the second and third term of Labour to promises of tougher asylum and immigration targets, fears of Islam and blaming black youth for violence. Ruth Kelly, Education Secretary from 2004 to 2006, claimed that white Britons were not comfortable seeing their shops and restaurants in town centres changing owner, which left the public wondering if she had ever ordered an Indian takeaway. The community cohesion and citizenship agenda supposedly supporting an ethnically diverse society was at odds with more punitive immigration and asylum and then terrorist legislation. In 2004 David Goodhart, editor of the journal *Prospect*, made familiar right-wing claims that it was 'progressive liberals' who supported diversity, and that sharing welfare benefits with diverse groups led to tension and fears. He argued that newcomers should adapt to their new country (Goodhart, 2004), and was supported in 2005 by Trevor Phillips, Chair of the Commission for Racial Equality (CRE) and from 2007 Chair of the Equality and Human Rights Commission (EHRC), who claimed that 'multiculturalism suggested separateness' and that the country was 'sleepwalking into segregation' (Tomlinson, 2008: 161). Comments in the media suggested that minority communities deliberately segregated themselves, ignoring data which by then indicated that despite discrimination, the outer suburbs had an increase in minority residence, and it was low incomes and/or low-paid jobs that tended to keep people in inner-city areas.

In 2005 Michael Howard ran a losing general election campaign vilifying immigrants, with a Labour MP commenting that he 'escalated the dangers of immigration beyond Enoch Powell's wildest dreams' (Hattersley, 2005). But in July 2005, four young Muslim men, born and educated in England, blew themselves and 56 people up in London, wounding over 700 others including Muslim citizens. Two weeks later there was an attempted London bombing by four more men, originally refugees but educated in English schools. The full force of the British intelligence and security services was then directed at gathering information on, and preventing, terrorist activities. In education, a Prevent programme was instigated, in which teachers in educational institutions were expected to check and report any suspicious activity on the part of the children and students (Gearon, 2015). This programme escalated over the years to become part of Contest – a government counter-terrorism strategy – which, as a *Telegraph* article pointed out, 'managed to alienate just about everybody' (Murray, 2010). The government commissioned a report on the teaching of Islamic studies in British universities that reported in 2007 with suggestions for a more modernised Islamic curriculum (Siddiqui, 2007). This was regarded by some students as another attempt to police Muslims. Blair changed from being relaxed about immigration – he had supported the inclusion of eight more countries into the EU in 2004, believing then that economic immigration was profitable – to telling the Labour Party Conference in 2006 that terrorism and immigration were major public concerns. In August 2005, when a young black man was axed to death in a public park in Liverpool, he had made no comment. In October, after riots in Birmingham between black and Asian young people in which one man was killed, Blair blamed 'Black culture', especially absent fathers and a lack of black role models. It was then disclosed that a third of all young black men were on a police DNA data base, and a Violent Crime and Reduction Act allowed school staff to search children for knives.

During New Labour's time in office, 3,600 new criminal offences were introduced and the prison population reached a record high, with an over-representation of young black men. To demonstrate that eugenic views were still in operation, in 2006 Frank Ellis, a lecturer at the University of Leeds, was suspended for claiming that black people were intellectually inferior to whites, writing in an article in the *Leeds Student* that 'multiculturalism is doomed to failure because it is based on the lie that all people, races and cultures are equal', and he added that he was an 'unrepentant Powellite' (Asthana and Salter, 2006). Later in the year a lecturer at the London School of Economics and Political Science (LSE) published a paper claiming that the causes of poverty and poor health in African states could be traced to lower intelligence (Campbell, 2006). In higher education, assumptions were that students on university courses would be free from racist views despite most having come through schools where issues of empire, race and racism were seldom discussed. This assumption was demonstrably false, as evidence (discussed in Chapter Nine) began to accumulate of the racism shown by white students towards minority students. After his initial burst of enthusiasm for a multiracial, multicultural society, Blair never commented on growing racial conflicts during his time in office, apart from condemning immigrants, terrorists and black young men. It was perhaps not surprising that he was not much mourned as he left office. David Marquand, as noted above, drew attention not only to the illiberal policies around immigration and Islam after 9/11, but also the wealth gaps that tax cuts and tuition fees did nothing to alleviate as far as social inequality was concerned. Even Neal Lawson, initially an ardent Blairite, wrote that, 'A decade of Blair has left the Labour Party on its knees' (Lawson, 2007).

Brown's woe's

While academics like to keep up with the times, it is often a mistake to rush into print while events are still unfolding. Written just before Brown finally took over as Prime Minister in July 2007, Labour government adviser and former head of the LSE, Lord Anthony Giddens, published *Over to you, Mr Brown* (Giddens, 2007). He was upbeat about the success of New Labour over its 10 years in office, especially its market-friendly policies and the benefits to citizen-consumers. He particularly extolled the City of London that 'Contributes a rising proportion of GDP. It is one of the great success stories of the British economy' (Giddens, 2007: 5). It was unfortunate that the world was about to enter its largest economic down-turn since the 1930s – the British economy would go into recession and the City banks and bankers were about to become pariahs.

Early environmental woes for Brown took the form of torrential flooding in Britain in July 2007, followed by an outbreak of foot-and-mouth disease. June 29 had seen an attempted terrorist attack at Glasgow airport by men angry at wars in the Middle East, but foreign policy in August meant a trip to the USA to assure George

Bush that Britain was still with him in a war alliance.[2] Then home again to find that in October, two discs containing the names and addresses of 25 million parents and children making claims for child benefit had been lost in the post! In the same month he decided not to call an election. In December he was so busy that he did not arrive on time in Lisbon where leaders of all the EU countries had gathered to sign the Lisbon Treaty that consolidated previous EU Treaties. Foreign Secretary David Miliband did the actual signing, and the Treaty came into effect in 2009. By 2009 Brown had to deal with the embarrassment of *The Daily Telegraph* revelations over MPs' expense claims that had taken some bizarre, greedy and illegal turns over the years for which taxpayers were footing the bills. Their journalists had obtained information on the expenses claimed by all 646 MPs. The most well known were claims for renovating a duck house by Conservative Sir Peter Viggers, among his £23,083 other expenses, and claims for biscuits from Labour Austin Mitchell, among £23,000 for other expenses. The most worrying were the claims made by Alistair Darling, Chancellor of the Exchequer, at the time dealing with the banking crisis. He had claimed second home allowances on four properties, which led to demands that he resign. Sir Christopher Kelly was appointed to examine the claims (Kelly, 2009), and improvements in the system were made. Labour Jeremy Corbyn was the only MP to make no expense claims.

The banking crisis began with the collapse of Northern Rock. From Newcastle-upon-Tyne to Redhill in Surrey people queued to get their cash out of this bank. Brown claimed he did not know about international banks' practices and wrote in his memoirs, 'I now found to my horror that a vast shadow banking system made up of banking affiliates that were not bound by the rules which applied to banks but which acted like banks – trading in dubious financial instruments' (Brown, 2017: 299). He also found that during 2008, some 50 trillion dollars 'more than the entire income of everyone in the world' was pledged across financial companies 'without ever being properly declared' (Brown, 2017: 299). Both Brown and Chancellor Alistair Darling have documented in their memoirs the steps they took to inject money into the banks and to save the careers of most of the bankers.

They also both claim they saved the world from a great recession. Darling wrote that he deeply regretted that in the 2010 General Election the government 'failed to capitalise on our successful handling of the financial crisis' (Darling, 2011: 323), but in his last budget he announced that confidence had not returned to business or consumers. This set the stage for the future coalition government to blame the Labour government for the banking crisis and to instigate an era of austerity, which impacted severely on the poor and on public services, including education.

Education policy from Blair to Brown

Education under Tony Blair and his advisers continued the evangelical emphasis on improving the nation's economic competitiveness through testing, inspection and centralisation. There was more support for a diversity of secondary schools, academies being the flagship schools, with specialist schools and trust schools added to the mix, and faith schools being encouraged. As Chancellor of the Exchequer, Brown had increased funding for education from 2002, with an extra £15 billion made available over three years, and funding per pupil increased. A Building Schools for the Future programme, with money from the Private Finance Initiative (PFI), was supported from 2003, and school buildings and facilities improved considerably, although at long-term cost to taxpayers. The Education Act 2005 overturned an historic funding agreement for schools with local authorities, and all funds would now come from the Secretary of State to all maintained schools.

Despite constant and often contradictory policies and initiatives, public education continued its long, slow improvement in terms of young people actually being taught, and entering for and passing tests and examinations, with the government taking credit for improvements and blaming schools and teachers where improvements did not occur, especially in urban schools attended by minority pupils. The language of failing was superseded by a competitive language of 'outstanding' or 'requires improvement'. Parental competition for 'good' schools intensified, as did the increased selection of children by overt and covert means for different and unequally resourced schools. The support for faith schools of all kinds continued to create problems, with an *Observer* Comment (2007) that, 'Faith has now become another word for race' (*The Observer*, 2007), and a *Times* article headed, 'Sneaky, unfair, divisive: Welcome to church schools' (Miles, 2007), claiming that church schools were used as covert forms of social and racial selection by the middle classes.

The flow of reports on the comparative achievements of various minorities compared to white pupils continued, with some laudable suggestions for raising performance in tests, but as noted earlier, with the goal posts being moved and levels of 'success' raised. Teaching literacy and numeracy and then traditional subjects in secondary schools was a focus for debate, with reports commissioned on the National Curriculum and on primary education. But what was actually being taught and tested received minimal attention. Most publishers had by this time recognised the nature of the multicultural society, and children's books and comics contained more than the token minority presence, as did some television programmes. The question of how far schools could combat public influences continued, with MP Jack Straw criticising Muslim dress again, this time objecting to the few women who chose to wear the *niqab* (face covering). There seemed to be no institution willing to combat the offensive racism such as that directed at the two tennis players, Venus and Serena Williams, who, from their arrival at Wimbledon in 2003, were subject to racist slurs from commentators and the media in England for all their careers (Jacques, 2003). Ken Livingstone, as Mayor of London, in 2007, did his best to raise awareness of racism by apologising for slavery on the bi-centenary of the abolition of the slave trade, and HM Treasury later boasted that many years ago, in 1833, it had paid reparations for the trade. It later transpired that the money, around £16 billion in today's money, had actually been paid to 46,000 slave owners to compensate them for losing their 'property'. From 2007, Labour's Harriet Harman had worked on bringing together all the various equality and anti-discrimination legislation into one Act, an Equalities Act passed in 2010. This Act consolidated 116 pieces of legislation into one Act on gender, race, disability, sexual orientation and employment.[3] Local councils in high minority areas began to be better represented, with minority members elected.

Academies

The Academies Programme continued to develop. By 2006, 46 had opened with plans for another 200. In his book defending academies, Andrew Adonis boasted that when he was made Minister for Schools in 2005, he could personally take decisions about the opening and organisation of these 'independent state schools' that would have dynamic sponsors taking control of their management. He had been grateful that he was sponsored at his private boarding school and had escaped the 'vast adolescent jungle' of Borehamwood School, a multiracial comprehensive school. Despite his subsequent Oxford History degree, he did not apparently see any imperial connotations with the jungle metaphor. The first chapter of his 2012 book was taken up with insulting Hackney Downs that had been demolished (see Chapter Five of this book). He extolled Mossbourne Community Academy built on the site at the cost of £28 million. He claimed Hackney Downs was one of the hundreds of failing comprehensives that constituted a 'cancer at the heart of English society' (Adonis, 2012: xii). In his book, villains opposing academies were egalitarian head teachers, teacher unions, local authorities, further education colleges, obstructive officials, some ministers and education professors, especially well-loved Professor Ted Wragg who had once referred to Adonis as 'Lord Barmy of Bedlam'. Heroes included strong head teachers, rich businessmen, property developers, consultancy firms, the churches and philanthropists (including an evangelical car salesman). The remedy for school improvement was apparently removing schools from local authority control and any democratic accountability. A number of private schools opted to become academies, and taxpayers rather than parents paid the fees. The Anglican Church's United Learning Trust quickly became a major sponsor of 20 schools. One of the donors to this Trust was multimillionaire Muslim Mahmoud Khayani, who also donated to the Labour Party. An Oasis Christian Trust, set up by the Baptist Church, planned academies based on 'core Christian values' that included opposition to homosexuality. The Catholic Church and other faiths expressed intentions to open academies, along with more business interests and sports clubs. Evidence quickly accumulated that these independent state schools were actually increasing social and racial segregation overall, and not improving results when compared with similar local authority-controlled schools.

Despite his troubled agenda, Brown was more interested in children than Blair. He visited schools in Tower Hamlets to read to Bangladeshi pupils, changed the Education Department into a Department for Children, Schools and Families, and created a Department for Universities, Innovation and Skills, which was short-lived. A Children Plan in 2007 encouraged children to enjoy their childhood and be prepared for adult life (DCSF, 2007). This proposal was repudiated by future Education Secretary Michael Gove, who told a conference at Brighton College in 2008 that the Conservatives would re-instate traditional styles of fact-based learning, and there would be none of this pupil-centred learning. He also began to consolidate his reputation for holding teachers and 'experts' in contempt. Although Blair, in 2004, had turned down suggestions by former head of Ofsted, Mike Tomlinson, that all pupils work towards a diploma at the age of 18, which would have abolished GCSEs and A-levels (DfES, 2004), Brown was more sympathetic to vocational education and apprenticeships. The Education Act 2006 suggested 14 vocational diplomas be set up, although this exacerbated an academic–vocational divide and the diplomas were another short-lived idea. His major battle was over tuition fees for higher education, but after the five-finger incident with Blair, he came round to the idea of supporting student repayment of fees through a type of graduate tax. In 2009 he allowed Peter Mandelson to appoint a friend, Lord Browne, former Director of British Petroleum, to undertake a review of fees. His report suggested an increase to £9,000. Brown was relieved that after the Labour General Election defeat in 2010, this was not his problem (see Brown, 2017: 239).

British values and the curriculum

Whatever Gordon Brown's problems, he did demonstrate some serious thinking about the notion of 'Britishness'. As a Scot he was aware that the United Kingdom was four nations and claimed rightly that over the past 50 years internal unity had frayed. Although he wrote that in a global era, identities were likely to be multiple, and he supported a 2007 report that suggested that cross-curricular themes in the Key Stage 3 curriculum should include identity and cultural diversity and community participation (QCA, 2007), he remained apparently unaware of the extent of racial divisions and hostilities in Britain. His remedy for conflict was a commitment to supposed British values of tolerance, liberty, fair play and social responsibility, and he suggested setting up an Institute for Britishness (Brown, 2017: 396). This plan was never implemented. In 2009 he agreed to write an introduction to a book on *Being British* edited by journalist Matthew D'Ancona, with contributors from the left and right of politics (D'Ancona, 2009). Michael Gove, then Shadow Education Secretary, contributed a chapter in which he attacked Brown for supporting Britishness to further his career, and accused him of poor history and partisan politics. Brown replied that for political reasons the Conservative Party seemed determined to prevent Labour from being identified with patriotic British values. Gove's contribution did not go unnoticed; one blogger later wrote that the Gove contribution to D'Ancona's book was 'The least attractive contribution ... a tedious tone-deaf piece in which the strange little man has a go at Gordon Brown and the European Union' (Reggie's blog, 2011). Gove had previously produced a book, *Celsius 7/7* (Gove, 2006), in which he likened some parts of Islam to fascist and communist ideologies, but the man and his version of British values came to dominate English education once the Conservatives returned to power.

An amended National Curriculum was to be in place from 2008, with teachers to be allowed more input into the design of courses. The History curriculum was to focus less on Henry VIII and his wives and more on recent topics, including the European Union. A study of the British Empire was to be minimally covered in Key Stage 3, and schools were to teach more foreign languages. In 2007, Black History Month celebrated 20 years of reminding schools of the realities of empire, although there were loud voices complaining that most of history was White history. Right-leaning groups had not given up their attacks on curriculum developments, the think tank Civitas claiming that 'traditional subjects have been high-jacked to promote fashionable causes such as gender awareness, the environment and anti-racism, and teachers are expected to achieve the Government's social goals instead of imparting a body of knowledge' (Civitas, 2007).

Summary

This chapter has suggested that during the last years of a Blair government and the subsequent years of Prime Minister Brown there was little evidence of the early claims to support a multiracial and multicultural society and a fairer education system. The war in Iraq and continuing war in Afghanistan led to acts of terrorism by some young men and women and anxiety on the part of all Muslims in Britain that they were now all regarded as the enemy within. The Prevent programme, about to be escalated by an incoming government, was regarded with suspicion by communities and teachers, and an increase in Eastern European immigration had led to more xenophobia in all social classes. Brown did not help his claim of commitment to values of tolerance and diversity in a speech he made in 2009 demanding 'British jobs for British workers' to placate workers striking over the employment of more Eastern European construction workers (Summers, 2009). Young black men continued to be regarded as less educable and more likely to be criminal. Education policy followed an agenda of choice, diversity and creeping privatisation, with an escalation of social and racial segregation, and a steady removal of local authority democratic oversight. A sustained focus on testing and assessment left little room for consideration of what was actually being taught. In May 2010, after an election campaign in which Brown unfortunately called one of his supporters a 'bigoted woman', the General Election delivered a hung Parliament, with the Liberal Democrats eventually joining the Conservatives in a coalition government. Brown resigned and Ed Miliband was elected as Shadow Labour

Leader, narrowly beating his brother David. As a final comment on the New Labour 'project', Rawnsley noted that at the last conference before the General Election they sang 'The red flag' and 'Jerusalem' to the accompaniment of violins, and 'the melancholy strains of the strings added to the feeling that the light was fading on the project which had once had the world at its feet' (Rawnsley, 2010: 679). But notions of a less xenophobic multicultural society and a fairer education system were about to be tested to destruction.

Notes

[1] Blair had his youngest son baptised in the River Jordan in 2000. The ceremony dates back to the days of John the Baptist. The subservience of some British Prime Ministers to Rupert Murdoch, owner of influential right-wing newspapers and described as 'one of the most powerful people in the world' (Davies, 2014: xiii), was well known. He and his companies survived a phone-hacking scandal after 2011, and continue to influence politics and politicians.

[2] The Alliance had been at war in Afghanistan since 2001. It was Britain's fourth Afghan War. The three previous wars in 1839-42, 1878-80 and 1919 had all ended in humiliating defeat. Brown regretted sending more troops to fight the Taliban after 2006. Continuing conflict is the major reason for Afghan asylum-seekers arriving in Britain, often trying to enter illegally from Calais.

[3] The 2010 legislation brought together the Equal Pay Act 1970, Sex Discrimination Act 1975, Race Relations Act 1976 and Race Equality Act 2000, Disability Discrimination Act 1975, Employment Equality (Religion) Act 2003 and Employment (Sexual Orientation) Act 2006.

8

A divided society: Race, class and education, 2010-16

> The materialistic and selfish quality of contemporary life is not inherent in the human condition. Much of what appears "natural" today dates from the 1980s: the obsession with wealth, the cult of privatisation and the private sector, and the growing disparities between rich and poor. (Judt, 2010: 2)

> More damage was done to Britain's schools and universities in the few years from 2010 to 2016 than at any other period in British history, albeit most of this damage was enacted in England. (Dorling, 2018: 10)

Even in rich developed countries inequality and the poor are apparently always with us. But, as Judt has pointed out, this is not natural at all. The Poor Laws in 1834 had one answer to poverty – people had the 'choice' to work for miniscule wages or face the workhouse. The UK in the 20th century eventually managed to follow some social democratic ideas of equality similar to those of its European neighbours, and by the 1970s had become one of Europe's most equitable countries. From 1980, that all changed. Governments in the UK, led by Thatcher, Blair and Brown, and from 2010 to June 2016, by David Cameron, followed policies that increased inequalities, the justification being that free markets and privatisation encouraged enterprise and wealth creation. There was never any acknowledgement that Britain had previously become rich by exploiting the wealth and labour of the Empire. With the British Empire gone, politicians claimed that the country would benefit from economic globalisation that increased flows of capital, labour, goods and services around the world, resulting in higher living standards for all. The World Trade Organization (WTO) was established in 1995 to fix fairer trade rules between countries, which would supposedly solve future global trading problems.[1] What actually happened in the UK was that free markets and shrinking state institutions increased the gap between the rich and poor, and by 2016 wealth and income inequalities were the highest in Europe. As Danny Dorling pointed out in his book *Inequality and the 1%*, by 2014, to qualify for being in the top 1%, a childless couple would need an income of £160,000 a year, the average income being £23,000 (Dorling, 2014). The poor, as Ken Loach's film *I Daniel Blake* illustrated, could die in job centre lavatories after having their rightful state benefits taken away (Loach, 2016). There could be no argument that the UK had become a society divided into rich and poor, with education helping this along, and with racial divisions and inequalities continuing to expand.

It was not until some five years later that it became common knowledge that the Home Office, under Home Secretary Theresa May, had, in 2013, instigated a 'hostile environment' policy intended to deter and deport illegal migrants, one result of which was the deportation of legal citizens, including some from the Windrush generation.

This chapter covers the period of the coalition government of Conservatives and Liberal Democrats to 2015 and then Cameron's Conservative government until the June referendum on leaving the EU in 2016. It was a period dominated by claims that the only way to reduce the 'structural deficit' was by a programme of austerity, which meant cutting money for public services, including education, with massive increases in fees for higher education. There was more privatisation of public services, and no wage increases. The resulting inequalities and lowered living standards felt by the middle and working classes were blamed on the unemployed, benefit scroungers, EU regulations and above all, immigrants. Racial and religious antagonisms were fuelled by riots in urban areas in August 2011, by fears of Islam and 'extremism' as the Trojan Horse affair in Birmingham schools in 2014 demonstrated, and, well before the Brexit vote, sustained campaigns against immigrant workers. One response from the DfE was a requirement to promote 'traditional British values' in schools (DfE, 2014).

The education system, with its academies, free schools and faith schools, competitive ethos and increasingly elaborate testing regimes furthered by the Blair–Brown and Cameron governments, continued to polarise children and families. An elite educated in private schools characterised the Cameron government, and most of his Cabinet had been educated at private schools and had then gone on to Oxford. Denigration of schools and teachers in schools attended largely by poor and minority children continued. Privatisation of various kinds continued in both the school and university sectors with an unprecedented rise in fees for students in higher education. A rhetoric of 'excellence', helping all children to reach their 'potential' and more social mobility, were weasel words used in education documents. Poor children and students were reassigned to the intractable category of 'disadvantaged'. The entire board of a Social Mobility Commission set up in 2011 resigned en masse in 2017, with the chair lamenting how divided the nation had become by income, geography and generation. In 2010 the Department for Children, Schools and Families (DCSF) presided over by Labour Ed Balls reverted to being a simple Department for Education again. Michael Gove took office as Education Secretary, with a background of threatening the 'education establishment' and denigrating Islam. The language of diversity continued, sometimes meaning schools, mostly meaning children and young people with darker skins, non-European languages and non-Christian faiths, but with white European migrants added to the mix. Yet another review of the National Curriculum further entrenched a traditional subject-centred curriculum with minimal information on the British Empire, Commonwealth and the EU, and no explanation as to why the society was multicultural and multiracial. Hostility towards black and Muslim young people intensified, and those MPs and MEPs determined to force the UK to leave the EU intensified their efforts.

Significant events

2009	Conservative leader David Cameron rules out a referendum on EU membership
2010	General Election, and Conservatives form a coalition government with the Liberal-Democrats led by Nick Clegg; Gordon Brown resigns and Ed Miliband is narrowly elected Labour Party leader; Theresa May is appointed Home Secretary
2010	(July) Academies Act – all schools are allowed to become academies; (November) White Paper *The importance of teaching* (DfE, 2010) includes a chapter on bad behaviour of working-class white and black pupils; Pupil Premium suggested; free schools to be established; Building schools for the Future programme, General Teaching Council and the Education and Maintenance Allowance are all abolished
2010	(October) Lord Browne's Review of higher education fees is published; the cap on fees is lifted, with students repaying fees when they earn £21,000; (November) David Willetts suggests fees of £9,000 per annum with any university charging over £6,000 to offer scholarships; (December) Parliament votes and agrees to the fee increase; Labour is opposed but the Liberal Democrats agree
2011	Education Act legislates for White Paper proposals; Wolf Review of vocational education published; review of the National Curriculum; historians Niall Ferguson and Simon Schama advise Gove; report by Graham Allen MP claims the defective brains of children in dysfunctional families cost the taxpayer money
2011	(Week of 5 August) Following the shooting of Mark Duggan by the police, riots break out in London, spreading to Salford, Manchester, Birmingham and Nottingham; Cameron returns from his Tuscan holiday to condemn the rioters; *Financial Times* article celebrates public school teenagers holidaying in Corfu
2011	Report of the Eminent Persons Group to the Commonwealth Heads of Government notes that trade between Commonwealth countries is 2.3% of world trade and Commonwealth trade preferences no longer exist
2013	(January) Cameron gives Bloomberg speech promising a referendum after fundamental reform of the EU; (February) UKIP comes second in a by-election in Eastleigh; the Home Office under Theresa May instigates a 'hostile environment' policy and sends vans around London boroughs telling 'illegal migrants to go home or face arrest'; Boris Johnson gives third Margaret Thatcher Memorial Lecture and claims that 'human beings are far apart in raw ability' and 'greed is a valuable spur to economic activity'; Dominic Cummings claims that scores in National Curriculum tests show 60-70% dependence on heritability (Cummings, 2013)
2014	(March) Trojan Horse affair in Birmingham; (May) Immigration Act notionally to remove illegal immigrants; in European elections, UKIP wins 2.6% of the vote; (November) DfE issues *Promoting fundamental British values* to be part of the spiritual, moral, social and cultural (SMSC) curriculum
2014	Michael Gove loses his job after criticising the Home Office slow stance

on 'Islamic terrorism'; he was replaced by Nicky Morgan, but policies continued as before; Michael Wilshaw is appointed as head of Ofsted; Child Poverty Action Group (CPAG) reports that 3-5 million children are in poverty, and forecasts 4-7 million by 2020

2015   Conservatives win the General Election with the first Tory majority since 1992

2015   GCSE subject curriculum revisions; in English Literature 20% marks for spelling and grammar; Grades A-G to be replaced by Grades 1-9; multiplication tables and handwriting to be tested at Year 6; Education and Adoption Bill allows more rapid conversion to academy status for schools; (December) MPs vote against lowering the voting age to 16

2016   (March) DfE paper *Educational excellence for all* signals the end of the local authority democratic role in English schools; a Chartered College of Teaching is proposed with a National Teaching Service

2016   (23 June) Referendum to leave the EU is won by 52%:48%; (24 June) Cameron resigns as Prime Minister; (25 June) Michael Gove tells Boris Johnson he will back him for the Tory leadership, then changes his mind and stands as a candidate himself; a further Immigration Act fuels the hostile environment; schools are told to record the birthplace and nationality of migrant children

Posh politics and austerity

David Cameron, born into a wealthy family with, as he said of himself, 'two silver spoons in his mouth' (Ashcroft and Oakshotte, 2015: 9), took over from Michael Howard as Conservative Leader in 2005, with backbencher David Davis thinking of challenging him. The then MP for Henley-on-Thames, Alexander Boris de Pfeffel Johnson, in disgrace for lying over an extramarital affair, would soon campaign to be Mayor of London for 2008-12. He was re-elected for 2012-16. He was also elected as MP for Uxbridge and South Ruislip in 2015. In the coalition led by Cameron, 60% of the members of his Cabinet had been educated in private schools. He claimed that his later 2015 Cabinet was a blue-collar Cabinet, but over 50% of its members had attended Oxford or Cambridge Universities and both Cabinets included several millionaires, notably George Osborne, Chancellor of the Exchequer. In 2009 it was reported that Osborne had been involved in an argument with (later) Labour Lord Peter Mandelson while holidaying on the luxury yacht of a Russian oligarch Oleg Deripaska, which made the public somewhat suspicious when he and Cameron announced a programme of austerity, claiming 'we are all in it together'.

The coalition government with Cameron as Prime Minister and Liberal Democrat Nick Clegg as Deputy agreed that eliminating the 'structural deficit' (debt) in the country should be a major aim. Thus the first budget cut public spending by £6 billion and promised the biggest reduction in public spending since the end of the Second World War. In the 2015 manifesto another £12 billion cuts were promised. The effects of cuts in public spending have been well documented (O'Hara, 2015; Atkinson, 2018; Dorling, 2018), and by 2015 the UK spent a lower proportion of GDP on public services than any other government in Europe.

Especially noted has been the rise in child and maternal mortality, an increase in child poverty and homelessness, a lowered life expectancy and a rise in people claiming incapacity benefits (renamed Employment Support Allowance) but being 'sanctioned' frequently by benefit officials and receiving no money to live on. Food began to be distributed to poor people via food banks, surpassing even Victorian ideas of keeping the poor alive to work if possible. More people developed mental health issues, and suicides and drug-related deaths rose. Work became more precarious, with an increase in zero-hours contracts, and spending on health and education was gradually reduced despite rising demand. There was a creeping privatisation of medical services, schools and especially universities. Even veteran Tory MP Kenneth Clarke, appointed as Justice Secretary in 2010, expressed surprise that as the consequences of the 2008 financial crash became more apparent, and the outrageous conduct of individuals and institutions that had led to the credit crunch and credit crash more obvious, those responsible were never held to account (Clarke, 2016). People were becoming angry with their lives and feared for their children's future, but still, as in previous years, blamed immigrants for taking low-paid work and supposedly putting pressure on housing, education and medical services.

It was eventually noted that 'the 2010 Government pursued austerity measures that inflicted great cruelty for no apparent economic benefit' (Dorling, 2018: 16). Austerity was justified by blaming the previous Labour government for over-spending, trade unions making irresponsible demands, and poor people for claiming too many welfare benefits. Geographically the country was becoming more divided than ever into richer and poorer areas, especially in London, and social class was increasingly defined by money and postcode. Meanwhile, the lives of 'posh' politicians and their friends appeared to carry on regardless. Cameron and his friends relaxed with what eventually became known as the 'Chipping Snorton set', a reference to the fact that they lived near the country town of Chipping Norton, and drug-taking among the party-goers was a fashionable recreation. One party-goer recalled a Conservative fund-raising party held at the home of millionaire Lord Chadlington, where 'there was a huge marquee full of ladies with big hair and even bigger jewellery.… Jeremy Clarkson's opening line to Dave was "come on, let's face it, no one in this tent could care less about comprehensive schools … everyone here sends their kids to private schools"' (Ashcroft and Oakshotte, 2015: 5-6).

The Camerons frequently entertained newspaper tycoon Rupert Murdoch and his family and Rebekah Brooks, one of Murdoch's editors, until she was sacked after her paper's phone-hacking scandal. Murdoch and his papers gave considerable support to Cameron during the 2010 election campaign, and a week after he became Prime Minister, Murdoch was entertained with tea in Downing Street. In recounting the story of the phone hacking by News Corp journalists and the Cameron government's involvement, Nick Davies commented that neoliberalism and the entwined powers of government, business and media elites led to the public being treated with contempt. Cutting taxes for the rich and welfare benefits of the poor manufactured deep layers of inequality and poverty, and 'all of this is cloaked in the twisted language of the power elite in which the ways of the wealthy have been disguised as a service for the needs of the poor' (Davies, 2014: 406).

All change about the EU

As Conservative Leader, Cameron was subject to continued demands from a small number of MPs and Nigel Farage's UKIP that the country should leave the EU. Standing firm at first, Cameron announced in 2009 that there would be no referendum on the issue. But as UKIP gained votes in the 2010 General Election and his Eurosceptic MPs continued their pressure, he made attempts to placate the anti-EU lobby by working for changes in EU regulations. In February 2013, in a by-election in Eastleigh, UKIP came second to the Liberal Democrats, taking 27.8% of votes cast. The Conservative candidate Marie Hutchings came third, although she was on record claiming that she wanted Britain to leave the EU. Cameron made a speech at the London headquarters of the Bloomberg financial firm, claiming that although as an island nation 'geography has shaped our psychology' and he was passionate about sovereignty, the EU rules needed an up-date. While setting out five changes that were needed, he was apparently also passionate for a Single Market for trade between EU states, and claimed that 'Britain is at the heart of a Single Market and must remain so' (Cameron, 2013). The speech was regarded as giving an all-clear for a referendum, and by 2015 a promised referendum was in the Conservative election manifesto. His government did not appear to take much notice of a report by an Eminent Persons Group set up to report on the Commonwealth countries and issues of trade and migration, which was finalised in 2011. Claims after Brexit that leaving the EU would make it easier to trade with the Commonwealth were already rebuffed in the report, which noted that Commonwealth trade preferences (with the UK) no longer existed: 'Many Commonwealth countries have developed close trading links with neighbouring countries and States' (Eminent Persons Group, 2011: 76). The report also noted that larger countries were poaching skilled workers and keeping unskilled workers out.

Race, class and riots

In a study of the educational experiences of black, middle-class parents in their dealings with schools, one respondent, a professional woman of Jamaican heritage, was asked by a white work colleague, 'Do you think that Jamaicans are genetically predisposed to violence?' (Rollock et al, 2015: 27). While the study noted that the black middle classes have relatively more power to respond to this kind of racial ignorance and covert racism, Cameron and his government continued to espouse the views that black and white working-class young people were more inclined to violence and rioting. This was evident in the response to rioting that occurred in August 2011 in London boroughs and other cities. The trigger, as in other previous cases, was the shooting in his car in Tottenham on 4 August of a young black man by police officers who were later exonerated from wrong doing. His family and friends went to Tottenham police station on 6 March to demand explanations and violence broke out. Rioting and looting then occurred in other parts of London and in other cities.

Cameron returned from his summer holiday in Tuscany to condemn what he called 'sickening violence', and chaired meetings of Cobra, the committee called together in cases of national emergencies (Lewis et al, 2011). He gave a speech in his Witney constituency on 15 August, claiming that the riots were not about poverty, but bad behaviour, and 'there is a slow motion moral collapse in some parts of our country ... the welfare system encourages the worst in people' (Cameron, 2011). Analysis of the causes of the riots showed a complex mix of motives, but it also transpired that a majority of 'rioters and looters' were under the age of 16 and a third had special educational needs. Despite this, Cameron blamed black gangs who earned money through drugs, and announced that Home Secretary Theresa May would join with the Work and Pensions Secretary Iain Duncan Smith to 'work on gangs as a national priority', and 'no phoney human rights concerns would get in the way of action' (Watt et al, 2011). Former Prime Minister Tony Blair weighed in, dismissing explanations of income inequalities between rich and poor, and blaming rioting on 'people from families that are profoundly dysfunctional, operating on different terms to the rest of society ... many of them shaping up that way by the time they are in primary or even nursery school' (Blair, 2011). Most young people were brought before the courts for trivial offences, although draconian prison sentences were handed out. Fines were imposed on people who had no means of paying.

In contrast, on 6 August, while some black and white working-class young people were engaged in disturbances, the *Financial Times Magazine*, which publishes advertisements of expensive goods for rich people to buy, included an article on 'The villa holiday' (Wry Society, 2011). This detailed the exciting holiday of a family in Corfu, whose children sent out a 'clarion call for all like-minded teenagers in the area … the English public school seems a common thread' (Wry Society, 2011: 57), and their swimming, boating, picnics, barbecues and other entertainments, which the young people and their parents enjoyed in their 12th year running in Corfu. Meanwhile, back in London, some young people were not as fortunate and did not leave their homes in Hackney. Among the children were Candy, aged 14, who sleeps under a coat on a bare mattress, looks after her mum who has depression, and reports that 'sometimes' they don't have enough food. There is also Joe, excluded from school but no one has tried to get him back, and Victoria, 11, playing in a small tarmac square for her holiday while keeping her eye on the younger children. Hackney had its youth funding cut by 75% and 8 out of 13 youth clubs closed (McVeigh, 2011). Subsequent claims by Cameron of a crusade to mend poor parenting and broken social values rang hollow with such stark evidence of inequalities (Elliot-Major, 2011).

Dysfunctional families

The Labour Party under Ed Miliband did not provide much effective opposition to the coalition austerities and appeared to support beliefs in a dysfunctional poor. Labour Graham Allen MP, who had previously written papers with Iain Duncan Smith for his Centre for Social Justice, authored a paper for the Cabinet Office on *Early intervention, smart investment, massive savings* (Allen, 2011). The cover showed a picture of a small, supposedly 'deprived brain' under a picture of a 'normal' brain. The point of the paper was to demonstrate that brains are formed by early experiences; poor dysfunctional families are not able to supply the right brain experiences, and their children are thus are a cost to the taxpayer later in life. The research on which this paper was based showed no such thing. Duncan Smith, briefly Conservative Party Leader, then Work and Pensions Minister in the Cameron governments, was largely responsible for carrying out austerity policies and creating a Universal Credit system that even in early stages had left poor people poorer. He always believed that there were 'a growing number of dysfunctional families cut off from what you or I might consider the normal process of education, aspiration, and work' (quoted in Gentleman, 2010), and opened a Centre for Social Justice to help reverse social breakdown, producing reports on *Breakdown Britain* (Centre for Social Justice, 2006). For Duncan Smith pathways to poverty were due to individual deficiencies rather than economic or wage policies. His plans to restrict Child Benefit to two children were intended to limit the family size of the poor; he himself has four children.

All this was and continues to be chillingly reminiscent of Victorian eugenic beliefs, when elite white men and some white women in the USA and UK espoused beliefs in the inferior intelligence and abilities of lower classes and racial groups. A theme in this book is that these views never disappeared, and have continued to underpin educational policies and public views. A new 'progressive eugenics' was developing, claiming evidence from advances in genetic research. Beliefs that differences in ability are largely due to genetic inheritance seemed again to be influencing policy on school selection and separation. Governments were searching for 'better brains' to enhance national economic competitiveness. Dominic Cummings was educated at Durham School and Oxford, and then spent three years in Russia. He then worked for Iain Duncan Smith. He later became an adviser to Michael Gove and produced a paper in 2013, quoting studies that supposedly showed that 60–70% of success in National Curriculum tests depend on heritability. Programmes such as Sure Start, focusing on the health and education of children aged 0–3, were apparently useless (Cummings, 2013). Indeed, many Sure Start Centres were later closed down in the government's austerity measures. Cummings later turned his attention to organising the 'Vote Leave' campaign for the EU referendum, being credited with inventing the slogan 'Take back control', and was reported in 2018 to claim that Westminster would become a smoking ruin if the Brexit supporters did not get what they wanted (Barnett, 2018). Boris Johnson, eventually a vociferous Leave supporter, also believed that 'human beings are very far apart in their raw ability ... as many as 16% of our species have an IQ below 85 ...

while 2% have an IQ above 130.' Announcing this in the third Margaret Thatcher Annual Lecture, he also claimed that 'greed is a valuable spur to human activity' (Johnson, 2013). He clearly believed he was in the top 2%.

The enemy within all over again

While those black and white nursery school toddlers from dysfunctional families were a worry to Blair and the coalition government, more urgent problems were posed by the possible radicalisation of young Muslims. The demonisation of Muslims and Islam as a world religion reached peak proportions during the coalition and Cameron governments, which discouraged sensible debate and information about national security. While British imperial involvement in Middle Eastern countries from the 19th century has been noted in previous chapters, the anger felt by people of all faiths at the outcome of the Bush–Blair Iraq War in 2003, and the lies told in support of military intervention, were likely to be regarded as an incentive for possible retaliation.

The bombings in London in 2005 by young men educated in English schools, as noted in Chapter Seven, was a catalyst for blanket condemnation of Muslims and Islam. In 2006 Michael Gove MP, future Education Secretary, but then a journalist and writer, produced his book *Celsius 7/7* (Gove, 2006) with the introduction 'It's the ideology, stupid'. The book detailed his views of Islam, which he claimed was a good historic faith, to be separated from Islamism – a totalitarian ideology using tactics of advancement similar to those used by fascists and communists. It included a chapter on 'The Trojan Horse', supposedly describing how fundamental Islamists spread their ideology. As a supporter of Israel, he likened Palestinian claims for land to the 1939 Munich agreement when the then Prime Minister Chamberlain capitulated to the Nazi government in Germany. The book never mentioned the historical role of the British and French in the Middle East, especially the Sykes–Picot Agreement and the Balfour Declaration (see Chapter One of this book). As a founder member of the Henry Jackson Society, a right-wing group set up after the 7/7 bombings, Gove lectured to the Society alongside media owner Rupert Murdoch. The Assistant

Director of this group was journalist Douglas Murray, who later wrote that 'Europe is committing suicide' by encouraging the settlement of migrants, and claimed that multiculturalism was a failed project (Murray, 2017). Given Gove's later importance as Education Secretary, then briefly as Justice Secretary, and also putting himself forward as leader of the Conservative Party in 2016, it is surprising that not more is known about his own ideologies. In 2016 a book, *Michael Gove: A biography*, was withdrawn from publication.[2]

In combating the possible radicalisation of young people, the Prevent strategy, initiated by the Blair government, was extended. A review was completed in 2011 (Francis, 2011). The review noted that extremism is defined as active opposition to fundamental British values that include democracy, the rule of law and mutual respect and tolerance of different faiths and beliefs. Schools and universities were expected to recognise and report signs that young people were being drawn into radical ideologies. This became more urgent with the rise (and fall) of the so-called 'Islamic state' (Isis), and the coalition government made Prevent one of the four elements of Contest, the government's counter-terrorism strategy. The Counter-Terrorism and Security Act 2015 extended the expectations on schools, universities, prisons and other institutions to 'prevent people being drawn into terrorism' (Gearon, 2015: 272). Teachers had a statutory duty to report signs of non-violent extremism with children as young as three apparently being referred, and Muslim religious leaders criticised the programmes as divisive and 'spying on young people' (Ramesh, 2015). It was also notable that cases of Islamic terrorism were matched by attacks by right-wing groups and individuals on Muslims and migrants. By 2017 a third of referrals to the Prevent strategy involved such groups.

Trojan horses revisited

Government panic ensued over a supposed Islamic takeover of schools in Birmingham in 2014, when a letter originally sent to the City Council in November 2013 was leaked to the media in March 2014 (Shackle, 2017). The letter outlined a supposed strategy named 'Operation Trojan Horse' to influence the placement of teachers and governors in 21 schools, replace head teachers and impose an Islamist curriculum. The letter was quickly discredited as a forgery, but the allegations were taken up by the media as an Islamist plot. The use of the term 'Trojan Horse' to suggest Islamic infiltration had been used not only by Michael Gove but also in other anti-Muslim writings, and was used by the neo-Nazi Norwegian Anders Behring Breivik who murdered 77 people in Norway in July 2011. The Trojan Horse affair escalated when, in April 2014, Gove appointed a former head of the Metropolitan counter-terrorism division to investigate the claims. Twenty-one schools were inspected by Ofsted and some teachers suspended. One school, Park View, had formerly been judged 'outstanding' in a previous inspection, but as the school had become an academy in 2010, the local authority had no control over the school or its curriculum.

The Insted Consultancy (2014) documented the competing narratives of the affair, as did Holmwood and O'Toole (2014), among others. The outcome after legal representations was that there had been no plot and teachers had been unfairly sacked. The affair also raised issues of the lack of accountability in academies. A further outcome was that that at a lunch with *The Times* owners and the then Home Secretary Theresa May, Gove criticised the Home Office handling of extremist issues and was forced to apologise (Walters, 2014). He was sacked as Education Secretary in July and replaced by Nicky Morgan. A telling comment on the issue was that 'A great deal of damage has been done by politicians who whip up hostility towards migrants coming to this country and towards the Muslim community. Viewing the problems of governance in Birmingham schools through the prism of culture wars was bound to leave many casualties' (Yaqoob, 2014). Another comment from barrister Andrew Faux was, 'what has the Trojan Horse affair achieved? Have great swathes of British Muslim children been saved from a path that inexorably leads to terrorism. Well, no. Because they weren't on that path in the first place' (Faux, 2017).

A hostile environment

Dealing with immigration issues had been outsourced to a Border Agency, but it had become so chaotic that in 2013, Home Secretary May took the Agency back into the Home Office. It was not until 2018 that more information began to be made public about policies that were intended to create a hostile environment, notionally for illegal immigrants, but which eventually resulted in the deportation and denial of public services to legal and settled citizens, including those of the Windrush generation. An enthusiastic strategy of being tough on immigration was, as always, considered to be a vote winner, and was embraced by Theresa May. She told *The Daily Telegraph* in 2012 that her policy was to create a really hostile environment for illegal migrants, and promised to reduce immigration to the 'tens of thousands', a policy, which, as Elgot later reported, 'brought anguish to a generation with every right to live their lives in Britain' (Elgot, 2018). It emerged that officials in Caribbean countries had alerted the Foreign Office from 2013 that older Caribbean residents were being classed as illegal immigrants but no action was being taken (Gentleman, 2018a). The Home Office created 'Operation Vaken', curiously naming it after a poem promoting fascism in 1930s Germany, and vans were sent around London boroughs with billboards saying 'Go home or face arrest (106 arrests in your area last week) Text Home to 780070 for free help and advice'. Apparently 63% of enquiries about free help were hoaxes and only 11 people left the country. Posters were also placed in minority newspapers, and in mosques and temples urging people to 'Go home'. Detention of immigrants increased, although four in ten appeals against detention were successful.

The Immigration Act 2014 was intended to make it easier to remove those 'with no right to be here', as the Act put it, and landlords, banks, driving instructors, NHS workers and even vicars were expected to check on people's legal status. Taylor later remarked that this Act removed legal protection from Windrush people immigrant in the 1960s and 1970s, but who had no legal documentation (Taylor, 2018). It later transpired that the Home Office had destroyed documents and landing cards that proved their status (Roundtree, 2018). A further Immigration Act in

2016 fuelled the hostile environment, with the DfE instructing schools in December 2016 to record the nationality, language and birthplace of children, although claiming the data would not be sent to the Home Office to check immigration status. This led some parents who feared deportation if their status was not confirmed to keep their children from school. As McInnery commented, 'What society lets families fear deportation for sending their children to school?' (McInnery, 2016). May also insisted that overseas students who came to study in Britain should be counted in immigration numbers and that, as she told the Conservative Party Conference in 2015, 'far too many of them are not returning home as soon as their visa runs out' (Stewart, 2017). In fact, as the ONS demonstrated, 97% of overseas students went home and only 3% overstayed. It appeared that even before the vote to leave the EU, the British Home Office under Theresa May was hostile both to legal settlers in the UK and those from both inside and outside the EU.

British values

The imperial assertions that British traditions and values were somehow superior to the rest of the world had been severely shaken by the end of the British Empire, the independence of former colonial countries and the inclusion of former colonial subjects with different and often denigrated cultures and ways of living into the country. The imperial social system was one in which all social classes in Britain assumed the superiority of what passed for British values, which were essentially the values of elite groups and initially included the subordination and deference of lower classes. While working-class struggles for equality persisted from the 19th century, all classes united in the exploitation of colonial people and in defence of any supposed threats from groups from former colonial societies. The Trojan Horse incident and fears of the radicalisation of young Muslims into pseudo-religious violence appeared to be one such threat. One response of government was the production of a policy requiring all schools to 'actively promote' 'fundamental British values'. Non-statutory guidance issued by the DfE (2014) required schools to promote values of democracy, the rule of law, individual liberty and mutual respect and tolerance of those with different faiths and beliefs. Teachers were expected to do this through the SMSC aspects of the curriculum. Ofsted was expected to police the teachers, who were told by Teachers Standards that they must not undermine British values. There was minimal information on how schools and teachers had responded to requirements to promote these values, but Carol Vincent studied how teachers were going about the task of producing good citizens imbued with the appropriate values. She noted that when people are asked to describe British values, they are often restricted to mentions of the Queen, tea, fish and chips and queuing (Vincent, 2019).

The most obvious question was whether the values to be promoted were just British values, or could also be European, Canadian, American, Australian, Indian or any other country that claimed to be a democracy. The Indian Constitution of 1949 explicitly supported democracy, the rule of law, liberty and tolerance, with the added advantage of declaring the country secular, despite numerous religions. Schools in England were to be at the frontline of ideological and religious wars of the 21st century, but contradictions were obvious. By 1998 faith schools of all kinds were allowed under English law – Anglican, Roman Catholic, Greek Orthodox, Jewish, Muslim, Hindu, Buddhist – but they were now required to give priority to secular law while still teaching their own religious beliefs. Academy schools were free of local authority control, which gave governing bodies more opportunity to influence the curriculum, a charge made in the Trojan Horse saga.

By 2016 a withdrawal from the EU, possible break-up of a United Kingdom and the end of the British Empire still a cause for regret, what actually constituted British values had become a crucial question. Lord Swann's 1985 report had pointed out that in a post-colonial world, offering all students a relevant education would entail considerable change to a curriculum that still reflected ethnocentric values, some of which were highly questionable in terms of democracy, tolerance and social and racial justice. There were problems in explaining that in the UK democratic beliefs in racial justice are often ignored. Whether schools are actually able to overcome religious intolerance is questionable. The separate religious schools in Northern Ireland, where intolerance between Protestants and Catholics continues, suggest that this is difficult. There are problems for schools in explaining why the British government regards countries that have no regard for democracy and support punitive religious laws as friends and allies, and even sells them arms, Saudi Arabia and the Gulf States being obvious examples. An important issue in the second decade of the 21st century was recognised as the decline of democracy. Populist movements around the world were finding increased support, especially from those who felt they had no influence over their lives. As Yascha Mounk and others have pointed out, people became disillusioned with liberal politics, and turned to authoritarian populists who could easily become elected dictators, and the survival of liberal democracy itself is then in question (Mounk, 2018).

Undemocratic education

Sustaining democracy in nation-states that include minorities and immigrant groups has always proved difficult. Education in developed countries was usually regarded as a means of unifying and including diverse groups, despite disagreements about retaining languages, cultures and religions. The English education system was slowly working its way towards inclusive comprehensive schooling, with partnerships between central and local government and with parents actually wanting good local schools. By 2010 the idea that education should have democratic input finally disappeared. Schooling became a 'national system nationally administered' (Ainley, 2001), with no input from democratically elected local councillors or teachers. Conservative policy from the 1980s was directed to ending local authority participation in maintaining local schools; teachers were to become a workforce to be managed in school businesses. The creation of a plethora of different kinds of schools to be available for competitive parental choice further consolidated undemocratic advances.

Private schooling remained the choice for parents who could afford it, for around 7% of children. Of all those taking A-levels, 26% were from private schools and there was an over-representation of these students in the 'top' universities.

Education services were privatised as far as possible, with as much out-sourcing to agencies as possible. School meals were supplied by private companies and supply teachers employed through agencies. University education was to be effectively privatised, the Lord Browne Review on fees was published in October 2010, and Minister David Willetts introduced legislation to raise the fees up to £9,000 a year (Browne, 2010). The assumption was that universities would obligingly sort themselves into a hierarchy of desirability, with some charging lower fees. But no vice-chancellors were about to advertise their institutions as second class. The fee increase was agreed in December, which eventually ended the parliamentary career of Liberal Democrat Nick Clegg, who had previously vehemently opposed fee increases. Students were to take out loans, the Student Loans Company was privatised, and interest charged on loans. The Conservatives later claimed that despite fee increases, more working-class young people had entered higher education, although with jobs disappearing and repayment of the loan being far distant, the decisions were not difficult. Top universities were consistently noted for taking fewer black and minority students. The peak of achievement apparently was to enter the Universities of Oxford and Cambridge. Only 40 out of 80,000 poor children receiving free school meals after 2010 were claimed to reach this pinnacle. Gove was worried that although 'schools should be engines of social mobility', more children from public schools made it to the top universities than the entire population of young people eligible for that 'basic benefit' (Gove, quoted in DfE, 2010: 6). Feeding children was now apparently a benefit.

Academies, free schools, grammar schools, studio schools, special schools, alternative provision schooling, remaining local authority-maintained schools, sixth form colleges and university technical colleges were supposedly choices in the secondary area, with further education colleges offering enhanced vocational training and overseeing a revived apprenticeship system (Wolf, 2011; Tomlinson, 2013). Academies, free schools, grammar and maintained schools could also be faith schools. 'Choice' of school led inexorably to division and inequality by area, by social class and by ethnicity. The 164 remaining grammar schools quietly increased their intakes and could expand by allowing annexes to the schools. Beliefs in selective education and the social mobility of a few working-class children continued to underpin policy. Money taken from other parts of the education budget was given to schools as a Pupil Premium for their disadvantaged children, but the end result of the coalition and Cameron governments was a system with gross inequalities, heavily under-funded, assessment and curriculum centrally controlled and with children, young people and teachers experiencing unprecedented levels of poor mental health. The Institute for Fiscal Studies estimates that between 2011 and 2015 there was a 13% cut in education spending. The School Cuts organisation noted that at the end of 2015 there had been £3 billion of cuts per annum affecting 91% of schools, with more cuts to follow (see https://schoolcuts. org.uk).

Undemocratic schools

The stated policy aims of the coalition government were to reduce attainment gaps between the rich and poor, increase social mobility and improve England's place in international comparisons and in economic competitiveness. The 2010 White Paper, presented by Education Secretary Michael Gove, claimed 'what really matters is how we are doing in comparison with our international competitors ... and for too long we have tolerated the accepted correlation between wealth and achievement at school.' But the gap between rich and poor was apparently not pre-ordained, as 'Chinese girls on Free School Meals significantly out-perform the national average' (Cameron and Clegg, 2010: 4). Although there were very few Chinese girls on free school meals in the cohort, the message was clear – poverty is no excuse, and if teachers smartened up, schools made more accountable and local authority influence removed, scores in the PISA tests would improve – as would economic competitiveness with other countries. Structures were to be improved by an accelerated Academies Programme. These were set up, as noted in previous chapters, by the Labour government through the Learning and Skills Act 2000, with the first academies opening in 2002.

The initial policy that academies should have external sponsors contributing to the funding quickly disappeared, and the

Academies Act was the first Act of the coalition government in July 2010. This allowed all schools to become academies, 'converting' without a sponsor and with no need to consult the local authority. Up to that time there were fewer than 300 academies. By 2015 there were over 4,000, with primary schools also allowed to change their status. Academies were directly funded from central government, inspected by Ofsted and eventually, eight regional commissioners were appointed by the government to oversee academies in their area. Although some schools under local authority control had developed partnerships with other schools, academies run as trusts with boards of trustees were encouraged to form chains, and eventually multi-academy trusts (MATs). By 2015 there were 846 MATs in England, with varying numbers of schools included, and with considerable scope for corruption, with unaccountable finance, large payments to CEOs of trusts, employment of family members, and all the problems that big businesses exhibit.[3]

The 2010 Act also created 'free' schools that were actually state schools funded from central government and operating under academy rules. Gove had visited Sweden before the election and was impressed by the Swedish *friskolor*, which were private schools run with public money. By 2011 there were over 250 applications for free schools, from parental, community and religious groups. The parental applications were mainly for free special schools, and religious groups included Muslim, Hindu, Sikh, Jewish and even a Maharishi school. Whether more religious schools could help heal social divisions or even raise school standards was never discussed. By 2015 some 500 free schools were in operation, but by then the Swedish free schools, many of which had become for-profit schools, were in trouble. As in English free schools and academies, Swedish free schools could employ unqualified teachers, and the declining Swedish scores in the PISA international comparisons were blamed on this and on the introduction of parental choice of a variety of schools (Weale, 2015: 13).

By 2013 child poverty had risen in poorer areas, with fewer schools in these areas gaining the Ofsted classification of 'good', and official anxiety was focusing on the lower achievements of white working-class boys. The Labour Party, under its leader Ed

Miliband, had been too embarrassed to oppose reforms, having created academies in the first place with claims that they would lead to higher standards. By 2013 Labour was becoming nervous at the lack of democratic input and the possible effects on a working-class vote. David Blunkett was deputed to undertake a review of structures, funding and achievements, and in 2014 made 40 recommendations for improvements. While in his opinion there was no way the current system could revert to local authority control, he suggested community trusts to oversee groups of schools with better trained governors to avoid Trojan Horse debacles, and with a National Director of School Standards (Blunkett, 2014). The government instead appointed a National Schools Commissioner to accelerate the academy agenda.

Gove's curriculum

The White Paper, *The importance of teaching* (DfE, 2010), and the subsequent 2011 Act set out the coalition's ideas for raising educational standards. A traditional subject-centred curriculum with continual assessments were the tools. The paper claimed that teachers were to be freed from bureaucracy and their professional status raised, a promise that rang hollow over the years as teachers were even more tightly controlled by assessment requirements. An EBacc of five traditional subjects, denoting successful schooling and further test and assessment regimes, was introduced. History was to be taught chronologically, and there was to be an emphasis on facts. Especially problematic was the introduction of Progress 8, a score given to schools on the basis of improvement in eight subjects at secondary school. By 2018 vulnerable pupils – the code for working-class and black pupils with learning difficulties – were being forced out of mainstream schools due to accountability measures and a narrow curriculum (Whittaker, 2018). A chapter in the 2010 paper focused on bad behaviour, suggesting that black and working-class boys were more likely to behave badly in school and to be excluded or truant. Teachers were to have the power to search pupils for weapons, pornography and tobacco, and head teachers given more powers to exclude pupils. Separate schooling for the problem children, if not in special schools and units, was ensured in alternative provision schooling outside of mainstream schools.

The National Curriculum, although not mandatory in academies, was intended to 'embody children's cultural and scientific inheritance', but should not try to cover all human learning or 'become a vehicle for imposing passing political fads on our children' (DfE, 2010: 41). It no longer needed to be spelled out that 'fads' included a discussion of race, racism, multiculturalism, immigration and even gender issues. A curriculum review in 2013 resulted in an even more tightly controlled curriculum, with content and assessment published subject by subject. Gove's adviser for the History curriculum was Niall Ferguson, noted in the introduction of this book as a believer in the 'greatness' of the British Empire'. The rationale for all this was set out in a speech Gove made to the Social Market Foundation in which he claimed that a 12-subject National Curriculum, but with the five EBacc subjects denoting high attainment, was intended for 'the cultivation of habits of proper thought' (Gove, 2013a). Whether a GCSE English curriculum including a mandatory Shakespeare play, poetry since 1789 and a work from the 19th and 20th centuries, fiction but excluding the popular book *To kill a mockingbird* (Lee, 1960), which teachers had found most useful in discussing racism, would cultivate proper thought, has proved questionable. In 2018 a group of white students at Nottingham Trent University who had recently studied the Gove curriculum were recorded chanting racist abuse outside a black female student's room. Included in the chants were 'We hate the Blacks' and 'Sign the Brexit papers' (Rawlinson, 2018).

Gove's views were further clarified in his 2013 speech, in which he declared that 'state schools should offer a 9 to 10 hour day including after-school sports matches, orchestra rehearsals, debating competitions, coding clubs, cadet training, Duke of Edinburgh awards and inspirational careers talks' (Gove, 2013a). While this all sounds like Gove's own private school day in the 1970s and 1980s, it does beg questions such as who pays teachers for a 10-hour day, where are sports matches to be played now that state school sports grounds have been sold off, who plays in orchestras now that schools and local authorities can no long provide instruments, who runs the cadet corps and who gives the inspirational careers talks now that careers services have been cut?

Gove did not take kindly to criticism of his curriculum plans. He described 100 professors and teachers who had signed a letter to *The Independent* in March 2013 as 'Enemies of promise ... a set of politically motivated individuals who have been actively trying to prevent millions of our poorest children from getting the education they need', and he 'refused to surrender to these Marxist teachers hell-bent on destroying our schools' (Gove, 2013b). Grave charges indeed.[4] The last White Paper produced before Cameron resigned after the EU referendum was labelled *Educational excellence everywhere* (DfE, 2016), which was intended to move as much teacher training as possible into schools, and to diminish university influence.

Summary

This chapter has documented some of the activities of the governments between 2010 and 2016, which had the effect of increasing hostility towards settled migrants from former colonial countries, and immigrants from EU countries; a hostile environment that eventually encompassed thousands of legal settlers who might be liable for deportation became official policy. Young black people and Muslims continued to be demonised. Despite a rhetoric of social mobility and helping the disadvantaged, the country became more divided than ever by wealth, income, geography and life chances through education. Poor people continued to be treated with contempt and blamed for their individual and family deficiencies. The government succeeded in its aim of removing democratic accountability in schooling, ensuring semi-privatised school structures that encouraged segregation by class and ethnicity.

The curriculum was further narrowed, and testing and assessment in subjects and content decided by central government became the norm. Teachers were expected to teach 'British values' that were and are debatable. Criticism was met by accusations that critics were 'Marxists'. Schools and teachers were more intensely policed by inspection and cuts in funding for schooling defended as part of austerity measures. Private schooling for the children of richer parents continued, and the consequences of an increase in fees for university education are still being assessed. There was evidence of an increase in mental health problems and suicides among students. What was learned by children and young people in schools was still influenced by historical, imperial understandings. A government-controlled curriculum ensured ignorance of even basic understandings of the post-colonial past and present. Ignorance of the EU and its actual functions was not addressed in schooling, or in the wider public, and antipathy towards the Union encouraged by Eurosceptic politicians and the media. It was not surprising that the vote to leave the EU, documented in the next chapter, was influenced by all these events.

Notes

[1] The WTO grew out of GATT, the General Agreement on Tariff and Trade (1945-94). On 1 January 1995 it became the WTO and met in Doha in 2001 to try to agree world trading rules. Talks were always difficult, especially in 2008 when there were arguments over agricultural trade between the USA, India and China, and further meetings have met disagreements. There is no guarantee that trading under WTO rules will be easy. The organisation itself notes that making trade agreements is complex and lengthy as they are legal texts. In 2018 President Trump declared tariffs on certain goods coming into the USA, and supported a protectionist agenda; China and other countries retaliated in kind.

[2] The book, *Michael Gove: A biography*, by Alistair Cathcart Sloan, was under contract with Biteback publishers in 2016, when the book contract was cancelled. Gove's views are changeable. In *Celsius 7/7* he complained that the Saudi Royal family were funding London's Central Mosque, and 'Saudi funding is clearly linked at the very least to leaving the door open to Islamists and extremist ideologies' (Gove, 2006: 113). By March 2018 he was part of a government welcoming the Crown Prince of Saudi Arabia, which is a major importer of arms manufactured in Britain, and at war with Yemen, a former British Protectorate.

[3] The expanding academy agenda, intended to semi-privatise all schools, has only been in operation for some 18 years. Research collecting evidence on the rapidly changing school structure has necessarily been limited and fragmented. Journalists have detailed much of the evidence of malfunctions and corruptions, especially in MATs, for example, the work of journalist Warwick Mansell, and those writing in the journal *Schools Week*. While large amounts of money are given to academics from an Education Endowment Fund to find 'what works' in schools and classrooms, funding is not available for critical study or alternative suggestions.

[4] Gove likened the 'enemies of promise' who signed the newspaper letter (the author was one signatory) to those quoted in a book by writer Cyril Connelly, who, in the 1930s, had complained that 'enemies of promise' stopped him from working. If Gove had read the book he would have found that Cyril's enemies were his rich friends who distracted him from his writing. Gove described the signatories as 'The Blob', a label first used by Chris Woodhead, the unpopular head of Ofsted in the 1990s. Gove also used the article to attack teaching unions and the Labour Party.

9

A dog's breakfast Brexit,
2016-18

We cannot be a colony of the EU for two years from 2019 to 2021.... That is not leaving the EU. That is being a vassal state of the EU. (Rees-Mogg, 2017; see also Mackie, 2017)

Britain should turn to Saudi Arabia after Brexit for new trade and investment opportunities, and not a backward looking Commonwealth, a Saudi Minister said. (Wintour, 2018)

Comic Relief this year focused on Malawi and Uganda. I didn't see any acknowledgement that Britain had been the Colonial power in the past.... Thanks for the gold, lads, Thanks for the diamonds. We had a whip round and got you a fishing rod. (Boyle, 2015)

There can be no conclusions to this book, as negotiations continue on what sort of United Kingdom, if the four nations stay together, will develop after it leaves the European Union, assuming that in some form it will. Nor can there be conclusions as to whether and how the nations' education systems will change to incorporate the new circumstances. It will take a decade or more before the reality of a Britain on its own in a globally trading world, with government instability and one of the highest inequalities of wealth in the developed world, becomes clearer. One certainty is that Britain cannot rely on its imperial past or on the fidelity of a Commonwealth. Even as a divided government planned to take the country out of the EU, it became obvious that there had been a massive failure to educate several generations about what the British Empire and the EU actually were or what they did. What did the Empire do for its subjects and how are the consequences of empire now affecting the future of a Britain out of the EU? It took a comedian to make a suitable ironic comment on the failure to acknowledge that former colonial countries had their wealth stripped under imperialism and are now regarded as places for charitable enterprises (Boyle, 2015). How inclusive is our national sovereignty when long-settled citizens are still not acceptable, people from European countries are no longer welcome, and refugees and asylum-seekers are treated with suspicion and hostility? It could also be asked how inclusive the nation was when, despite Prime Minister May asserting that she wanted 'a country that works for everyone' (May, 2016), there were more food banks, an increase in homelessness, cuts to disability allowances and adult social care, with life expectancy actually decreasing in the UK compared to other European countries.

Early Brexit years

The years following the Brexit vote were surely some of the most turbulent in British political history, as parties and individuals slugged it out to present some kind of a Brexit to the British public. The British are fond of their dogs, so dog metaphors appeared to be in order to describe the Brexit negotiations by the end of July 2018, when a final deal on leaving the EU was intended to be agreed on by the following November. The old slang term used in Glasgow of a 'dog's breakfast', meaning that something was a complete mess and was not going the way it was intended, seemed appropriate. *The Sunday Telegraph* of 22 July 2018 compared the 'glaring shambles' of the Brexit negotiations plus a very hot summer with the 'dog days of Ancient Greece' that were associated with intense heat and drought that made dogs and men go mad and 'lose their marbles' (Booker, 2018).

Those whose job it was to provide an exit from the EU at first appeared to have little understanding of the future, with civil servants joking that an 'Empire 2.0' could be created for trade. After Labour Party splits and several leadership elections, Jeremy Corbyn, although a life-long Eurosceptic, emerged to lead the Labour Party towards what had been labelled a 'soft Brexit' – keeping the UK in a Customs Union with the EU, if not in a

Single Market. A similar plan eventually devised by Theresa May and her advisers to keep a version of a Customs Union and solve the problem of the Irish border was criticised almost immediately by her own 'Brexiteers', notably Boris Johnson, who resigned as Foreign Secretary over the issue on 11 July 2018. The main Leave members of Parliament, Boris Johnson, Michael Gove, Liam Fox and, jumping later on to the bandwagon, Jacob Rees-Mogg, were all telling Prime Minister May that it was a 'hard Brexit' or 'no deal'.

Meanwhile, US President Donald Trump started a global trade war in 2018 by putting tariffs on goods from abroad, which made more questionable assertions that British trade with the USA and the rest of the world outside the EU would be easy. Trump's contribution to the Brexit debate came after a brief 'working visit' to Britain on his way to Russia, when he claimed that, 'The EU is my foe' and an enemy of the USA in trade terms. He also suggested Theresa May sue the EU rather than negotiate over leaving terms (Roth et al, 2018). Ten days later he had changed his mind and agreed a large trade deal with the EU. The assumption that Britain and the USA were in a kind of special relationship over trade and defence, that had endured from the end of the Second World War, was now in doubt.

What the EU did for the UK may be a question for the future, when we will find it actually did a great deal. Since the 1992 Maastricht Treaty, as Andrew Geddes has pointed out, the EU has worked its way into British politics, and its economy has been deeply integrated with other EU countries. What did we share with the EU by the second decade of the 21st century? We shared security policies, nuclear and other energy policies; employment and social policy; citizenship and free movement; a Single Market and Customs Union; agriculture issues; fishing rights; border checks; asylum and immigration; civil and criminal justice; transport; aviation agreements; tax; economic policies; health policies; university and other research including educational research and student exchange programmes; consumer protection; industrial policy; environment issues, commercial and financial provision; and much more (Geddes, 2013: 7). Britain also used the European Court of Justice (ECJ) that Eurosceptics had always regarded as taking legal decisions away from British courts.[1]

The negotiations between representatives of the EU and the British government over leaving the EU and the legalities and trading arrangement started in June 2016, when a referendum to leave the EU resulted in 52% voting to Leave and 48% to Remain. Arguments ensued about which social, geographical, racial, gender or age groups voted most to Leave or Remain. It finally appeared that the main Leavers were older Tory voters who were not from the richest of the Tory areas, some working-class people in both southern and northern areas, and voters in coastal towns with few migrants. Young people were mainly in favour of Remaining (Moore, 2016). The 52% voting to Leave was only 37% of those eligible to vote. The Conservative Party, never particularly united before the vote, indulged in party antagonisms more hostile than any previous internal squabbles over the Party's leadership and what leaving the EU would mean.

There were no reminders of the words of the French Minister Jean Monnet, sometimes described as the Father of Europe, who, in 1945, forecast that, 'There will be no peace in Europe if States rebuild themselves on the basis of national sovereignty, with its implications of prestige politics and economic protection.... The countries of Europe are not strong enough individually to be able to guarantee prosperity and social development for their peoples. The States of Europe must therefore form a federation or a European entity that would make them into a common economic unit' (Monnet, 1945). As Former US Secretary of State Madeleine Albright pointed out, by 2018 the EU was the world's largest economy after the USA, with 14 of the world's wealthiest countries in Europe (Albright, 2018).

By 2017 contenders for the Conservative Party leadership were using imperial references to colonies and vassal states, with Boris Johnson copying Rees-Mogg's claim that Britain should not go from a member state to a vassal state (Johnson, 2017b). Perhaps older people remembered 'doing' the Vikings in primary school, which taught that after much looting and pillaging, these foreign invaders attempted to turn parts of Britain into vassal states. Perhaps that is what both these men remembered from their public school education at Eton. While the Norman invaders, descendants of the Vikings, eventually managed to take over Britain, subsequent wars were to keep or take over large parts of the European continent. By the late 1500s, as the Introduction to this book noted, the process of turning over a quarter of the world into vassals of a British Empire had begun. The notion that Britain would become a vassal state of the EU was nonsense, as both men knew. But neither were they willing to concede that after leaving the EU there was no chance of a 'Great' post-imperial Britain emerging. While older people who presumably remembered the Second World War had largely voted to leave the EU, it seemed that they had forgotten that the wars that had dominated the European continent for over 600 years were less likely to occur in a union of the countries.

A negative effect of the Brexit vote in 2016 was an escalation of xenophobia, race hatred and a strengthening of beliefs in a national sovereignty that excludes 'foreigners'. This included black, Asian and other settled citizens. Also included are those from outside the EU, European citizens and migrant workers, asylum-seekers and refugees. Even before rules to limit the free movement of workers had been formulated, there were attempts to remove settled European or non-EU citizens who had been in the UK for years, working and paying taxes, often married or partnered with British citizens. Colour and cultural racism was joined by anti-European and global racism. While a closing of national borders was becoming common in other European countries as far-right politicians were elected, British nationals living and working in European countries began taking their claims to remain European citizens to the courts (O'Carroll, 2018). The problems of Gibraltar's sovereignty and the Irish border were only just beginning. Both Gibraltar and Northern Ireland had voted to remain in the EU, and both have borders with an EU country.

In England, while schools were constrained by the 'traditional curriculum' imposed by Gove and his fellow believers, some university students and staff were beginning to question a Eurocentric bias, demanding a decolonisation of the curriculum. More academics and writers were documenting the reality of black and minority experiences in the UK, and the racism unleashed in the USA after the election of Donald Trump. The

Black Lives Matter movement in the USA was influential in raising racial justice issues in the UK (McVeigh, 2016). But the 'heirs' to Enoch Powell are convinced, as Conservative academic Roger Scruton wrote, that 'Brexit will give us back pride in our island roots' (Scruton, 2017). These roots had been nurtured by imperialism. Moral panics over racial and cultural differences underpinned escalating antagonisms and race hate (Goodhart, 2017).

Concern that universities might actually be discussing Brexit with their students was questioned by a Conservative MP, Chris Heaton-Harris, who, in October 2017, wrote to all vice-chancellors asking for the names of professors who might be including such a discussion in their lectures. Fortunately no vice-chancellors obliged. But the consequences of an ethnocentric school curriculum were beginning to be apparent in the racist behaviour of some white university students.

Significant events[2]

2013	David Cameron makes the Bloomberg speech, promising reforms to the EU and a referendum on staying in the EU; UKIP comes second in the Eastleigh by-election, taking 27.8% of the vote
2014	UKIP wins 2.6% of the vote in European elections; Nigel Farage stays on as an MEP despite campaigning to leave the EU
2015	(May) General Election, Conservatives win a majority and Cameron promises a referendum by 2017; in October the 'Vote Leave' and the 'Britain Stronger in Europe' campaigns are launched; in December 'Labour in for Britain' campaign starts
2015	Labour leader Ed Miliband resigns and Jeremy Corbyn wins a leadership contest and wins again after a further challenge
2016	(February) Cameron secures an agreement in Brussels including reducing benefits for migrants; Michael Gove and Boris Johnson both back Leave; (May) Gove and Johnson write to Cameron accusing him of 'corroding public trust'; (16 June) MP Jo Cox is murdered
2016	(23 June) Referendum vote to leave the EU by 52% to 48% (or 17,400,000 million to 16,300,000); (24 June) Cameron resigns as Prime Minister; Gove tells Johnson he will back him in a leadership vote; (30 June) Gove says Johnson is not ready to be Prime Minister and puts himself forward instead
2016	(5 July) Theresa May leads in Conservative leadership campaign; (13 July) May becomes Prime Minister; (24 July) Jeremy Corbyn is re-elected Labour Leader with 62% of the vote; Amber Rudd is made Home Secretary; (October) Casey review on *Opportunity and integration*
2016	(October) May says she will trigger Article 50 on leaving the EU by March 2019; (November) High Court rules that only Parliament, not the

government, has the power to trigger Article 50; *Daily Mail* newspaper calls the judges 'enemies of the people'; Donald Trump is elected 45th President of the USA and asks for Nigel Farage to be made British ambassador in Washington

2017   (January) May makes a speech at Lancaster House announcing a 'hard Brexit'; May meets and holds hands with Donald Trump at the White House in Washington; (February) Article 50 Bill passes in the House of Commons; Tony Blair urges Britons to rise up against Brexit

2017   (29 March) May signs letter triggering Article 50; the UK is to leave the EU by 29 March 2019; (April) May announces a General Election

2017   (June) Conservative Party lose their overall majority in the General Election; Labour gains 30 seats; with no overall majority, May does a deal with the Northern Irish DUP to secure their votes; (13 June) Grenfell Tower fire in London kills over 70 people, most of them minorities; (November) black MP David Lammy's Review on minorities in the criminal justice system

2017   (May) Boris Johnson enthuses about a trade in whisky with India while in a Sikh temple; (15 September) Johnson publishes an article in the *Daily Mail* criticising Prime Minister May; (22 September) in a speech in Florence, May says she will seek a two-year transition period to Brexit; (4 October) May, suffering from a heavy cold, makes a disastrous speech to the Conservative Party Conference

2017   (October) Tory MP Chris Heaton-Harris writes to all university vice-chancellors asking for the names of professors teaching European studies with particular reference to Brexit; (November) Roger Scruton writes in *The Times* that 'Brexit will give us back pride in our island roots'; (December) Rees-Mogg and Johnson make 'vassal state' claims

2018   (February) Corbyn makes a speech supporting a Customs Union with the EU; (March) May makes a speech at the Mansion House London supporting a 'hard-line Brexit but with special arrangements'

2018   (March) Communities Minister Sajid Javid publishes *Integrated communities strategy: Building stronger, more united communities*

2018   (January) Theresa May makes a poorly attended speech at Davos on Britain's proud history; (19 March) Prime Minister May and David Davis make a provisional agreement on finally leaving the EU on 31 December 2020. In the first week of April at the Heads of Commonwealth Meeting in London, May turns down a request to discuss Caribbean deportations with the Heads as the 'staggering heartlessness' of the treatment of the Windrush generation becomes apparent; Home Secretary Amber Rudd denies deportation targets, then admits to them and resigns on 30 April; Sajid Javid is appointed Home Secretary

2018   (21 June) Annual day of celebrations for the Windrush generation inaugurated, held in Westminster Abbey

2018   (Friday 6 July) May holds a Cabinet Day at Chequers and thinks a 'soft Brexit' pro-business plan has been agreed; (Monday 10 July) David Davis resigns as Brexit Secretary and Dominic Raab is appointed; (Tuesday 11 July) Boris Johnson resigns as Foreign Secretary, saying Britain is headed for 'colony status' and Jeremy Hunt is appointed – he resigns in October and a third Brexit Secretary is appointed; (17 July) White Paper published on the future relationship between the UK and EU; (18

2018

July) Johnson makes a resignation speech criticising the Brexit plan; Michael Barnier, head of the EU negotiating team, also criticises the White Paper

(26 July) Parliament goes into summer recess with no plans agreed on Brexit; May takes control of Brexit negotiations; concerns over food, medical and other supplies after a possible 'hard Brexit' emerge; (10 December) Theresa May announced that a Bill to Withdraw from the EU, expected to be voted on by Parliament, would be delayed until the New Year, and set off to visit other European leaders.[3]

Politics of self-interest

Politics is a fractious business and people who enter Parliament do so with a variety of motives. The Attlee government of 1945-51 took over after a war that had decimated the economy. The country in the 1930s had reached a peak of gross economic and social inequality. Despite personal antagonisms, this Labour government managed to develop a welfare state that benefited the whole society (Dorling and Tomlinson, 2017). Since 2010 and especially from 2015 Britain has suffered from governments and politicians who have appeared more concerned with furthering their own careers, fighting their fellow MPs and protecting their own wealth and importance than working for a fair and equal country. It was becoming clearer that by March 2019, when Brexit is due to occur with a transitional period to December 2020, the country is likely to continue to be economically and socially unequal. According to playwright David Hare, it would also see 'government handed over to spiteful misfits' (Hare, 2016).

In 2015 the Cabinet was dominated by rich men who had attended public school, several from Eton and then Oxford, and who were long-time supporters of the market ideologies of Margaret Thatcher. Prime Minister David Cameron will eventually be known in history as the man responsible for the EU referendum and its consequences. He left Parliament in 2016 to enjoy his wealth of over £10 million, with millions more to come in family inheritance, to write his memoirs in his £25,000 garden shed. He was noted as a man who saw the world through 'the narrowing prism of a social set and sectional interests' (Toynbee and Walker, 2015: 2).

In 2010, together with wealthy Chancellor George Osborne, they developed the policy of austerity, slashing spending on health, education, housing, social security and local government, which led to some £14 billion cuts in government spending over five years. This was hailed as a success in reducing the national debt, but leaving, as Ann Pettifor put it, 'our social fabric in tatters' (Pettifor, 2018). Benefit recipients, apart from pensioners, were labelled as idle scroungers, and 'social cohesion was subverted' as housing and other benefits were removed and low-paid jobs segregated poor people into the cheaper parts of towns (Toynbee and Walker, 2015).

From 2015, schools were expected to make £3 billion in savings, with the ultimate irony being an announcement in 2018 that school breakfast clubs, many of which had already disappeared, would be given £26 million, but the money would come from a tax on soft drinks.[4]

Cameron never appeared enthusiastic about the EU, but a referendum to leave the EU had been in the 2015 election manifesto. He was worried by the rise of the UKIP vote in European elections in 2014. Nigel Farage, MEP, then UKIP Leader, was financed by rich donor Arron Banks, and was determined the UK should leave the EU. Cameron was apparently surprised to win the 2015 General Election and he did his best to prevent a referendum by travelling in Europe to persuade the European Commission to change some of the rules on migration and benefits. He managed to negotiate a temporary brake on welfare benefits for EU migrants, but this was not sufficient to placate his increasingly Eurosceptic colleagues.

Theresa May, appointed in 2010 as Home Secretary, proceeded to be very hostile to immigrants. She suggested migrants should be refused entry to the country unless they had a job, while Sajid Javid, then Business Secretary, suggested only migrants from richer countries as measured by their GDP should travel freely – visas were only available for rich people, with a Tier 1 visa allowing an immigrant to settle permanently in the UK if they invested £10 million. In early 2018, wealthy Chinese people had been given 146 out of 355 investor visas. The referendum went ahead on 23 June 2016, and there was a majority vote to leave the EU. There were subsequent claims, notably by former Prime Minister Blair, Liberal Democrat Leader Nick Clegg, previous Labour leadership contender Owen Smith, and many others, that the referendum could be run again and might produce a different result. But the 'Department for Exiting the European Union' had already started negotiations, and even 'Brenda from Bristol' was upset at the prospect of more voting (Oakley, 2017). Moves towards leaving the EU continued, the arguments, demands, conciliations and insults documented daily in all newspapers and in the media and social media.

Brexit lies and wishful thinking

The political arguments and campaigns before the referendum, the outright lies told during the campaign, and the jockeying for leadership of the Conservative Party after June 2016 have been presented in detail in two books by the political editor of *The Sunday Times* (see Shipman, 2016, 2017) and in other books produced quickly after the Brexit vote.[5] The Leave campaign, led by former education adviser Dominic Cummings, who had spent three years in Russia and perhaps knew something about disinformation, posted an online video that claimed 'every week the United Kingdom sends £350 million of taxpayers' money to the EU ... Vote leave, let's take control' (Shipman, 2016: 55). The money claim was a lie but appeared on the Leave bus that toured the country in 2016, with Boris Johnson loudly supporting the claim that the money would go to the NHS. Michael Gove, former Education Secretary and a key figure in the 'Vote Leave' campaign, claimed that Turkey and four other countries would soon join the EU, leading to a possible 5.2 million more migrants into Britain with visa-free travel open to 77 million Turkish citizens. In 2018 he admitted the Leave campaign should not have 'stoked up fears' about Turkish migration (Sabbagh, 2018). On 27 July the House of Commons Digital, Culture, Media and Sport (DCMS) Committee published a report on their enquiries into the misinformation used by the Vote Leave campaign through the use of social media, notably Facebook, and concerns about the funding of the Leave campaign. The Committee concluded that data abuses and the disinformation spread constituted a risk to democracy (Waterson, 2018).

The 'Stronger in' campaign found it hard to combat the misinformation and present a positive view of the EU. The subsequent negotiations over the way the country would leave the EU was eventually described as a 'war', with the ministerial group meeting to decide the future of the country described as a 'war cabinet' (Montgomerie and Pancevski, 2017). The way ministers and their advisers actually conducted themselves between June 2016 and the 2017 General Election and subsequently was perhaps more reminiscent of toddlers fighting, with, according to Shipman, a great deal of bad language and insults. Boris Johnson had made no secret of his wish to become Tory leader and Prime Minister, and his friend Michael Gove promised to support his candidacy when Cameron resigned on 24 June 2016 and a leadership contest ensued. Colleagues opposing Johnson had previously formed an 'Anyone but Boris' group (Shipman, 2016: 508). On 30 June Gove suddenly announced he was not supporting Boris but standing himself for the leadership. In the event, 'While the boys were fighting among themselves the leading woman in the Tory Party was quietly going about her business' (Shipman, 2017: 546). Theresa May was elected leader and became Prime Minister. Husband Philip May has money in an offshore island tax haven left over from the Empire.[6]

May and Machiavelli

As Prime Minister, May had grasped that any discussion of the future of Britain after Brexit must depend on new trade partners, if the £44 billion trade done annually with the EU was to disappear. Her first foray was to the USA to congratulate President Donald Trump on his election in November 2016, then to rush over as his first overseas visiting Prime Minister to beg for trade deals, and be photographed holding his hand. Other ministers, notably Liam Fox, were sent off to attempt to make trade deals with India and China. Selling arms had long been a major trade for Britain and this was to continue, often to countries with poor records of human rights and little regard for civilian populations, In March 2018, the Crown Prince of Saudi Arabia was welcomed by May, and deals to sell more fighter planes and other arms agreed, although Saudi Arabia was at war with Yemen, a former British Protectorate. The Saudi Arabia Energy Minister claimed a new partnership, and 'Britain should regard the Kingdom as your gateway to Africa, one of the next frontiers' (Wintour, 2018). The irony that a continent still suffering from the effects of imperialism should be regarded as a new frontier was not remarked on.

Other problems were likely to be with the Commonwealth countries, noted in the previous chapter as being less enthusiastic over trade deals. Much was to be made of hosting the Commonwealth Heads of Government Conference in London in April 2018, where it was hoped trade would be an important topic. The Commonwealth countries were actually less interested in trade deals than in their debts, and especially in climate change. The Conference was originally scheduled to meet in Vanatu (colonised in 1887, independence given in 1980), but had to move as tropical storms and floods affected the island. The countries had also given notice that in the event of the Queen's death they wanted to discuss her successor as Head of the Commonwealth, as it was by no means agreed on who should be the next Head (Roy and Bowcott, 2018). Eventually, it was reported that at the prompting of the Queen, the Heads of Governments agreed that Prince Charles should take over as Head after her.

May had a particularly difficult time as Prime Minister, although following Italian nobleman Machiavelli's advice from the 16th century, she endeavoured to keep her enemies closer by appointing them to her Cabinet, while aware that he also said 'one can make this generalisation about men: they are ungrateful, fickle, liars and deceivers, they shun danger and are greedy for profit' (Machiavelli, quoted in Bull, 1961: 96). Her Foreign Secretary Boris Johnson was regarded with amazement by the global diplomatic world for his gaffes and ignorance, and his eventual resignation from the post in July 2018 was reported to have been greeted with cheers and champagne in the Foreign Office. Her friend, Philip Hammond, as Chancellor of the Exchequer, remained sensible to the eventual need, as Machiavelli had insisted, to placate the population, by eventually suggesting an end to some aspects of austerity. She gave in to the campaign led by Gina Miller, noted in the Introduction to this book as being vilified as a 'bloody immigrant', when High Court judges ruled that Parliament should eventually have a vote on the terms of leaving the EU. An independent judiciary was apparently in some danger when the *Daily Mail* newspaper denounced the judges as 'enemies of the people' (Slack, 2016). On 29 March 2017 May finally signed the letter triggering Article 50 of the 2009 Lisbon Treaty, which allowed for withdrawal of a member state from the EU. Despite speeches at Lancaster House and in Florence suggesting a 'hard Brexit' and more plotting by her colleagues to remove her from office, she made a poor speech at the Conservative Party Conference in October 2017. By March 2018 she and Brexit Secretary David Davis had signed a provisional agreement with the EU over leaving terms. Michael Gove, now Environment Minister, was immediately upset about the fate of British fish in the agreement.

Politics of exclusion

There were many reasons why 17.4 million people voted to leave the EU. As this book has suggested, one reason was a mindset of empire, a nostalgia for an imperial past nurtured by a desire for a British national sovereignty unencumbered by the presence in this country of those 'black and brown inferiors' that Victorian England tolerated, providing they toiled oversees. But around 13% of the population are the descendants of these 'toilers' who came post war to work, some taking the jobs the white workers did not want to do. As Afua Hirsch eloquently noted, colour of skin or foreign-sounding name brings the question, 'where are you from?' to which in their imagination is 'a mythical darkie country' (Hirsch, 2018: 32). The language of a 'Great' Britain spoke of a colonial past when a quarter of the world 'belonged to us'. An inability to come to terms with what the end of the British Empire actually meant in terms of population movements, the economy and global trade was part of the mindset. As noted, the doctrine of what became 'Powellism' – Enoch Powell's views of national sovereignty, anti-immigration and Euroscepticism – surfaced regularly over the years (Tomlinson, 2018). It nurtured the assumption by governments and the public that a Great Britain with a former Empire had no need of closer union with its European neighbours, even as that Empire was disintegrating. This book records that there has been a massive failure in the education system to teach truthfully about empire and its consequences or about the EU.

While the country had been attempting to join the EEC from the 1950s, by the 21st century it had become deeply integrated with other member states, especially in trade and investment and security issues.[7] But public opinion surveys, as Geddes noted in 2013, 'show that British people declared less knowledge of interest in and confidence in the EU than citizens of the other EU states' (Geddes, 2013: 6). The proportion of the electorate who thought the EU was an important issue was rarely above 5%. Claims that leaving the EU would result in less immigration led to settled citizens, EU workers, refugees and those 'foreigners' being targeted for open and covert hate crime and that familiar message, 'Go home'.

The most shocking hate crime happened the week before the Brexit vote on 16 June, when Labour MP Jo Cox was murdered in her Yorkshire constituency by a man with links to the far-right neo-Nazi group Britain First. The police recorded a 57% rise in reported race crime incidents after the vote, including the murder of a Polish man in Harlow, Essex in September 2016. The Polish ambassador visited the town and expressed shock at the murder and the rise in xenophobic attacks following the Brexit decision (Weaver, 2016). A 16-year-old Polish girl was found hanged at her school a month after the 2016 referendum having been bullied at school and told to go back to her own country (Press Association in *The Guardian*, 20 July 2016).

In education, the organisation Reclaiming Schools documented children being subject to racist abuse by adults and other children, with five-year-olds asking their teachers when they would 'be forced to leave' (Reclaiming Schools, 2016). While journalists, and academic and voluntary organisations, quickly collected evidence of racial and xenophobic attacks, especially on Muslim women,[8] journalist Aditya Chakrabortty encapsulated the situation in an article, 'After a campaign scarred by bigotry it is now OK to be racist in Britain' (Chakrabortty, 2016). He also noted that during the campaign Boris Johnson and Michael Gove had falsely claimed that Turkey and its 77 million Muslim citizens would join the EU, Nigel Farage claimed that Syrian refugees would put British women at risk of sexual assault, Polish school children were given cards calling them vermin and telling them to leave the EU, and people made such comments as 'we've got the country back' and 'blow up that f★★cking mosque' (Chakrabortty, 2016: 33). Labour's successful candidate for Mayor of Manchester, Andy Burnham, stirred up the antagonisms, making a speech in December 2016 claiming that a reluctance to discuss immigration was undermining communities and 'the safety of our streets' (Burnham, 2016). The history of the previous 120 years demonstrates that far from any reluctance, immigration had always been a persistent and often vicious topic of discussion.

After the 2017 General Election, Prime Minister May was moved to express horror at the racist, sexist and anti-Semitic attacks on candidates. Long-serving Labour MP Diane Abbott received racist abuse every day, and Conservative candidate Ameet Jogia found graffiti in the voting booths reading 'keep Pakis out of politics' (Mason, 2017). On 13 June 2017 a horrendous fire engulfed Grenfell Tower, a London tower block of flats, with over 70 people killed. Although the block was in one of the richest boroughs in London, the residents were mainly poor and/or minorities. A national newspaper concluded in an article entitled 'Behind this disaster lies a brutal indifference to the lives of the poor' that the government and local councils were indifferent and uncaring about them (*The Observer*, 2017).

After years of attempts to 'kick racism out of football', open racism against black, minority and European footballers and referees surfaced again with the chair of the Football Association and their technical director accused of failures to tackle racism and sexism in the game (Taylor, 2017), and a Northern Irish footballer apologising for his wife's racist tweet against the Romanian referee, 'Romanian Gypsy c★★t, to actually think Northern Ireland has probably homed one of his smelly relatives' (Hunter 2017). Some targets for hate were off limits. Meghan Markle, the mixed race fiancé of Prince Harry, later his wife, was certainly not to be targeted by racist slurs, as the *Daily Mail* announced in January 2018, after the partner of Henry Bolton, the current UKIP leader, claimed that 'Meghan's seed will taint our Royal Family' (Owen, 2018). Bolton lost his job and his partner was forced to apologise. With the documentation of such hate, indifference and exclusion, government pronouncements on social integration ring hollow.

Integration all over again

But governments over the years have persisted in producing papers and policies examining the barriers to an ill-defined notion of integration. Chapter Three showed that post-war immigration from former colonial countries was met with much hostility, despite the migrants filling labour needs. Settlement was in inner cities or northern town where the jobs were. White flight from areas where minorities settled was highest during the later 1960s, but by the 1970s those remaining in the area did mostly so for economic reasons. If employment disappeared they would still be there because of friends and relatives and low-cost housing.

A plethora of government and academic literature on the themes of assimilation, integration and living in culturally plural societies appeared, much of it naive and lacking a historical context. Eventually the language of integration became the favourite way of complaining that black and minority ethnic groups and recent migrants were reluctant to be absorbed into what was assumed to be a homogeneous majority culture and way of life. The 2011 Census showed 81% living in the country defining themselves as White British, with 5.4% White Irish or White Other, 7.1% Asian, 3.1% Black, 2% Mixed Race and 0.9% Other. Most settled minority citizens lived in London, Manchester and the West Midlands and also in northern towns, where owners of textile mills had used their labour and then closed the mills if they became unprofitable. The settlement of newer migrants and refugees was largely determined by government policies of dispersal, to Glasgow and Gloucester, for example, while EU migrant workers went where the work was – potato picking in Lincolnshire – or moved into urban areas where other minorities lived in low-cost housing. The familiar complaints surfaced continually over the years, that migrants took jobs, houses, medical services and overwhelmed schools. By the early 21st century and after the events of 9/11 in the USA, particular hostility was directed at Muslim communities, and, as Tahir Abbas noted, politicians, the media and public views across the political spectrum blamed Muslims for cultural separatism and self-imposed segregation (Abbas, 2005). The idea spread that 'politically correct' multiculturalism had fostered fragmentation rather than integration and 'Britishness'.

The successive reports blaming minorities for segregation continued to lack background history or mention of the great white ghetto that comprised most of Britain. Riots in northern towns in 2001 were blamed on Asian segregation in the reports by Ted Cantle and others, and in 2005 Cantle set up an Institute for Community Cohesion and the iCoCo Foundation, which was claimed as the leading authority on community cohesion. In 2016, at the instigation of David Cameron, Dame Louise Casey published a review, *Opportunity and integration* (Casey, 2016), which again, with no historical context, complained that people felt overwhelmed by demographic shifts in their communities and blamed harmful community practices and possible terrorism. Communities with poor English and not enough adherence to 'British values' were blamed again. In 2017, Ted Cantle, worried that the government had not responded to the Casey Review, chaired another group reporting on *Integration and demonisation* (APPG, 2017). His All-Party Parliamentary Group included Chukku Umunna MP and the Bishop of Oxford, and it acknowledged that demonisation and xenophobia were impediments to integration. The government eventually responded to the Casey Review with a Controlling Migration Fund, and in 2018, produced yet another *Integrated communities strategy Green Paper* (HM Government, 2018). Sajid Javid, then Housing, Communities and Local Government Minister, complained in a Foreword that his Pakistani mother and elderly ladies like her could not speak English. This report also noted that there was a lack of social mixing, high unemployment among minorities, with more of them in prisons, as a report by David Lammy MP had indicated, and there was a need to promote 'the values that unite us'. Evidence seemed to suggest that these values were more connected to exclusion, xenophobia and racism than to democracy, tolerance and even the rule of law.

Windrush and a hostile environment again

It was noted in Chapter Eight that in 2010 Theresa May was appointed Home Secretary, and Prime Minister Cameron decided that 'a tough stance on immigration was a flagship party offering'. Although this had been party policy for years, it was enthusiastically taken up by May (Malik, 2018). In 2012, she promised to create a 'really hostile environment' to illegal migration and reduce legal migration to what became a mantra of 'the tens of thousands'. As noted, she insisted on counting international students as immigrants, insisting that many did not return home after their studies. Even when research demonstrated that 97% of university students coming to study did return to their home countries, she continued this policy. But immigration Acts in 2014 and 2016 fuelled a hostile environment, with policies restricting healthcare, bank accounts, renting, marriage and other rights for suspected illegal migrants, with landlords, doctors and NHS staff, teachers, vicars and others expected to check on immigration status. Schools were told in December 2016 to record the nationality and birthplace of migrant, refugee and asylum-seeking children, although they were told the information would not be sent to the Home Office. Campaign groups challenged this and eventually the DfE announced collection would cease in September 2019, but the collected data retained. Immigration detention increased, but 40% of appeals to immigration judges against detention were successful.

All this helped fuel a scandal when it became clear that many people without regular documentation, which included Caribbean arrivals as children of the Windrush generation, had been targeted for deportation. The issue was raised in 2013 in response to a parliamentary question and the government admitted that there was a problem with undocumented migrants (Gentleman, 2018a). By April 2018, the treatment of many of the Windrush generation was reported daily in the media. Cases included the denial of cancer treatment to a man who had lived and worked in England for 44 years, and the attempted deportation of a woman who had lived in the country for 50 years and who worked as a cook in the House of Commons (Gentleman, 2018b).

It emerged that people who had arrived as children from Jamaica had been deported if they had no regular documentation. In 2016, The Jamaican *Gleaner* reported that over 9,000 people had been sent back to the island, mainly from the UK. A National Organisation for Deported Migrants (NODP) had been set up in Jamaica in 2016, supported by the British High Commission, and booklets given to deported arrivals (to a country they had never lived in) with such nonsensical instructions as, 'try to speak Jamaican' and 'keep your wallet safe' (Saunders, 2016). As noted, the Home Office had actually destroyed thousands of landing cards and other documents of Caribbean migrants that would have proved entitlement to citizenship (Roundtree, 2018). Amber Rudd MP, appointed Home Secretary after May became Prime Minister, first denied the Home Office had targets for deportation, and then had to resign after admitting she had misled Parliament over deportation targets (McCann and Mendick, 2018). She issued an apology for the 'appalling actions' of her own Department towards those deported. Sajid Javid was appointed Home Secretary in her place, and together with the Prime Minister, attended an annual day of celebrations for the Windrush generation and their descendants in Westminster Abbey on 22 June. Despite all this, a YouGov poll in the last week of April 2018 found a majority of those polled supported a 'hostile environment' policy towards immigrants (Nevett, 2018). Rudd was returned to government as Work and Pensions Secretary in October 2018.

Schools, universities and the curriculum

In 1969 two Americans published a book, *Teaching as a subversive activity* (Postman and Weingartner, 1969) in which they described American education at the time as like 'driving a multimillion pound car and screaming faster, faster, while peering into the rear-view mirror'. This possibly describes the current English school curriculum in both state and private schooling, albeit with some valiant attempts by heads and teachers to create the subversive strategies. Chapter One of this book noted that a curriculum at all levels in education is mainly the product of the values and decisions of dominant social and political groups.

The curriculum from the 1980s, and especially from 2010, had largely become a vehicle for government-approved learning, obsessed with a traditional model of transmitting approved 'knowledge'. In 2018 A-level History candidates were presented with a module in which post-war history began in 1951 and ended in 1997, thus missing out the Attlee government's creation of the welfare state and ending before the first Blair government (Abrams, 2018). The curriculum was in no way changed to overcome the dishonest presentation of a history of colonialism and its consequences, or relationships with Europe and the rest of the world. Book publishers realised from the 1980s that books should include some minority characters, but it was found in 2018 that only 1% of children's books had a main black or minority character (Flood, 2018). While there is limited research on how Michael Gove's curriculum, imposed in 2013, has affected schools, the consequences can be assessed by examining the views of students in higher education who have experienced the recent curriculum. To date, the picture is bleak. The Director of the South Asian Centre at the LSE noted that:

> Students arrive at university completely ignorant about the Empire, that vital part of history. When we talk of Syria they have no knowledge of Britain's role in the Middle East over the last century ... they have no clue about the history of immigration. They don't understand why people of other ethnicities came to Britain in the first place, they haven't learned about it in school. (Mohsin, 2016)

Perhaps this is why 32 medical students were suspended at Cardiff University in 2017 for performing in a play that mocked one of their lecturers by blacking up and wearing a dildo, portraying him as a 'stereotypical hyper-sexualised black man'. When African students complained, they were told they were being unduly sensitive (Morris, 2017). The university produced a report that included the familiar rhetoric that issues relating to equality and diversity were taken very seriously. At the University of Exeter a law student posted screenshots of his fellow law students calling people 'paki' and 'nigga sluts', and signs saying 'Rights for

Whites' had been found on the campus (Motavali, 2018). Those Nottingham students chanting 'We hate Blacks' and 'Sign the Brexit papers' were noted in Chapter Eight. In May 2018, 11 students at the University of Warwick were suspended for their rape and racist 'jokes' made on a Facebook Chat. These included comments such as 'Rape 100 girls' and 'Love Hitler … hate Jews and Corbyn' (Bushey, 2018). Comments on the incidents by other students included claims that free speech was being eroded, as private conversations were being criticised.

Not all students have succumbed to such stupidity, although objecting to a racist past or present would never be easy. Attempts by students at Oxford to remove the statue of Cecil Rhodes from Oriel College and at Cambridge to return a golden cockerel stolen from Nigeria were frowned on by the university administrations. Suggestions that the English curriculum at Cambridge could be 'decolonised' by including a diversity of literature was met with racist and sexist abuse, especially directed at Lola Olufemi, the Cambridge Student Union woman's officer, with *The Daily Telegraph* claiming white authors would be replaced by black authors (Khomami and Watts, 2017). At least the *National Geographic* magazine acknowledged, on the 50th anniversary of the assassination of Martin Luther King Jr in the USA, that in the past its coverage of black and minority ethnic groups had been historically racist, by promoting caricatures of the noble savage and presenting 'White teenage boys with pictures of brown bare breasts', with Westerners always fully clothed (Greenfield, 2018).

During the Brexit negotiations there was apparently some suspicion in government that universities were actually discussing Europe and the vote to leave the EU. Chris Heaton-Harris, MP for Daventry and a former MEP and chair from 2010-16 of the Eurosceptic European Research group, wrote to all university vice-chancellors in the UK. He wanted to know the names of academics lecturing on Brexit. His request was described by Lord Patten, Chancellor of the University of Oxford, as 'idiotic and offensive Leninism', and no vice-chancellors obliged (*Private Eye*, 2018). In July 2018, after the Brexit Secretary David Davis and his Deputy resigned, Dominic Raab was appointed as the new Brexit Secretary with Heaton-Harris as his Deputy.[9] Raab resigned in November 2018 and a third Brexit Secretary was appointed.

Summary

This book has mainly covered the period from the height of the British Empire in the 1880s to late 2018. The withdrawal from the EU in June 2016, known as 'Brexit', was due to take effect in March 2019, with a proposed two-year transitional period. On 10 December Prime Minister May told Parliament that she was delaying a vote on a Withdrawal from the EU Bill, and returned to discussions with other European leaders. Trying to understand the past and present entails reading social and imperial history, economics, politics and policy-making, education policy, and literature on developments in education, race and ethnicity. The persistence of post-imperial ideologies and claims that a post-Brexit future will 'give us back our island roots' and make Britain 'Great' again are directed at populations already ageing, angry at their economic situation, and willing to blame immigrants and 'foreigners' for their situation. Whatever kind of Brexit is agreed, a hard crash out of the EU, a softer landing with some trade, borders and other relationships agreed on, or even a change of mind about leaving, there is certainly agreement that, since the referendum, government over the past two years has been chaotic and driven more by political self-interest than for the good of the country. By the end of July 2018, *Telegraph* journalist Booker referred to 'the glaring shambles that is the Brexit negotiations' (Booker, 2018). *Financial Times* writer Stephens wrote that 'Today's nostalgia (for the past) has become an engine of nationalism, it thrives on the economic and cultural insecurities thrown up by globalisation, we look backwards for a safe identity' (Stephens, 2018). This identity would be the white identity of the 1950s with its assumptions that immigrants and foreigners were somehow responsible for social and economic ills. Dire predictions for the future have been raised, with suggestions for stock-piling food and medicine in the event of a 'hard Brexit' (Jack, 2018), and Timothy Garton-Ash writing that, 'Over the next year or two we could witness the emergence of a rancid angry Britain, riven by domestic divisions and economic difficulties, let down by its ruling classes and fetid with humiliation and resentment' (Garton-Ash, 2018).

There have been limited attempts over the years to develop a more realistic education system that presents young people with the truths of the past and present of Britain's position in the world, and leaves behind the whitewashing of the past. Myths and misinformation still imbue the curricula in schools and higher education. Those in government, their advisers and their academic supporters persist with this. The ideological commitment of those currently in power prevents any serious questioning or debate on what kind of future there will be for Britain in a post-Brexit world, in which popularism, nationalism and protectionism in trade are challenging democracy and global engagement.

The overt racism and xenophobia, always there but unleashed after the Brexit vote, will continue to damage the country unless governments work towards a democratic and inclusive country. No amount of teaching questionable 'British values' will prevent scepticism about whose values are being promoted. There is no future in continuing to blame minorities and migrant workers for taking jobs, taking unemployment benefit when they lose their jobs, taking low-cost housing, sending their children to schools in the area they live in, and refusing to 'Go home'. There is no future in encouraging some working-class voters or elderly Tory voters to believe that their lives would improve if only immigrants would disappear. As long as ignorance of the past and the presentation of a mythological future are perpetuated by a fragmented, divisive, unchanged education system, and by politicians who are in disagreement over the future good of their country, a Britain without an Empire will not be 'Great' any more. Outside a European Union as a third country, Britain will be globally diminished.

Notes

[1] The EU European Court of Justice (EJC) is often confused with the European Court of Human Rights (ECHR). The latter is overseen by a Council for Europe, founded in 1949 after a suggestion by Winston Churchill that all countries in Europe should work more closely together. There are currently 47 member states. The Council for Europe oversees

a European Court of Human Rights enforcing a European Convention on Human Rights. The EU, which has 28 members (27 after Brexit), oversees the EJC.

[2] Events between 2013 and 2017 are documented in a timeline in Tim Shipman's two books (Shipman, 2016, 2017).

[3] *The Guardian* newspaper reported on 11 December that 'Theresa May is to embark on a frantic round of European diplomacy in a final attempt to salvage her Brexit deal and her premiership' (Sabbagh and Boffey, 2018).

[4] In 2014, a school in Cardiff, with its funding cut and the head having to close the club that fed children who came without breakfast, stayed open because the 'dinner ladies' on low wages themselves decided to pay for the breakfast food out of their own money (McInch, 2018).

[5] Several dozen books quickly appeared in bookshops in the years following Brexit. See, for example, Bennett (2016), Clegg (2017), Macshane (2017), Seidler (2018) and Dorling and Tomlinson (2019).

[6] In 2017 the Paradise Papers, a series of documents held by a law firm in Panama, showing the use of tax havens by wealthy people, including many Conservative ministers and party donors, were leaked to newspapers. Beneficiaries of those finding (legal) ways to minimise their tax payments in the UK by using off-shore accounts included David Cameron's father, Philip May, Arron Banks, Michael Ashcroft, Jacob Rees-Mogg, and many others (Garside et al, 2017).

[7] The importance of security links with the EU were demonstrated when, in March 2018, a former Russian spy living in Salisbury, England, was poisoned with a nerve gas thought to come from Russia. Eventually, after requests from the British government, the EU did condemn the poisoning and recalled the EU ambassador from Russia, with other countries following suit.

[8] Some of the organisations collecting evidence of racism and xenophobia were the Oxford Centre Compass, the Institute of Race Relations, The Runnymede Trust, Tell Mama, Stop Hate UK, True Vision, Breaking Views and the *Huffington Post*.

[9] In 2012, Dominic Raab co-authored *Britannia unchained: Global lessons for growth and prosperity* (Kwarteng et al, 2012). The book claimed that British workers were the worst idlers in the world, and that small business owners should be exempt from paying the Minimum Wage. He also chaired the Eurosceptic European Research Group.

References

Abbas, T. (ed) (2005) *Muslim Britain: Communities under pressure*, London: Zed Books

Abrams, F. (2018) 'A-levels: If history starts in 1951 did the Tories "blue-wash" the syllabus', *The Guardian* (Education), 19 June

Adonis, A. (2012) *Education, education, education. Reforming England's schools*, London: Biteback

Ainley, P. (2001) 'From a national system locally administered to a national system nationally administered: The new Leviathan in education and training', *Journal of Social Policy*, 30, 457-76

Akomaning, L. (2018) 'The educational experiences of young people of Ghanaian origin in England', PhD thesis, Chelmsford: Anglia Ruskin University

Albright, M. (2018) *Fascism: A warning*, New York and London: William Collins

Allen, G. (2011) *Early intervention, smart investment, massive savings, The second report from Graham Allen MP*, London: HM Government

APPG (All-Party Parliamentary Group on Community Cohesion) (2017) *Integration and demonisation, Report of the APPG on Community Cohesion*, London: House of Commons

Apple, M. (1999) 'The absent presence of race in educational reform', *Race, Ethnicity and Education*, 2, 1, 9-16

Archbishop of Canterbury (1985) *Faith in the city*, London: Church House Publishing

Ashcroft, M. and Oakshotte, I. (2012) *Call me Dave: The unauthorised biography of David Cameron*, London: Biteback

Aspden, P. (2018) 'The art of war', *Financial Times* (Life and Arts FT Weekend), 7 July

Astbury, K. and Plomin, R. (2014) *G is for genes: The impact of genetics on education and achievement*, London: Wiley

Asthana, A. and Salter, J. (2006) 'Campus storm over racist Don', *The Observer*, 5 March

Atkinson, A.B. (2018) *Inequality: What can be done?*, Cambridge, MA: Harvard University Press

Attlee, C. (1961) *Empire into Commonwealth* (The Chicele Lectures), Oxford: Oxford University Press

Avon NUT (National Union of Teachers) (1980) *After the fire*, Bristol: NUT

Ball, S.J. (2007) *Education plc*, London: Routledge

Barber, M. (1995) 'The school that had to die', *Times Educational Supplement*, 17 November

Barber, M. (1996) *The learning game*, London: Gollanz

Barber, M. (2001) 'High expectations and standards for all, no matter what: Creating a world class education service in England', in M. Fielding (ed) *Taking education really seriously: Four years hard labour*, London: Routledge Falmer

Barnett, A. (2018) 'How to win the Brexit civil war: An open letter to my fellow remainers', *Open Democracy*, 6 June

BBC Four (2018) [television] *The women who saved the NHS*, 2 July

BBC News (2002) 'Blunkett stands by "swamping" remark', Politics

Beck, U. (2000) *What is globalisation?*, Malden, MA: Polity Press

Beck, U. (2016) *The metamorphosis of the world*, Cambridge: Polity Press

Beckett, F. (2007) *The great city academy fraud*, London: Continuum

Benewick, R. (1969) *Political violence and public order*, London: Allen Lane

Benn, C. and Chitty, C. (1996) *Thirty years on*, London: David Fulton

Benn, T. (1994) *Years of hope 1940-1962*, London: Arrow

Bennett, O. (2016) *The Brexit club*, London: Biteback

Best, N. (1979) *Happy Valley: The story of the English in Kenya*, London: Secker & Warburg Ltd

Bew, J. (2016) *Citizen Clem: A biography*, London: Riverrun Press

Bhambra, G.K. and Narayan, J. (eds) (2016) *European cosmopolitanism: Colonial histories and post-colonial societies*, London: Routledge

Bhopal, K. (2018) *White privilege*, Bristol: Policy Press

Bishop, A.J. (1993) 'Culturizing mathematics teaching', in A.S. King and M.J. Reiss (eds) *The multicultural dimension of the National Curriculum*, London: Falmer Press, 32-48

Blair, T. (1996) Twentieth Anniversary Lecture, Oxford: Ruskin College, University of Oxford

Blair, T. (1997a) Speech to the Labour Party Conference, Brighton, October

Blair, T. (1997b) Speech to the European Socialists Congress, Malmö, Sweden, 6 June

Blair, T. (1998) *The third way: New politics for a new century*, Pamphlet no 588, London: The Fabian Society

Blair, T. (1999) The Prime Minister's New Year Speech, given at Trimdon Community Centre, Durham, County Durham, 29 December

Blair, T. (2003) Speech at meeting with President George Bush, The White House, Washington, DC, 31 January

Blair, T. (2007) Resignation speech, Trimdon, Sedgefield, 10 March

Blair, T. (2010) *A journey*, London: Hutchinson

Blair, T. (2011) 'Blaming a moral decline for the riots makes good headlines but bad policy', *The Observer*, 21 August

Bloom, J. (2017) 'Free trade area, single market, customs union – what's the difference?', BBC Business News, 14 August

Blunkett, D. (2014) *Education structures, funding, and raising standards for all*, Policy Review, London: Labour Party

Board of Education (1927) *Report of the Consultative Committee on the education of the adolescent* (The Hadow Report), London: HMSO

Booker, C. (2018) 'The last word: The ever more glaring shambles that is the Brexit negotiations is now entering its dog days', *The Sunday Telegraph*, 24 June

Booth, M. (1993) 'The foundation subjects: History', in A.S. King and M.J. Reiss (eds) *The multicultural dimension of the National Curriculum*, London: Falmer Press, 78-90

Booth, R. (2017) 'The Ambassador, Kipling and Johnson', *The Guardian*, 30 September

Boulton, A. (2008) *Tony's ten years. Memoirs of the Blair administration*, London: Simon & Schuster

Bourke, D. and MacBride, I. (2016) *The Princeton history of modern Ireland*, Princeton, NJ: Princeton University Press

Bower, T. (2016) *Broken vows: The tragedy of power*, London: Faber & Faber

Boyle, F. (2015) 'Britain's criminally stupid attitudes to race and immigration are beyond parody', *The Guardian* (Comment is Free), 20 April

Brace, A. (1994) 'Is this the worst school in Britain?', *The Mail on Sunday*, 20 March

Breathnach, D. (2018) 'White Paper, A starting point for meaningful Brexit negotiations', Statement by Declan Breathnach, Ireland Spokesperson for North-South Bodies and Cross-Border Co-operation, Dublin, Ireland

Bratton, J.S. (1986) 'Of England, home and duty: The image of England in Victorian and Edwardian juvenile literature', in J.M. MacKenzie (ed) *Imperialism and popular culture*, Manchester: Manchester University Press, 73-93

Brendon, P. (2007) *The decline and fall of the British Empire 1781-1997*, London: Jonathan Cape

Bright, M. (1999) 'The loves and lies of Chris Woodhead', *The Guardian*, 11 April

British trades alphabet (1955) London

Brown, G. (2017) *My life, our times*, London: The Bodley Head

Brown, P., Lauder, H. and Ashton, D. (2011) *The global auction: The broken promises of education, jobs and income*, Oxford: Oxford University Press

Bull, G. (translator) (1961) Niccolo Machiavelli *The Prince*, London: Penguin Books

Bullock Report (1975) *A language for life: Report of the Committee of Inquiry into the teaching of reading and other uses of English*, London: HMSO

Burnham, A. (2016) Speech to House of Commons, 7 December

Burroughs, E.T. (1919) *Tarzan the untamed*, London: Methuen

Bushey, E. (2018) 'University of Warwick suspends 11 students over rape jokes and racist slurs', *The Independent*, 9 May

Cameron, D. (2011) Speech given in Witney constituency, Witney, Oxfordshire, 15 August

Cameron, D. (2013) Speech on the European Union, given in the Headquarters of the Bloomberg Company, London, 23 January

Cameron, D. and Clegg, N. (2010) 'Foreword by the Prime Minister and Deputy Prime Minister', *The importance of teaching*, Cmd 7980, London: Department for Education

Campbell, A. and Stott, R. (eds) (2007) *The Blair years: Extracts from the Alastair Campbell diaries*, London: Hutchinson

Campbell, D. (2006) 'Low IQs are Africa's curse, says lecturer', *The Observer*, 5 November

Cannadine, D., Keatman, J. and Sheldon, N. (2011) *The right kind of history: Teaching the past in twentieth century England*, London: Palgrave Macmillan

Cantle, T. (2001) *Community cohesion: Report of the Independent Review* Team (The Cantle Report), London: Home Office

Casey, Dame L. (2016) *Review into opportunity and integration*, London: Department for Communities and Local Government

Castle, S. (1993) 'Major says three in Cabinet are "bastards"', *The Independent*, 24 July

Castle, S. (2017) 'Defence Secretary quits over inappropriate conduct', *The New York Times*, 1 November

CEA (Conservative Education Association) (1992) *Choice and diversity: The CEA response to the White Paper*, London

Centre for Contemporary Cultural Studies (1982) *The Empire strikes back*, London: Hutchinson

Centre for Social Justice (2006) *Breakdown Britain*, London

Chakrabortty, A. (2016) 'After a campaign scarred by bigotry it is now OK to be racist in Britain', *The Guardian*, 28 June

Chantiluke, R., Kwoba, B. and Nkopo, A. (2018) *Rhodes must fall: The struggle to tear out the racist heart of Empire*, London: Zed Books

CIAC (Commonwealth Immigrants Advisory Committee) (1964) *Third report*, Cmd 2458, London: HMSO

Civitas (2007) *The corruption of the curriculum*, London

Clarendon Commission (1864) *Report of the Public Schools Commission* (4 vols), London: HM Government

Clark, A. (2018) 'Shared experience', *The Observer*, 4 February

Clarke, H. (2016) *Norman England 1066-circa 1100,* AQA GCSE History, Banbury: Hodder Education

Clarke, K. (2016) *A kind of blue: A political memoir*, London: Macmillan

Clegg, N. (2017) *How to stop Brexit*, London: The Bodley Head

Coard, B. (1971) *How the West Indian child is made ESN in the British school system*, London: New Beacon Books [reprinted in Richardson, 2005]

Cobain, I. (2016) *The history thieves: Secrets, lies and the shaping of a modern nation*, London: Portobello

Cobain, I. (2017) 'Files on Britain's most controversial episodes vanish from archives', *The Guardian*, 26 December

Cole, M (2018) 'Racism in the UK: Continuity and change', in M. Cole (ed) *Education, equality and human rights: Issues of gender, 'race', sexuality, disability and social class* (4th edn), London and New York: Routledge

Colenso, J.W. (1892) *Arithmetic: Designed for the use of schools* (2nd edn), London: Longman Green & Co

Collingham, L. (2017) *The hungry empire: How Britain's quest for food shaped the modern world*, London: The Bodley Head

Connolly, S.J. (2007) *The Oxford companion to Irish history*, Oxford: Oxford University Press

Cooke, A. (2014) 'Enoch Powell and Ulster', in Lord Howard of Rising (ed) *Enoch at 100: A revaluation of the life, politics and philosophy of Enoch Powell*, London: Biteback, 251-73

Cosslett, R.L. (2017) 'How sad that English-speaking parents fear their children being taught in Welsh', *The Guardian*, 27 June

Coupland, R. (1954) *Welsh and Scottish nationalism*, London: Collins

Cox, B. (1991) *Cox on Cox: An English curriculum for the 1990s*, London: Hodder & Stoughton

Cox, C.B. and Boyson, R. (1977) *Black Paper 1977*, London: Temple-Smith

Craig, G. (2007) *Sure Start and Black and ethnic minority populations*, Nottingham: DfES Publications

CRE (Commission for Racial Equality) (1988) *Learning in terror: A survey of racial harassment in schools and colleges*, London

Crick, B. (1998) *Education for citizenship and the teaching of democracy in schools, Report of an Advisory Group on Citizenship*, London: Department for Education and Skills

Crossman, R. (1975) *The diaries of a Cabinet Minister 1964-70*, London: Hamish Hamilton and Cape

Crouch, C. (2003) *Commercialisation or citizenship: Education policies and the future of public services*, Fabian Ideas 606, London: The Fabian Society

Cummings, D. (2013) 'Some thoughts on education and political priority', Paper presented to the Secretary of State for Education, London, October

Currie, E. (2002) *Diaries 1987-1992*, London: Biteback

Curtis, L.P. (1968) *Anglo-Saxons and Celts*, Bridgeport, CT: Bridgeport Press

Dalrymple, W. (2015) 'The original corporate raiders', *The Guardian*, 4 March

D'Ancona, M. (2009) *Being British: The search for values that bind a nation*, London: Transworld Publications

Darling, A. (2011) *Back from the brink*, London: Atlantic Books

Davies, N. (2014) *Hack attack: How the truth caught up with Rupert Murdoch*, London: Chatto & Windus

DCSF (Department for Children, Schools and Families) (2007) *The Children's Plan: Building brighter futures*, London: The Stationery Office

Department for Exiting the European Union (2018) *The future relationship between the United Kingdom and the European Union*, White Paper, London: Cabinet Office

Derbyshire, H. (1994) *Not in Norfolk: Tackling the invisibility of racism*, Norwich: Norfolk and Norwich Racial Equality Council

DES (Department of Education and Science) (1965) *The education of immigrants*, Circular 7/65, London: HMSO

DES (1971) *The education of immigrants. Education Survey 13*, London: HMSO

DES (1974) *Educational disadvantage and the needs of immigrants*, London: HMSO

DES (1977) *Education in schools: A consultative document*, London: HMSO

DES (1978) *Special educational needs: Report of a Committee of Inquiry into the education of handicapped children and young people* (The Warnock Report), London: HMSO

DES (1981) *West Indian children in our schools* (The Rampton Report), London: HMSO

DES (1985) *Better schools*, Cmd 9469, London: HMSO

DES (1991a) *Draft orders for the National Curriculum in geography*, London

DES (1991b) *History in the National Curriculum (England)*, London

DfE (Department for Education) (1992) *Choice and diversity: A new framework for schools*, London

DfE (2010) *The importance of teaching*, Cmd 7980, London

DfE (2014) *Promoting British values as part of SMSC (social, cultural, spiritual and moral values) in schools*, London

DfE (2016) *Educational excellence for all*, London

DfES (Department for Education and Skills) (2004) *Curriculum and qualifications reform 14-19: Final report* (Mike Tomlinson Report), Nottingham

DoE (Department of the Environment)/Home Office (2003) *The Victoria Climbié Inquiry, Report of an inquiry by Lord Laming*, London: The Stationery Office

Donegan, L. (1995) 'Muslim leaders warn of other cities on verge of violence as police give up', *The Guardian*, 16 October

Dorling, D. (2010) *Injustice: Why social inequality persists*, Bristol: Policy Press

Dorling, D. (2014) *Inequality and the 1%*, London: Verso

Dorling, D. (2017) *The equality effect: Improving life for everyone*, Oxford: New Internationalist Publications

Dorling, D. (2018) *Peak inequality: Britain's ticking time bomb*, Bristol: Policy Press

Dorling, D. and Thomas, B. (2016) *People and places: A 21st century atlas of the UK*, Bristol: Policy Press

Dorling, D. and Tomlinson, S. (2017) 'Is Corbyn as lacking in drive and personality as Attlee? Let's hope so', *The Guardian*, 9 May

Dorling, D. and Tomlinson, S. (2019) *Rule Brittania: Brexit and the end of Empire*, London: Biteback

Dorras, J. and Walker, P. (1988) 'Two-way culture shock', *Times Educational Supplement*, 19 February

Duncan Smith, I. (2012) 'Foreword', in Lord Howard of Rising (ed) *Enoch at 100: A re-examination of the life, politics and philosophy of Enoch Powell*, London: Biteback, xvii–xxiii

Eddo-Lodge, R. (2017) *Why I'm no longer talking about race*, London: Bloomsbury

Egerton Commission (1889) *Report of the Royal Commission on the blind, deaf, dumb and others, of the United Kingdom* (4 vols), London: HMSO

Elgot, J. (2018) 'How May's "hostile environment" for migrants brought anguish to a generation with every right to live their lives in Britain', *The Guardian*, 18 April

Elliot, L. and Atkinson, D. (2007) *Fantasy island: Waking up to the incredible economic, political and social illusions of the Blair legacy*, London: Constable

Elliot-Major, L. (2011) 'Do wrongs make a riot', *Society Now*, Autumn

Eminent Persons Group (2011) *Report of the Eminent Persons Group to the Commonwealth Heads of Governments*, Commonwealth Secretariat, Perth, Scotland, October

Evans, A. (2017) 'Evans apologises for wife's racist outburst at referee', *The Guardian*, 11 November

Evans, R. and Lewis, P (2013) 'Their son was killed by racists. So why did the police spy on them?', *The Guardian*, 24 June

Eysenck, H.J. (1971) *Race, intelligence and education*, London: Temple Smith

Faith in the City (1985) Report of the Archbishop of Canterbury's Commission, London: Church House

Faux, F. (2017) 'How Gove's "brain flip" poisoned the extremist debate', *The Guardian*, 4 July

Fawcett, R. (ed) (1948) *Empire Youth Annual 1948*, London: P.R. Gawthorne Ltd

Ferguson, N. (2004) *Empire: How Britain made the modern world*, London: Penguin

Field, F. (1990) 'Britain's underclass: Countering the growth', in C. Murray (ed) *The emerging British underclass*, London: IEA Health and Welfare Unit, Institute for Economic Affairs, 37-42

Finnemore, J. (1902) *Men of renown: King Alfred to Lord Kitchener*, London: A & C Black [2nd edn, 1916]

Fletcher, C.R.L. and Kipling, R. (1911) *School history of England*, Oxford: Oxford University Press

Flood, A. (2018) 'Only 1% of children's books have BAME main characters, study finds', *The Guardian*, 17 July

Foot, P. (1969) *Immigration and race in British politics*, Harmondsworth: Penguin

Francis, M. (2011) '2011 Prevent Strategy', London: HM Government (www.radicalisationresearch.org/research/2011/)

Fremeaux, J. and Maas, G. (2015) 'Colonization and globalisation', in K. Nicolaïdis, B. Sèbe and G. Maas (eds) *Echoes of empire: Memory, identity and colonial legacies*, London and New York: I.B. Tauris, 383–92

Fryer, P. (1984) *Staying power: The history of Black people in Britain*, London: Pluto Press

Galton, F. (1869) *Hereditary genius*, London: Macmillan

Gardiner, J. (1997) 'Blunkett to continue shaming', *Times Educational Supplement*, 14 November

Garside, J., Osborne, H. and MacAskill, E. (2017) 'The loud voices of the Brexit campaign who put their money offshore', *The Guardian*, 10 November

Garton-Ash, T. (2018) 'A humiliating deal risks descent into Weimar Britain', *The Guardian* (Journal), 27 July

Gaskell, E. (1855) *North and South* [1995 edn published by Penguin Books, London]

Gaythorne-Hardy, D. (1977) *The public school phenomenon*, London: Hodder & Stoughton

Gearon, L. (2015) 'Education, security and intelligence studies', *British Journal of Educational Studies*, 63, 3, 263–79

Geddes, A. (2013) *Britain and the European Union*, London: Palgrave Macmillan

Gentleman, A. (2010) 'Life on the edge', *The Guardian* (Society), 11 April

Gentleman, A. (2018a) 'Warnings of Windrush scandal date back to 2013', *The Guardian*, 19 July

Gentleman, A. (2018b) 'Rudd tells MPs: we were wrong over Windrush citizens', 'Rudd's U-turn. At last, an end to the staggering heartlessness', *The Guardian*, 17 April

Gibbon, E. (1781) *The history of the decline and fall of the Roman Empire* (6 vols, 1776-1788) [cited in Brendon, 2007, using the 1994 edition, Penguin, Harmondsworth]

Giddens, A. (2007) *Over to you, Mr Brown*, Cambridge: Polity Press

Gillborn, D. (2007) 'Tony Blair and the politics of race in education', *Oxford Review of Education*, 34, 6, 713–25

Gillborn, D. (2010) 'The white working class: Racism and respectability: Victim, degenerates and interest convergence', *British Journal of Educational Studies*, 58, 1, 2-25

Gillborn, D., Demack, S., Rollock, N. and Warmington, P. (2017) 'Moving the goalposts: 25 years of the Black/White achievement gap', *British Educational Research Journal*, 43, 5, 848-74

Gilley, B. (2017) 'The case for colonialism', *Third World Quarterly*, 15 August

Gilroy, P. (1987) *There ain't no Black in the Union Jack*, London: Hutchinson

Gilroy, P. (2004) *After Empire: Melancholia or convivial culture*, London: Routledge

Goldberg, D.T. (2009) *The threat of race: Reflections on racial neoliberalism*, Malden, MA and Oxford: Wiley-Blackwell

Goodhart, D. (2004) 'The discomfort of strangers', *The Guardian*, 24 February

Goodhart, D. (2017) *The road to somewhere: The populist revolt and the future of politics*, London: Hurst

Gould, S.J. (1981) *The mismeasure of man*, London: Penguin Books

Gove, M. (2006) *Celsius 7/7: How the West's policy of appeasement has provoked more fundamental terror and what is to be done*, London: Weidenfield & Nicolson

Gove, M. (2013a) Speech to the Social Market Foundation, London, 23 August

Gove, M. (2013b) 'I refuse to surrender to the Marxist teachers who are hell-bent on destroying our schools; Education Secretary berates "the new enemies of promise" for opposing his plans', *Mail Online*, 23 March

Graham, D. with Tytler, D. (1993) *A lesson for us all: The making of the National Curriculum*, London: Routledge

Greenfield, P. (2018) 'National Geographic admits racist reports', *The Guardian*, 14 March

Guest, A. (1910) 'Social ideals: The Earl of Meath', *Court Journal*, 16 February

Hall, S. (ed) (1978) *Policing the crisis*, London: Macmillan

Hall, S. (1991) 'Old and new identities; old and new ethnicities', in A. King (ed) *Culture, globalisation and the world system*, London: Macmillan

Hansard (1992) Cols 149-202, London: House of Commons

Hare, D. (2016) 'Like all revolutions, it will eat its own', *The Guardian*, 2 July

Hargreaves, D. (1993) 'Preface', in S.A. King and M.J. Reiss (eds) *The multicultural dimension of the National Curriculum*, London: Falmer Press

Hastings, M. (2007) 'Premiership of Tony Blair tainted with mendacity', *The Guardian*, 12 April

Hattenstone, S. (2018) 'Why was the scheme behind May's "Go Home" vans called Operation Vaken', *The Guardian*, 16 April

Hattersley, R. (2005) 'Even Enoch Powell did not stoke fears like this', *The Guardian*, 25 April

Hawkes, N. (2012) 'Nicolas Hawkes 1955-1957', in C. Shindler, *National Service*, London: Sphere

Hayward, K. and Komarova, M. (2018) 'Brexit on the border', QEB Institute for Peace, Security and Justice Belfast, Belfast: Queen Elizabeth University

Heath, E. (1970) Letter to Bexley Community Relations Council, Bexley, Kent, June

Heath, D. (2010) *Purifying Empire*, Cambridge: Cambridge University Press

Hechter, M. (1975) *Internal colonialism: The Celtic fringe in British national development 1536-1966*, London: Routledge & Kegan Paul

Henderson, J. (2017) Video of interviews with adults bussed as children in Huddersfield in the 1960s, Huddersfield: University of Huddersfield

Hennig, B. and Dorling, D. (2016) 'The EU Referendum: Political insights', *The Spectator*, 1 September

Herbertson, A.J. (1910) *Commercial geography of the world*, Edinburgh: W & R Chambers [2nd edn, 1916]

Herrnstein, R. and Murray, C. (1994) *The bell curve: Intelligence and class structure in American life*, New York: Free Press

Hirsch, A. (2018) *Brit(ish): On race, identity and belonging*, London: Jonathan Cape

HM Government (2018) *Integrated communities strategy: Building stronger more united communities*, Green Paper, London: Department for Communities and Local Government

Hobsbawm, E. and Ranger, T. (1983) *The invention of tradition*, Cambridge: Cambridge University Press

Holmwood, J. and O'Toole, T. (2014) *Countering extremism in British schools: The truth about the Trojan Horse affair*, Bristol: Policy Press

Home Affairs Committee (1981) *Racial disadvantage*, Cmd 6234, London: HMSO

Home Office (1965) *Immigration from the Commonwealth*, Cmd 2739, London: HMSO

Honeyford, R. (1982) 'Multiracial myths', *Times Educational Supplement*, 19 November

Hoque, A. (2015) *British-Islamic identity: Third generation Bangladeshis from East London*, London: IOE Press

Hughes, K. (2015) 'Dorm feasts and red-hot pashes', *The Guardian*, 14 February

Hughill, B. (1987) 'Dramatic steps that will carry Britain forward', *Times Educational Supplement*, 16 October

Humphries, S. (1981) *Hooligans or rebels? An oral history of working class childhood and youth 1889-1939*, Oxford: Oxford University Press

IAAM (Incorporated Association of Assistant Masters in Secondary Schools) (1950) *The teaching of history*, London

Independent, The (1995) 'The Sleaze List', 22 July

Inglis, F. (1985) *The management of ignorance*, Oxford: Blackwell

Insted Consultancy (2014) *The Trojan Horse affair in Birmingham: Competing and overlapping narratives. March-May 2014* (www.instead.co.uk)

ITV (2017) [television] *Victoria*, London, Channel 3 [Serial in six parts]

Jack, I. (2018) 'Hoarding food now seems the only sensible thing to do', *The Guardian*, 28 July

Jackson, B. and Marsden, D. (1962) *Education and the working class*, London: Routledge & Kegan Paul

Jacques, M. (2003) 'Tennis racist – it's time we did something about it', *The Guardian*, 25 June

James, O. (1990) 'Crime and the American mind', *The Independent*, 22 May

Jeffcoate, R. (1979) *Positive image: Towards a multicultural curriculum*, London: Harper & Row

Jenkins, R. (1966) Address to a meeting of the Voluntary Liaison Committees, London, National Council for Commonwealth Immigration, 23 May

Jensen, A. (1969) 'How much can we boost IQ and scholastic achievement?', *Harvard Education Review*, 39, 1-23

John, G. (2010) 'The people of Grenada need answers', *The Guardian*, 10 October

Johnson, B. (2013) The 2013 Annual Margaret Thatcher Lecture, Centre for Policy Studies, London, 27 November

Johnson, B. (2017a) 'My vision for a bold, thriving Britain after Brexit', *The Daily Telegraph*, 16 September

Johnson, B. (2017b) 'Brexit mustn't leave us a "vassal state"', *Sunday Times*, 17 December

Joseph. K. (1986) 'Without prejudice: Education for an ethnically mixed society', *Multicultural Teaching*, 4, 3, 6-8

Judt, T. (2005) *Postwar: A history of Europe since 1945*, London: Vintage Books

Judt, T. (2010) *Ill fares the land*, London: Allen Lane

Kaletsky, A. (2000) 'Who do these worthy idiots think they are?', *The Times*, 21 October

Kampfner, J. (2003) *Blair's wars*, London: Simon & Schuster

Kappal, B. (2017) 'Why Brexiteers need to update their colonial history', *New Statesman*, 17 March

Karalsoglu, Y. and Luchtenberg, S. (2006) 'Islamophobia in Germany', *Lifelong Learning in Germany*, 3, 195-201

Kelly, E. and Cohen, T. (1988) *Racism in schools: New research evidence*, Stoke-on-Trent: Trentham Books

Kelly, Sir Christopher (2009) 'MPs expenses scandal: A time-line', *Daily Telegraph*, 4 November

Kelso, P. (2000) 'Prisoner killed in race hate attack', *The Guardian*, 25 October

Kennedy, C. (2000) *The future of politics*, London: HarperCollins

Khomani, N. and Watts, H. (2017) 'Coverage of call to decolonise the English curriculum made student "target" for abuse', *The Guardian*, 27 October

Kiernan, V.G. (1969) *The lords of humankind: European attitudes towards the outside world in the imperial age*, London: Weidenfield & Nicholson

King, A.S. and Reiss, M.J. (1993) *The multicultural dimension of the National Curriculum*, London: Falmer Press

Kingsley, C. (1863) *The water-babies: A fairy tale for a lost baby*, Oxford: Oxford University Press [reprinted 2003, Oxford Classics]

Kipling, R. (1940) *The definitive edition of Kipling's verse*, London: Hodder & Stoughton

Kipling, R. (1899) *Stalky and Co*, London: Hodder & Stoughton

Kirp, D. (1979) *Doing good by doing little*, Berkeley, CA: University of California Press

Kureishi, H., Roy, A., Shamsie, K. et al (2017) 'Open the doors and let these books in', *The Guardian Review*, 11 November

Kwarteng, K., Patel, P., Raab, D., Skidmore, C. and Truss, E. (eds) (2012) *Britannia unchained: Global lessons for growth and prosperity*, London: Palgrave Macmillan

Kynaston, D. (2007) *Austerity Britain 1945-1951*, London: Bloomsbury

Labour Party (1989) *Multicultural education: Labour's policy for schools*, London

Labour Party (1992) *Election manifesto*, London: Labour Party

Lawrence, D. (2007) *And still I rise: A mother's search for justice*, London: Faber & Faber [first published 2006]

Lawson, N. (2007) 'A decade of Blair has left the Labour Party on its knees', *The Guardian*, 19 April

Lawson Walton, J. (1899) 'Imperialism', *The Contemporary Review*, LXXV

Lawton, D. (2005) *Education and Labour Party ideologies 1900-2001 and beyond*, London: Routledge Falmer

Lee, H. (1960) *To kill a mocking bird*, New York: HarperCollins

Levy, A. (2004) *Small island*, London: Headline Publishing

Lewis. P., Newburn, T., Taylor, M. and Ball, J. (2011) 'Blame the police: Why the rioters say they took part', *The Guardian*, 5 August

Lloyd, T.O. (1984) *The British Empire 1558-1983*, Oxford: Oxford University Press

Loach, K. (director) (2016) [film] *I, Daniel Blake* (written by Paul Laverty) [Winner of the Palme D'Or Film Festival de Cannes]

Lord Browne (2010) *Securing a sustainable future for higher education: An independent review of higher education funding and student finance*, London: Department for Business, Innovation and Skills

Lord Howard of Rising (2014) *Enoch at 100: A re-evaluation of the life, politics and philosophy of Enoch Powell*, London: Biteback

Lord Hutton (2004) *Inquiry into the circumstances surrounding the death of Dr David Kelly*, HC 247, London: HM Government

Lord Jebb (1961) Speech to the House of Lords, London

Lord Meath (1910) 'Duty and discipline in the education of children', in Lord Meath (ed) *Essays on duty and discipline 9*, London: Cassell & Co

Lord Parekh (2000) *The future of multi-ethnic Britain* (The Parekh Report), London: Profile Books

Lord Rosebery (1900) 'Inaugural address on the conferment of title as Rector of Glasgow University', in *Records of the ninth jubilee of the University of Glasgow 1451-1901*, Glasgow: James Macalese and Son

Lord Scarman (1982) *The Brixton disorders 10-12th April 1982, Report of an Inquiry by Lord Scarman*, London: Penguin Books

Lord Swann and Committee of Inquiry into the Education of Children from Ethnic Minority Groups (1985) *Education for all: The report of the Committee of Inquiry into the Education of Children from Minority Groups* (The Swann Report), London: HMSO

Lord Whitelaw (1976) Speech to Leicester Conservative Party, Leicester, June

Maarstricht Treaty (1992) *The unseen treaty: Treaty on European Union Maarstricht 1992*, London: Foreign and Commonwealth Office

MacCleod, D. (1996) 'Clampdown on inner city schools', *The Guardian*, 7 May

MacDonald, I., Bhavani, T., Khan, L. and John, G. (1989) *Murder in the playground*, Manchester: Longsight Press

MacFarlane, R.A. (2007) 'Historiography of selected works on Cecil John Rhodes', *History of Africa*, 34

MacIntyre, D. (1991) 'Baker seeks extra police after riots', *The Independent*, 15 September

MacKenzie, J.M. (1984) *Propaganda and empire: The manipulation of British public opinion 1880-1984*, Manchester: Manchester University Press

MacKenzie, J.M. (ed) (1986) *Imperialism and popular culture*, Manchester: Manchester University Press

MacKenzie, J.M. (2015) 'Epilogue: Analysing Echoes of empire in contemporary context: A personal odyssey of an imperial historian', in K. Nicolaïdis, B. Sèbe and G. Maas (eds) *Echoes of empire: Memory, identity and colonial legacies*, London and New York: I.B. Tauris, 189-208

Mackie, T. (2017) 'UK cannot become a colony of the EU for two years', *Daily Express*, 16 December

Macpherson, Sir W. (1999) *The Stephen Lawrence Inquiry*, Cmd 4262, London: The Stationery Office

Macshane, D. (2017) *Brexit, no exit: Why (in the end) Britain won't leave Europe*, London: I.B. Tauris

Magraw, B.I. (1919) *The thrill of history* (4 vols), London [7th edn, 1959]

Malik, N. (2018) 'My joy was followed by a nausea of fury', *The Guardian*, 5 March

Mandelson, P. and Liddle, R. (1996) *The Blair revolution: Can New Labour deliver?*, London: Faber & Faber

Mangan, J.A. (1980) 'Images of Empire in Edwardian-Victorian public schools', *Journal of Educational Administration and History*, 1, 2, 1

Mangan, J.A. (1986) 'The grit of our forefathers: Invented traditions, propaganda and imperialism', in J.M. MacKenzie (ed) *Imperialism and popular culture*, Manchester: Manchester University Press, 113-39

Mansell, W. (2004) 'Make room for the Empire', *Times Educational Supplement*, 9 July

Manzoor, S. (2008) 'Black Britain's darkest hour', *The Observer*, 24 February

Marquand, D. (2009) 'The spirit of Thomas Paine could yet inspire Cameron', *The Guardian*, 9 September

Marshall, T.H. (1951) *Citizenship and social class*, Cambridge: Cambridge University Press

Marx, K. (1870) 'Letter to Siegfried Meyor and Augustus Vogt in New York, 9 August 1870', in D. McLellan, D. (1976) *Karl Marx: His life and thought*, London: Paladin, p 471

Mason, R. (2017) 'May calls for inquiry into abuse of politicians', *The Guardian*, 13 July

May, T. (2016) 'A country that works for everyone', in *Conservative election manifesto*, London: The Conservative Party

McCann, K. and Mendick, R. (2018) 'Rudd quits as leaked letter leaves her denials in tatters', *The Daily Telegraph*, 30 April

McCulloch, G. (2009) 'Empires and education: The British Empire', in R. Cowen and A.M. Kazamias (eds) *International handbook of comparative education*, Dordrecht: Springer, 169-79

McInnery, L. (2016) 'What society lets families fear deportation for sending their children to schools', *The Guardian* (Education), 18 October

McInch, A. (2018) 'Only schools and courses: An ethnography of working-class schooling in South Wales', PhD thesis, Cardiff Metropolitan University

McNeal, J. and Rogers, M. (1971) *The multiracial school*, Harmondsworth: Penguin

McVeigh, T. (2011) 'The message when youth clubs close: No one cares', *The Observer*, 14 August

McVeigh, T. (2016) 'Deaths are not just happening in the US: Why activists brought the Black Lives movement to the UK', *The Observer*, 7 August

Meyer, H.D. and Benavot, A. (2013) *Pisa, power and policy*, Didcot: Symposium Books

Miles, A. (2007) 'Sneaky, unfair, divisive: Welcome to church schools', *The Times*, 23 May

Ministerial Working Group on Public Disorder and Community Cohesion (2001) *Report to the Home Secretary*, London: The Home Office

Ministry of Education (1946) *The nation's schools*, London: HMSO

Mirza, H.S. (1998) 'Race, gender and the social consequences of a pseudo-scientific discourse', *Race Ethnicity and Education*, 1, 1, 111-28

Mishra, P. (2017) *Age of anger: A history of the present*, London: Allen Lane

Modood, T., Berthoud, R., Lakey, J., Nazroo, J., Smith, P., Virdee, S. and Beishon, S. (1997) *Ethnic minorities in Britain: Diversity and disadvantage. The Fourth National Survey of Ethnic Minorities*, London: Policy Studies Institute

Mohsin, M. (2016) 'Empire shaped the world, There is an abyss at the heart of dishonest history textbooks', *The Guardian*, 31 October

Monnet, J. (1945) 'There will be no peace', Speech to the French Committee of National Liberation, Paris, France, 5 August

Montgomerie, T. and Pancevski, B. (2017) 'May drafts Gove in to Brexit war cabinet', *The Sunday Times*, 3 November

Moore, M. and Ramsey, G. (2017) *UK media coverage of the 2016 EU referendum campaign, and voting patterns*, London: King's College, Study of Media and Communications

Moore, P. (2016) 'How Britain votes: Over 65's were more than twice as likely as the under 25's to have voted to leave the European Union', YouGov, 27 June

Moorhouse, G. (1984) *India Britannica*, London: Paladin

Morris, S. (2017) 'Play mocking lecturer led to medical school race segregation', *The Guardian*, 26 January

Motavali, A. (2018) 'Student who called out lad culture for what it really is', *The Observer*, 25 March

Mounk, Y. (2018) *The people vs democracy: Why out freedom is in danger and how to save it*, Cambridge, MA: Harvard University Press

Msimang, S. (2016) 'Boris Johnson is perfectly in tune with Britain's post-colonial lament', *The Guardian*, 19 July

Murray, C. (1990) *The emerging British underclass*, London: IEA Health and Welfare Unit, Institute for Economic Affairs

Murray, C. (1994) 'Underclass: The crisis deepens', *The Sunday Times*, 22 May

Murray, D. (2010) 'The Prevent Strategy, a textbook example of how alienate just about everybody', *Daily Telegraph*, 31 March

Murray, D. (2017) *The strange death of Europe: Immigration, identity, Islam*, London: Bloomsbury

Myers, K. (2015) *Struggles for the past: Irish and Afro-Caribbean histories in England*, Manchester: Manchester University Press

Naylor, F. (1988) 'Political lessons of Dewsbury', *The Independent*, 22 December

Nagesh, A. (2016) '11 things Boris has said to make him the perfect Foreign Secretary', *Metro*, 14 June

Nevett, J. (2018) 'Britains prefer tough immigration: Windrush crisis could benefit Tories in local elections', *The Daily Star*, 2 May

Newsinger, J. (2006) *The blood never dried: A people's history of the British Empire*, Stoke-on-Trent: Trentham Books

Newsom Report, The (1963) *Half our future: A report of the Central Advisory Council for Education*, London: HMSO

Nicolaïdis, K., Sèbe, B. and Maas, G. (eds) (2015) *Echoes of Empire: Memory, identity and colonial legacies*, London and New York: I.B. Tauris

Norton-Taylor, R. and Milne, S. (1999) 'Racism: Extremists led Powell's marches', *The Guardian*, 1 January

NUT (National Union of Teachers) (1993) *Union response to the proposals for the reform of initial teacher training*, London

Oakley, N. (2017) 'Brenda from Bristol sums up the mood of the nation in just four words after General Election results', *Daily Mirror*, 9 June

Obioma, C. (2017) 'Africa has been failed by Westernisation: It must cast off its subservience', *The Guardian*, 13 November

Observer, The (2007) 'Comment 29, The big issue: Segregated schools', 3 June

Observer, The (2017) 'Editorial: Behind this disaster lies indifference a brutal to the lives of the poor', 18 June

O'Brien, E. (1960) *The girl with green eyes*, London: Hutchinson [reissued in 1975 by Penguin]

O'Carroll, L. (2017) 'Gina Miller fears acid attack following months of threats', *The Guardian*, 10 August

O'Carroll, L. (2018) 'Dutch judge allows British expats to pursue EU citizenship rights', *The Guardian*, 8 February

O'Connor, M., Hales, E., Davies, J. and Tomlinson, S. (1999) *Hackney Downs: The school that dared to fight*, London: Cassell

O'Dowd, N. (2013) 'The era of no Blacks, Dogs or Irish is over but should not be forgotten', *Irish Central News*, 4 October

Ofsted (Office for Standards in Education) (1993) *Access and achievement in urban education: A report from HMI*, London: HMSO

O'Hara, M. (2015) *Austerity bites*, Bristol: Policy Press

Olusoga, D. (2016) *Black and British: A forgotten history*, London: Palgrave Macmillan

Olusoga, D. (2017) 'Empire 2.0 is dangerous nostalgia for something that never existed', *The Guardian*, 19 March

Osler, A. and Starkey, H. (2005) *Changing citizenship: Democracy and inclusion in education*, Maidenhead: Open University Press/McGraw-Hill

Owen, G. (2018) 'Vile racist attack on Meghan by mistress of UKIP chief', *Daily Mail*, 14 January

Owen, J. (2016) 'British Empire: Students should be taught colonialism was "not all good" say historians', *The Independent*, 22 January

Palmer, F. (ed) (1986) *Anti-racism: An assault on education and values*, Nottingham: The Sherwood Press

Parekh, B. (2000) *Report on the future of multi-ethic Britain*, London: Runnymede Trust

Patten, J. (1995) *Things to come: The Tories in the 21st century*, London: Sinclair-Stevenson

Paxman, J. (2012) *Empire*, London: Penguin/Random House

Pearce, S. (1986) 'Swann and the spirit of the age', in F. Palmer (ed) *Anti-racism: An assault on education and value*, Nottingham: The Sherwood Press 136-148

Perry, B. (2012) '1944-48', in C. Shindler (ed) *National Service*, London: Sphere

Pettifor, A. (2018) 'A triumph for Osborne austerity plan? Not when our social fabric is in tatters', *The Observer*, 4 March

Phillips, R. (1998) *History teaching, nationhood and the state: Study in educational politics*, London: Cassell

Pierce, A. (2008) 'Queen asks why no one saw it coming', *Daily Telegraph*, 5 November

Plowden Report, The (1967) *Children and their primary schools, A report of the Central Advisory Council for Education*, London: HMSO

Porter, B. (2015) 'Epilogue: After images of empire', in K. Nicolaïdis, B. Sèbe and G. Maas (eds) *Echoes of empire: Memory, identity and colonial legacies*, London and New York: I.B. Tauris, 393-406

Postman, N. and Weingartner, C. (1969) *Teaching as a subversive activity*, New York: Delta Books

Powell, J.E. (1959) Speech: Hola Camp, House of Commons, 27 July, in Lord Howard of Rising (ed) (2014) *Enoch at 100: A re-evaluation of the life, politics and philosophy of Enoch Powell*, London: Biteback, 54-62

Powell, J.E. (1961) Speech on nationhood to the St George Society, London, 22 April, in Lord Howard of Rising (ed) (2014) *Enoch at 100: A re-evaluation of the life, politics and philosophy of Enoch Powell*, London: Biteback, 143-6

Powell, J.E. (1968) Speech to the Annual General Meeting of the West Midlands Area Conservative Political Centre, Birmingham, 20 April, in Lord Howard of Rising (ed) (2014) *Enoch at 100: A re-evaluation of the life, politics and philosophy of Enoch Powell*, London: Biteback, 172-9

Powell, J.E. (1971) Speech on European Union to the Association des Chefs d'Entreprises Libre, in Lord Howard of Rising (ed) (2014) *Enoch at 100: A re-evaluation of the life, politics and philosophy of Enoch Powell*, London: Biteback, 35-46

Press Association (2016) 'Inquest into death of Polish-born schoolgirl returns open verdict', *The Guardian*, 20 July

Private Eye (2018) 'Prickly Heaton', No 14

Pyke, N. (1994) 'Patten is forced to apologise', *Times Educational Supplement*, 24 June

QCA (Qualifications and Curriculum Authority) (2007) *The National Curriculum: Statutory requirements for Key Stages 3 and 4*, London

Ramesh, R. (2015) 'Prevent Programme spying on our young people', *The Guardian*, 6 December

Ramsey, A. (2013) 'My public school days and the building of upper-class solidarity', Bright Green, 25 June

Ranson, S. (1984) 'Towards a tertiary tripartism: New codes of control and a 17+', in P. Broadfoot (ed) *Selection, certification and control*, London: Methuen

Rawlinson, K. (2017) 'Viscount jailed for offering money for killing of Gina Miller', *The Guardian*, 13 July

Rawlinson, K. (2018) 'Two arrested after complaints of racist chants', *The Guardian*, 9 March

Rawnsley, A. (2000) *Servants of the people: The inside story of New Labour*, London: Penguin Books

Rawnsley, A (2010) *The end of the party: The rise and fall of New Labour*, London: Viking Books

RCCCFM (Royal Commission on the Care and Control of the Feeble-Minded) (1908) *Report of the Royal Commission on the Care and Control of the Feeble-Minded* (8 vols), London: HM Government

Reclaiming Schools (2016) 'Brexit campaign leaves children scared', Reclaiming Schools.org, 30 June

Rees-Mogg, J. (2017) [television] *BBC News Night*, 15 December

Reggie's blog (2011) 'On being British', 1 October (https://medotutissimus.blogspot.co.uk)

Reinders, R.C. (1968) 'Racialism on the left: E.D. Morel and the Black horror on the Rhine', *International Review of Social History*, XIII, 2.

Rex, J. (1973) *Race, colonialism and the city*, London: Routledge & Kegan Paul

Rex, J. (1986) *Race and ethnicity*, Milton Keynes: Open University Press

Rex, J. (1996) *Ethnic minorities in the modern nation state*, London: Macmillan

Rex, J. (2004) 'Multiculturalism and political integration in modern nation states', in A. Gorny and P. Ruspini (eds) *Migration in the new Europe*, London: Palgrave Macmillan, 93-108

Rex, J. and Moore, R. (1967) *Race, community and conflict*, Oxford: Oxford University Press

Rex, J. and Tomlinson, S. (1979) *Colonial immigrants in a British city: A class analysis*, London: Routledge & Kegan Paul

Rich, P.S. (1986) *Race and empire in British politics*, Cambridge: Cambridge University Press

Richardson, B. (ed) (2005) *Tell it like it is: How our schools fail Black children*, London: Bookmark Publications/Trentham Books

Rizzo, M. (2006) 'What was left of the groundnut scheme? Developmental disaster and labour market in Southern Tanganyika 1946-1952', *Journal of Agrarian Change*, 6, 2, 205-38

Robbins Report (1963) *Higher education, Report of the Committee appointed by the Prime Minister under the chairmanship of Lord Robbins 1961-63*, Cmd 2154, London: HMSO

Roberts, A. (2014) 'Enoch Powell and the nation state', in Lord Howard of Rising (ed) *Enoch at 100: A re-evaluation of the life, politics and philosophy of Enoch Powell*, London: Biteback, 123–42

Roberts, R. (1971) *The classic slum: Salford life in the first quarter of the century*, Harmondsworth: Penguin

Rodrigues, J. (2017) 'From the archive: How *The Guardian* reported the partition of India 70 years ago', *The Guardian*, 14 August

Rollock, N., Gillborn, D., Vincent, C. and Ball, S.J. (2015) *The colour of class*, London: Routledge

Rose, E.J.B. and Associates (1969) *Colour and citizenship: A report on British race relations*, Oxford: Oxford University Press

Rose, H. and Rose, S. (2012) *Genes, cells and brains*, London: Verso

Roth, A., Smith, D. and Helmore, E. (2018) 'EU is my foe, says Trump as he heads for summit with Putin', *The Guardian*, 16 July

Roundtree, C. (2018) 'The new Windrush betrayal: Home Office shredded documents that proved Caribbean migrants came to the UK decades ago', *Daily Mail*, 17 April

Roy, E.A. and Bowcott, O. (2018) 'Commonwealth meeting "will discuss Queen's successor"', *The Guardian*, 13 February

Runnymede Trust, The (1993) *Racist attacks and harassment: The epidemic of the 1990s*, London

Rushdie, S. (1988) *The Satanic verses*, London: Viking Books

Rutter, M. and Madge, N. (1976) *Cycles of disadvantage*, London: Heinemann

Sabbagh, D. (2018) 'Gove says Vote Leave wrong to fuel fears over Turkish influx', *The Guardian*, 17 July

Sabbagh, D. and Boffey, D. (2018) 'Desperate May reveals her plan B: to buy more time', *The Guardian*, 11 December

Sabbagh, D., Stewart, H. and Elgot, J. (2018) 'May narrowly heads off defeat after caving in to the Brexit hard-liners', *The Guardian*, 16 July

Sampson, S. (1992) *The essential anatomy of Britain: Democracy in crisis*, London: Hodder & Stoughton

Saunders, A. (2016) 'Jamaicans deported over four years: 9425 sent back to Jamaica, mainly from the UK', *Jamaican Gleaner*, 8 September

Schools Inquiry Commission (1868) *The Taunton Commission*, London: HM Government

Scott Inquiry (1996) *Report on arms sales to Iraq by Lord Justice Scott*, London: The Stationery Office

Scruton, R. (1986) 'The myth of cultural relativism', in F. Palmer (ed) *Anti-racism: An assault on education and value*, Nottingham: The Sherwood Press, 127–35

Scruton, R. (2017) 'Brexit will give us back pride in our island roots', *The Times* (Weekend Essay), 18 November

Seeley, J.E. (1883) *The expansion of England*, London: Macmillan

Seidler, V.J. (2018) *Making sense of Brexit*, Bristol: Policy Press

Select Committee on Race Relations and Immigration (1973) *Education*, London: HMSO

Select Committee on Race Relations and Immigration (1977) *The West Indian community*, London: HMSO

Select Committee on Race Relations and Immigration (1969) *The problems of coloured school-leavers*, London: HMSO

Sennett, R. (2006) *The culture of the new capitalism*, New Haven, CT: Yale University Press

Shackle, S. (2017) 'What really happened in the Trojan horse schools?', *The Guardian* (The Long Read), 2 September

Shain, F. (2013) 'Race, nation and education: An overview of British attempts to manage diversity since the 1950s', *Education Inquiry*, 4, 1, 63–85

Sherman, A. (1979) 'Britain's urge to self-destruction', *The Daily Telegraph*, 9 September

Shindler, C. (2012) *National Service: From Aden to Aldershot: Tales from the conscripts 1946-62*, London: Sphere

Shipman, T. (2016) *All out war: The full story of Brexit*, London: William Collins

Shipman, T. (2017) *Fall out: A year of political mayhem*, London: William Collins

Shotte, G. (2002) 'Education, migration and identities: Relocated Montserratian students in London schools', PhD study, Institute of Education, London

Shukla, N. (ed) (2016) *The good immigrant*, London: Unbound

Siddiqui, A. (2007) *Islam at universities in England: Meeting the needs and investing in the future*

Simon, B. (1960) *Studies in the history of education 1780-1870*, London: Lawrence & Wishart

Simon, B. (1990) *Education and the social order 1940-1990*, London: Lawrence & Wishart

Slack, J. (2016) 'Enemies of the people: Fury over "out of touch" judges who have declared war on democracy by defying the 17.4 million British voters and who could trigger a constitutional crisis', *Daily Mail*, 3 November

Smith, D. (2013) 'Tony Blair plotted military intervention in Zimbabwe, claims Thabo Mbeki', *The Guardian*, 27 November

Smith, E. (2015) 'Communist attitudes towards Polish migration to post-war Britain', Hateful of History, Blog, 5 May

Smith, M. (2017) 'Myths about the EU since 1992', *Daily Mirror*, 9 October

Speed, B. (2016) 'How different demographic groups voted in the EU Referendum (The Lord Ashcroft Poll)', *New Statesman*, 24 June

Stembridge, J.H. (1939) *The world: A general regional geography*, Oxford: Oxford University Press [7th edn, 1956]

Stembridge, J.H. (1951) *New world geographies: Europe*, Oxford: Oxford University Press

Stephens, P. (2018) 'Nostalgia has stolen the future', *Financial Times* (Global Politics), 27 July

Stewart, H. (2017) 'Focus on students was a "stupid policy" based on bad data', *The Guardian*, 25 August

Stewart, H., Cregar, P. and Elgot, J. (2018) 'Johnson attacks "miserable" Brexit plan', *The Guardian*, 19 July

Summers, D. (2009) 'Brown sticks by British jobs for British workers remark', *The Guardian*, 30 January

Syal, R. (2013) 'Anger at "go home" message to illegal migrants', *The Guardian*, 26 July

Sylvester, R. (2000) 'The nine charmed lives of Stephen Norris', *The Telegraph*, 26 August

Taylor, D. (2017) 'Curt, almost implausible email puts FA chairman in firing line', *The Guardian*, 17 October

Taylor, D. (2018) 'UK removed legal protection for Windrush immigrants in 2014', *The Guardian*, 16 April

TES (*Times Educational Supplement*) (1990) 'Editorial', 23 June

Thatcher, M. (1993) *The Downing Street years*, London: HarperCollins

Thatcher, M. (1978) Interview for Granada Television, 30 January

Tilly, C. (1976) 'Reflections on the history of European state-making', in C. Tilly (ed) *The formation of nation states in Western Europe*, Princeton, NJ: Princeton University Press

Times, The (1849) 'Editorial'

Times, The (1919) 'Letters', Sir Ralph Williams, 14 June

Times, The (1919) 'Letters', Felix Hercules, 19 June

Times Higher Education Supplement (2017) Letter: 'Pro-colonialism paper: How did it get published?', 28 September, p 31

Tinker, H. (1982) *A message from the Falklands: The life and gallant death of David Tinker, Lieut RN, from his letters and poems*, London: Junction Books

Tiratsoo, N. (1997) *From blitz to Blair: A new history of Britain since 1939*, London: Weidenfield & Nicholson

Tomlinson, S. (1981) *Educational subnormality: A study in decision-making*, London: Routledge & Kegan Paul [reprinted in 2018]

Tomlinson, S. (1982) *A sociology of special education*, London: Routledge & Kegan Paul [reprinted 2012]

Tomlinson, S. (1983) *Ethnic minorities in British schools*, London: Heinemann

Tomlinson, S. (1990) *Multicultural education in white schools*, London: Batsford

Tomlinson, S. (1992) 'Disadvantaging the disadvantaged: Bangladeshis and education in Tower Hamlets', *British Journal of the Sociology of Education*, 13, 4, 437-46

Tomlinson, S. (1993) 'The multicultural task group: The group that never was', in A.S. King and M.J. Reiss (eds) *The multicultural dimension of the National Curriculum*, London: Falmer Press, 21-9

Tomlinson, S. (1995) 'Hit squad needs new set of rules', *Times Educational Supplement*, 22 December

Tomlinson, S. (1998) 'New inequalities: Education markets and ethnic minorities', *Race Ethnicity and Education*, 1, 2, 207-24

Tomlinson, S. (2005) *Education in a post-welfare society*, Maidenhead: Open University Press/McGraw-Hill

Tomlinson, S. (2008) *Race and education: Policy and politics in Britain*, Maidenhead: Open University Press/McGraw-Hill

Tomlinson, S. (2013) *Ignorant yobs? Low attainers in a global knowledge economy*, Abingdon: Routledge

Tomlinson, S. (2017) *A sociology of special and inclusive education: Exploring the manufacture of inability*, London: Routledge

Tomlinson, S. (2018) 'Enoch Powell, empires, immigrants and education', *Race Ethnicity and Education*, 21, 1, 1–14

Tomlinson, S. and Dorling, D. (2016) 'Brexit has its roots in the British Empire – So how do we explain it to the young?', *New Statesman*, 10 May

Touraine, A. (2000) *Can we live together?* (translated by David Macey), Cambridge: Polity Press

Townsend, H.E.R. and Brittan, E.M. (1973) *Multiracial education: Need and innovation*, London: Evans/Methuen

Toynbee, P. (2017) 'The Irish question may yet save Britain from Brexit', *The Guardian*, 28 December

Toynbee, P. and Walker, D. (2015) *Cameron's coup: How the Tories took Britain to the brink*, London: Guardian Books and Faber & Faber

Travis, A. (2015) 'How Cameron advisor helped thwart plan to aid young black people after 1985 riots', *The Guardian*, 30 December

Trevor-Roper, H. (1983) 'The invention of tradition: The Highland tradition of Scotland', in E. Hobsbawn and T. Ranger (eds) *The invention of tradition*, Cambridge: Cambridge University Press, 15–41

Troyna, B. and Smith, D.I. (1982) *Racism, school and the labour market*, Leicester: National Youth Bureau

Verkaik, R. (2018) *Posh boys: How the English public schools run Britain*, London: One World

Vincent, C. (2019) *Tea and the Queen: British values, education and citizenship*, Bristol: Policy Press

Vine, D. (2011) *Island of shame: The secret history of the military base on Diego Garcia*, Princeton, NJ: Princeton University Press

Wallace, W. (2004) 'History tells us we must nip it in the bud', *Times Educational Supplement*, 4 June

Walters, S. (2014) 'Tory bloodbath over Muslim schools fiasco', *The Mail on Sunday*, 8 June

Warmington, P. (2014) *Black British intellectuals and education*, London: Routledge

Warsi, S. (2017) *The enemy within: A tale of Muslim Britain*, London: Allen Lane

Waterson, J. (2018) 'Data abuses and fake news a risk to democracy', *The Guardian*, 28 July

Watson, D. (1996) 'Research note', *Historical Studies in Industrial Relations*, March [also in *Hansard*, 8 June 1948, col 1185]

Watt, H. (2013) 'Cash for questions: A scandal that should have changed the face of British politics', *Daily Telegraph*, 31 May

Watt, N., Laville, S. and Dodd, V. (2011) 'Too few, too low, too timid, Tories attack police over riots', *The Guardian*, 12 August

Weale, S. (2105) 'Swedish free schools: Famed for success and a beacon for Britain. So what went wrong?', *The Guardian*, 11 June

Weaver, M. (2016) 'Polish ambassador calls for unity against xenophobia as he visits scene of killing', *The Guardian*, 1 September

Whittaker, F. (2018) 'Progress 8 forcing schools to ask for more PRU places', *Schools Week*, edition 132

Whitty, G., Power, S. and Halpin, D. (1998) *Devolution and choice in education*, Buckingham: Open University Press

Wilby, P. (2011) 'Mad professor goes global', *The Guardian*, 14 June

Wilkinson, R. and Pickett, K. (2009) *The spirit level: Why more equal societies almost always do better*, London: Allen Lane

Williams, R. (1965) *The long revolution*, London: Penguin Books

Williams, S. (1988) 'Foreword', in G.K. Verma (ed) *Education for all: A landmark for pluralism*, London: Falmer Press

Williams, S. (2006) *Colour bar: A United Kingdom*, London: Allen Lane

Williams, S. (2011) *Who killed Hammarskjold? The UN, the CIA, war, and white supremacy in Africa*, London: Hurst & Company

Willis, P. (1977) *Learning to labour: How working class lads get working class jobs*, Farnborough: Saxon House

Winder, R. (2004) *Bloody foreigners*, London: Abacus

Wintour, P. (2018) 'Saudi Arabia wants more trade deals, says Crown Prince's team', *The Guardian*, 8 March

Wolf, A. (2011) *Review of vocational education* (The Wolf Report), London: Department for Education

Woodham-Smith, C. (1962) *The great hunger*, New York: Free Press

Worsthorne. P. (1982) 'Editorial', *The Sunday Telegraph*, 23 May

Wry Society (2011) 'The villa holiday', *Financial Times Magazine*, 12 August

Yaqoob, S. (2014) 'No need for ideology', *The Guardian*, 23 July

Younge, G. (2007) 'A decade of Blairism has left society more segregated, fearful and divided', *The Guardian*, 28 May

Zephaniah, B. (2005) 'Over and out', in B. Richardson (ed) *Tell it like it is: How schools fail our black children*, Stoke-on-Trent: Trentham Books, 156-8

Zimmern, A.E. (1926) *The third British Empire* (3rd edition 1934), London: Oxford University Press

Index

Page references for notes are followed by n

CPSIA information can be obtained
at www.ICGtesting.com
Printed in the USA
LVHW081348070721
691900LV00019B/236

9 781447 345848